"The biblical, theological and rational case against Calvinism has never been stated more clearly, concisely, irenically or convincingly."

ROGER E. OLSON,
Professor of Theology, George W. Truett Theological Seminary

"Walls and Dongell present an exceptional blend of careful scholarship, readable presentation, uncompromising conviction and graceful opposition in their forcefully argued book *Why I Am Not a Calvinist*. The book demonstrates well the often overlooked fact that the issues between Calvinism and Arminianism are not primarily exegetical but theological and even philosophical. This task is ably accomplished by the combination of an exegetical scholar and a theological philosopher in the authorial team—an ideal amalgamation for such a book.

The book clearly identifies and explains the most powerful problems for Calvinism—conceptual problems with the notion of freedom, logical consistency problems and problems of ingenuous application of Calvinist theology to Christian life. While clearly and unapologetically *non*-Calvinist, the authors are most assuredly not *anti*-Calvinist. Their treatment of Calvinism and Calvinists is always in the spirit of Christian love, acceptance, understanding and unity. The book is very timely, given the central debates in contemporary conservative and evangelical theology and the resurgence of pro-Calvinist sentiment over the last two decades."

JAMES F. SENNETT,
Professor of Philosophy and Interdisciplinary Studies,
Lincoln Christian College and Seminary

"Without the usual rancor, hysteria and triumphalism, Walls and Dongell offer a clear and forceful biblical and philosophical case for Arminianism. This book is a welcome and important contribution to the recent upsurge in discussions of Calvinism and Arminianism."

KELLY JAMES CLARK, *Professor of Philosophy, Calvin College*

WHY I AM
NOT A
CALVINIST

JERRY L. WALLS AND
JOSEPH R. DONGELL

IVP Books
An imprint of InterVarsity Press
Downers Grove, Illinois

InterVarsity Press
P.O. Box 1400, Downers Grove, IL 60515-1426
World Wide Web: www.ivpress.com
E-mail: email@ivpress.com

InterVarsity Press® is the book-publishing division of InterVarsity Christian Fellowship/USA®, a student movement active on campus at hundreds of universities, colleges and schools of nursing in the United States of America, and a member movement of the International Fellowship of Evangelical Students. For information about local and regional activities, write Public Relations Dept., InterVarsity Christian Fellowship/USA, 6400 Schroeder Rd., P.O. Box 7895, Madison, WI 53707-7895, or visit the IVCF website at <www.intervarsity.org>.

Design: Cindy Kiple

Images: North Wind Picture Archives

ISBN 978-0-8308-3249-1

Printed in the United States of America ∞

Library of Congress Cataloging-in-Publication Data

Walls, Jerry L.
  Why I am not a Calvinist/Jerry L. Walls and Joseph R. Dongell.
     p. cm.
  Includes bibliographical references and index.
  ISBN 0-8308-3249-1 (pbk.: alk. paper)
  1. Calvinism. I. Dongell, Joseph. II. Title.
  BX9424.3.W35 2004
  230'.42—dc22

                                                                    2003027947

P	23	22	21	20	19	18	17	16	15	14	13	12	11	10
Y	23	22	21	20	19	18	17	16	15	14	13	12		

To my wife, Regina, whose strength in the midst of weakness

has been for me a deep encouragement and a clear

proof of God's abiding presence.

JOE

To every member of Gen X and Y who has ever

joined in an argument about Calvinism

and thereby shown that interest in serious theological

issues is alive and well in your generation.

JERRY

CONTENTS

ACKNOWLEDGMENTS

Several persons deserve thanks for helping in various ways in the writing of this book. First of all, Scott Burson deserves credit for conceiving the idea for the book and writing the initial proposal. He originally planned to coauthor the book until illness forced him to pull out of the project. But without his energy and vision, this book would likely never have been written.

Among those who read portions of the material and offered helpful comments and suggestions are Jason Gillette, Yukie Hirose, Kimi Jehn, Brian Marshall and Stacey Patterson. Thanks are also due to Damon Gibbs and Dallas Pfeiffer for research assistance.

A special word of thanks to Terry Tiessen for his extensive critical comments on the entire manuscript. His work enabled us to clarify and strengthen our arguments at several points. Thanks also to Angela and Jonathan Walls for their interest in this subject and for their energetic participation in numerous conversations it has generated. Finally, thanks to Asbury Seminary for sabbatical support which enabled the writing of several of these chapters.

INTRODUCTION

The enormously popular sitcom *Seinfeld,* despite its aim to be a show about nothing, occasionally raised some very important questions. In one episode George Costanza, the character who could never quite get his life in order, finally appears to have everything going his way. But then, true to form, the plane he is on goes into a nosedive. As he sees his life passing before his eyes, he blurts out, "I knew God wouldn't let me be successful!" (In the end, the plane straightens out and George's life is spared. He does, however, wind up in prison by the end of the episode.)

We do not want to exaggerate George's theological insight, but he did manage to hit on an issue of extraordinary importance in his little outburst. In fact, we cannot imagine a more important issue than the one he suggests. The question, quite simply put, is whether there are persons, as George saw himself, whom God has chosen not to bless. Or can we be assured, regardless of our lot in this life, that God truly loves us, desires our well-being and wants us to have his ultimate gift of eternal life? This question is the driving force behind our decision to write *Why I Am Not a Calvinist.* And this is the primary question we seek to answer in this book.

THE LOCUS OF THE DEBATE: GOD'S CHARACTER

The debate between Calvinism and Arminianism is often framed by the concept of freedom, with God's sovereign right to do what he chooses with his creation on one side (Calvinism) and humanity's ability to shape its own destiny on the other (Arminianism). When the debate centers on freedom, the issue boils down to one of power. Is the sovereign Creator of the universe in control, or is sinful humanity in charge? Does God not have the right and ability to do what he pleases with his creation? It is easy to see the attraction of Calvinism when the debate is transformed into a court hearing with Calvinism defending the majesty of God and Arminianism representing the rights of humanity.

Although we would agree that a portion of the dispute swirls around the topic of sovereignty and human freedom, we contend that the truly fundamental dispute is not over power but rather over God's character. Our motivation for writing this book is not our desire to present a case for human liberty. Protecting the tree of liberty in such a way that Patrick Henry would be proud, which R. C. Sproul suggests is the main Arminian issue, is not in fact the crux of our concern.[1] The fundamental issue here is which theological paradigm does a better job of representing the biblical picture of God's character: which theological system gives a more adequate account of the biblical God whose nature is holy love?

In the chapters that follow, we will argue that Calvinism distorts the biblical picture of God and fails in other crucial ways that show its inadequacy as a theological system. Before proceeding further, let us identify the views we aim to scrutinize and analyze.

WHAT IS CALVINISM?

Calvinism derives its name, of course, from the great Protestant Reformer John Calvin (1509-1564). It is important to understand, however, that we are using the general term *Calvinism* to refer to a certain tradition in theology of which Calvin is the most famous proponent. It is called Calvinism because of Calvin's role in articulating the theology clearly and systematically. Before Calvin, however, the same basic views were defended by a number of important theologians, most notably

---

[1] R. C. Sproul, *Chosen by God* (Wheaton, Ill.: Tyndale House, 1986), p. 9. After employing the image of the tree of liberty, Sproul goes on to write, "The specter of an all-powerful God making choices for us, and perhaps even against us, makes us scream, 'Give me free will or give me death!' " Of course, Patrick Henry is famous for the line "Give me liberty or give me death!"

Augustine (354-430), although Augustine was not as clear or consistent as Calvin on these matters. Another important figure in this connection is Martin Luther, Calvin's great contemporary in the Reformation, who also follows Augustine and was essentially in agreement with Calvin on the points we discuss in this book.[2] And since Calvin, his system of theology has been further elaborated and refined by numerous theologians down to the present day.

We do not by any means intend to reject everything associated with Calvinism and Reformed theology. We have enormous respect and appreciation for Calvin and the heritage he defined and engendered. Calvinism has for centuries represented a vital tradition of piety that is intellectually and morally serious. Calvinists have set a standard for scholarship and cultural engagement that evangelicals of other traditions can readily admire and emulate. Scholars in the broadly Reformed tradition have developed distinct approaches to matters ranging from epistemology (the theory of knowledge) to political theory and cultural criticism that do not necessarily hinge on the aspects of Calvinism we will criticize.[3] Christians from other theological backgrounds can profit greatly from this rich body of work and even adapt it to their perspectives. Moreover, many Calvinists have been zealous evangelists and missionaries and have contributed powerfully to the cause of winning the lost for Christ. In their passion for the glory of God, Calvinists have played a leading role in the renewal of worship in this generation.

The aspects of Calvinism we will criticize, however, are central to historic Reformed theology and are where Calvinism diverges most sharply from Arminianism and from several other competing theological traditions. We have in mind certain Calvinistic claims about salvation and

---

[2]On Martin Luther's "Calvinism," see J. I. Packer and O. R. Johnston, "Historical and Theological Introduction," in Martin Luther, *The Bondage of the Will*, trans. J. I. Packer and O. R. Johnston (Westwood, N.J.: Revell, 1957), pp. 57-59. It would be more historically accurate to describe both Luther and Calvin as Augustinians, but this brand of theology is best known as Calvinism, so we will retain this term.

[3]For example, Alvin Plantinga, who has developed a Reformed approach to epistemology, holds an Arminian view of freedom.

how God bestows it on his fallen children. The issue of salvation is clearly at the heart of Christian theology; some of the most hotly contested disputes among believers arise over it. The distinctively Reformed account of salvation has been spelled out in five concise claims known for generations as the "five points of Calvinism." Indeed, these five points have been conveniently summarized in what is perhaps the most famous acronym in the history of theology, namely, the Calvinist "tulip":

Total depravity

Unconditional election

Limited atonement

Irresistible grace

Perseverance of the saints

Of course, no simple summary, no matter how time honored and historic, can do justice to the subtlety and sophistication of Reformed theology. But these five points remain a convenient overview of Calvinism, particularly for those approaching these matters for the first time. So let's consider these five points in the order they appear in the acronym.

Total depravity. Total depravity describes the desperate condition of fallen sinners apart from the grace of God. Sin has affected every facet of human personality to such an extent that we are incapable of doing good or loving God as we should. Our thinking is distorted, our emotions are deceptive and out of proportion, and our desires are unruly and misdirected. In this condition, we are bent on rebellion and evil and are completely unwilling to submit to God and his perfect will. Consequently, we deserve only God's wrath and eternal punishment. Sinners in this condition are so utterly helpless that they are accurately described as "dead in [their] transgressions and sins" (Eph 2:1). So pervasive and deadly is the effect of sin that they can no more respond to God or do his will than a corpse could respond if commanded to get up and walk.

On the matter of total depravity, Calvinists are in essential agreement with believers in many other Christian traditions. The differences arise when one asks how God deals with sinners in this desperate condition. The Arminian and Wesleyan answer is that the death of Christ provided grace for all persons and that, as a result of his atonement, God extends sufficient grace to all persons through the Holy Spirit to counteract the influence of sin and to enable a positive response to God (Jn 15:26-27; 16:7-11). The initiative here is entirely God's; the sinner's part is only to respond in faith and grateful obedience (Lk 15; Rom 5:6-8; Eph 2:4-5; Phil 2:12-13). However, it is possible for sinners to resist God's initiative and to persist in sin and rebellion. In other words, God's grace *enables* and encourages a positive and saving response for *everyone,* but it does not *determine* a saving response for *anyone* (Acts 7:51). Moreover, an initial positive response of faith and obedience does not guarantee one's final salvation. It is possible to begin a genuine relationship with God but then later turn from him and persist in evil so that one is finally lost (Rom 8:12-13; 11:19-22; Gal 5:21; 6:7-10; Heb 6:1-8; Rev 2:2-7).

Unconditional election. On all of these points, Calvinists beg to differ. It is their contention that God in his sovereign grace has chosen to rescue certain specific fallen sinners from their helpless condition while leaving the rest of humanity to perish eternally. It is important to emphasize that God's choice of whom to save is entirely unconditional; it does not depend in any way on his foreknowledge of a person's faith, obedience and the like.

Limited atonement. Limited atonement is the claim that Christ died only for the elect persons whom God has chosen unconditionally to save, rather than for all persons alike, as Arminians hold. Christ's death covers all the sins of the elect and is therefore effective to save all persons for whom he died. Since his atonement is effective in this way, if he had died for all, then all would actually be saved. But all are not saved, so his atonement is limited in this respect to the elect.

It is noteworthy that recently a number of Calvinists have expressed reservations, and in some cases outright disagreement, with the traditional notion of limited atonement. Some take exception to the phrase itself, preferring alternative formulations such as "particular atonement," and argue that it is actually the Arminians who limit the atonement since they do not believe salvation is guaranteed for all persons for whom Christ died. Others dispute the substance of the notion and argue that it is incompatible with clear scriptural teaching that Christ died for all persons. Those Calvinists who acknowledge this but still want to retain the essence of the traditional Reformed position argue that Christ died for the elect in a different sense than he died for the non-elect.

Irresistible grace. This brings us to the fourth point of Calvinism, namely, irresistible grace, which is closely related to the previous two points. If God unconditionally elects who will be saved as a matter of his sovereign will, and if the atonement of Christ is effective in that it ensures the salvation of all persons for whom Christ died, then it follows naturally that the elect will not be able to resist God's sovereign choice to save them. Those who are elect cannot fail to respond positively to God's grace.

It is tempting to conclude that if grace is irresistible in this way, then God forces himself on the elect and their freedom is destroyed in the process. Indeed, this is a common criticism of Calvinism. However, this criticism is usually a misguided one, for Calvinists typically deny that God forces himself on us and insist that human freedom is maintained throughout God's saving activity. God's grace does not violate our wills but rather changes them so that sinners willingly and gladly respond.

The coherence of these claims is one of the most vexed and difficult issues in this controversy. We will explore this issue in detail below, but for now it is sufficient to note that the notion of irresistible grace should not be understood as automatically ruling out human freedom.

Perseverance of the saints. If election is unconditional and the death of Christ is necessarily effective to save for all persons for whom he died, and if saving grace cannot be resisted by these persons, then it follows that those who are chosen will persist in faith. God in his sovereignty will sustain them in faith and accomplish the final salvation for which he elected them.

It is worth noting that the notion of the perseverance of the saints sometimes goes under the label "eternal security," and as such it is often affirmed by believers who are not full-blown Calvinists. In particular, Baptists of various stripes typically defend eternal security, although many of them reject unconditional election, limited atonement and irresistible grace. While the doctrine of the perseverance of the saints is most at home in a fully Reformed context, it is not necessarily inconsistent to affirm it while denying the middle three points of Calvinism. But those who hold to eternal security while rejecting the middle three points are not truly Calvinists but are rather a sort of Calvinist-Arminian hybrid.

Although these five points represent the core of what is distinctive about Calvinism, they are hardly exhaustive. Underlying them is a particular understanding of divine sovereignty that is also characteristic of Calvinism, an issue we will explore in more detail in chapter four. But for the purposes of this book, Calvinism will be defined in terms of these five points, with allowances for qualifications about limited atonement.

CALVINIST COMEBACK?

The dispute between Calvinism and its critics has raged throughout the centuries of church history at least since the time of Augustine. The details of this conflict are fascinating, but they are not our concern here. What is noteworthy, however, is that in the past several decades Calvinism seemed largely to have lost the battle, at least in the theater of American evangelicalism. Various forms of Arminian, Wesleyan and Pentecostal theology came to predominate in much of evangelicalism in the twentieth century. While Calvinism always had its articulate advocates and has continued to exert considerable influence through educational institutions, publishing houses and other organizations, it seemed to be fighting a losing battle in the modern and postmodern church.

Recently, however, Calvinism seems to be staging a remarkable comeback. Consider the words of popular author Dave Hunt, explaining why he chose to write a book on Calvinism despite the controversy it might cause.

> I had scarcely given Calvinism a thought for years. Then
> suddenly—or so it seemed to me—in the past two years Calvinism

began emerging as an issue everywhere. Perhaps I am just waking up, but it seems to me that this peculiar doctrine is being promoted far more widely and aggressively now than I was ever aware in the past.[4]

These comments resonate with the experience of the authors of this book. While some of our academic colleagues have wondered whether we are "beating a dead horse" in writing a book on Calvinism, we have observed an intense and growing interest in this issue among Christians of all ages. Not long ago we took part in a debate on Calvinism hosted by a local church. It was attended by nearly one thousand people—most of whom looked to be high school, college or seminary students.[5] Most stayed for the entire three-hour debate, and many even remained afterward to continue questioning the participants. So much for the widely alleged claim that Generation X has little interest in theology and doctrine!

Those seeking additional evidence of Calvinism's comeback need look no further than the Southern Baptist Convention, the largest Protestant body in the United States and a major force within the diverse entity known as evangelicalism. The Baptists are a particularly interesting case study because their theology is often a hybrid of Calvinism and Arminianism. Baptist theology certainly has some strong Calvinist roots, though from the beginning the Calvinist influence was moderated. Most Baptists today are Arminian except for their belief in eternal security.

For the past several years, however, several influential Baptist leaders,

---

[4]Dave Hunt, *What Love Is This? Calvinism's Misrepresentation of God* (Sisters, Ore.: Loyal, 2002), p. 15. It may seem that people everywhere are talking about Calvinism. But when Houston Astros power hitter Lance Berkman was asked about the best conversation he ever had with a catcher at the plate, he replied, "Benito Santiago is pretty good with the banter. It is not like we are discussing Calvinism versus Arminianism or anything." Apparently batters are not near catchers long enough to get a good discussion of the matter started! See "Dan Patrick Outtakes," *ESPN the Magazine*, May 12, 2003, p. 118.

[5]This debate was held at Southland Christian Church in Lexington, Kentucky, on April 12, 2002. The Calvinist representatives in the debate were Thomas R. Schreiner and Bruce A. Ware of Southern Baptist Seminary.

many of them young, have been calling for a revival of Calvinism.[6] They have observed that segments of their denomination, like much of American evangelicalism, have become theologically thin, spiritually superficial and morally confused. As these Baptist leaders diagnose the problem, Arminian theology is a major (if not *the* major) cause of these ills. In a recent work, Ernest C. Reisinger and D. Matthew Allen describe the situation as follows: "Southern Baptists are at a crossroads. We have a choice to make. The choice is between the deep-rooted, God-centered theology of evangelical Calvinism and the man-centered, unstable theology of the other perspectives present in the convention."[7] Whether this choice is fully free or is one determined by God these writers do not say, but as the title of their book indicates, they see the resurgence of Calvinism in their denomination as nothing less than a contemporary Reformation. And when the choice is posed in such terms, Calvinism seems like the obvious theology of choice.

Others see the matter quite differently. For instance, the eminent Baptist historian William R. Estep cites approvingly the view of Andrew Fuller, an earlier participant in the Calvinist controversy, who contended that if the Baptists had not moderated their views on Calvinism, they "would have become a perfect dunghill in society."[8] The present controversy, often carried out over the Internet, has been intense, with both sides leveling strong charges against their opponents.

It is worth underscoring that the resurgence of Calvinism among the Baptists is happening particularly among young leaders such as Albert Mohler, president of Southern Baptist Theological Seminary in Louisville. Moreover, Calvinism seems to have an appeal to persons younger still, especially college students, as indicated by the growing influence of

---

[6]See Keith Hinson, "Calvinism Resurging Among SBC's Young Elites," *Christianity Today*, October 6, 1997, pp. 86-87.

[7]Ernest C. Reisinger and D. Matthew Allen, *A Quiet Revolution: A Chronicle of Beginnings of Reformation in the Southern Baptist Convention* (Cape Coral, Fl.: Founders, 2000), p. 12.

[8]William R. Estep, "Doctrines Lead to 'Dunghill' Prof Warns," <http://www.founders.org/FJ29/article1.html.>.

such campus groups as Reformed University Fellowship. It is also worth noting in this connection that Calvinism has had a significant impact on contemporary Christian music and is embraced by a number of well-known singers and artists. Caedmon's Call, one of the most popular Christian bands among college students, is openly Reformed in terms of theological conviction. This band is characterized not only by a distinctive musical sound but more importantly by their lyrics, which are among the most theologically literate in the industry. And often those lyrics convey in memorable fashion a Reformed perspective. Derek Webb, the band's articulate former lead singer, described the focus of Caedmon's Call:

> We just try to be as true as we can to what we believe to be the Biblical angle of salvation. . . . Spiritual death is like a physical corpse—what can a corpse do to help itself rise from the dead? If the language of Genesis, Romans, and Ephesians is true (that the day we ate of the fruit, we died and we have to be made alive in Christ) what kind of choice does that give us?[9]

Not all musical comments on Calvinism are so positive, however. Another band known for its rich lyrics is Vigilantes of Love, fronted by songwriter and singer Bill Mallonee. In one of his recordings, Mallonee colorfully expresses a sentiment with which many others involved in this debate can identify: "God's love shines through a prism, I'm so confused by Calvinism."[10]

The difficulty and complexity of the issues in this historic debate make his confusion altogether understandable. But such references to Calvinism in popular music are another indication of how the younger generation is coming to this issue with renewed interest and passion.

Why is Calvinism making a comeback? What is its appeal? No doubt

---

[9]"The Call of Caedmon," interview by Dan Ewald, *All Access*, November 2000, p. 27.
[10]These lyrics appear in a bonus track on the Vigilantes' CD *Room Despair*. In a later recording of the song, the words were changed to "I'm so confused by television." Apparently Mallonee has become an Arminian and is no longer confused by Calvinism.

there are several factors involved here, but let us mention just two. First, part of Calvinism's attraction is surely that it represents a stark alternative to the superficial, seeker-sensitive theology that predominates in many churches in America. In such churches, God is often reduced to a "cosmic bellhop" whose only concern is to meet whatever needs contemporary people feel in their lives. The biblical picture of a God of holy love before whom we stand guilty and in need of salvation is obscured or even denied. Doctrine is dismissed as irrelevant, Scripture is used as a self-help manual, and worship is replaced by various forms of entertainment.

Many have tired of such novelties and have recognized that if there really is a God, he must be taken much more seriously than American Christianity appears to take him. Well, the God of Calvinism is far from a cosmic bellhop. He is not obliged to do anything for you except send you to hell, and if he chooses to do so, he is glorified by your damnation. Calvinism is, if it is anything, serious about doctrine, passionate about the Bible and zealous for the glory of God. As such, it appears to be the perfect antidote to the trivialities prevalent in the contemporary church.

Second, many see Calvinism as a liberating doctrine that breathes new life into sterile and legalistic devotional life. Seminary students Jennifer L. Bayne and Sarah E. Hinlicky highlighted this factor as one of the things that led them to embrace the Calvinistic account of predestination: "Ironic as it sounds, accepting predestination into our lives was the most freeing thing that has ever happened to us spiritually. We were free to be creatures again! We no longer had the burden of trying to be the Creator."[11]

ENGAGING THE ISSUES

If embracing Calvinism is the best way to take God seriously, to acknowledge our status as creatures and to experience spiritual liberation, then we want to be Calvinists too! Obviously we don't believe this is the case,

---

[11]Jennifer L. Bayne and Sarah E. Hinlicky, "Free to Be Creatures Again," *Christianity Today,* October 23, 2000, p. 44.

or we would not have written this book. But we appreciate the appeal of Calvinism and respect many of the motives that draw believers to embrace it. Moreover, we hold high regard for all those who are currently engaging this issue, whether as convinced advocates or as those who are still trying to make up their mind. There is a lot at stake in this controversy, and it is altogether understandable that its participants express strong feelings. What is at stake is nothing less than the question of how we are saved from our sins and granted eternal life—a question toward which no believer can rationally be indifferent. If we don't care about this question, we just don't understand! Indeed, the issue is deeper still, for it concerns the ultimate matter of how God is truly worshiped and glorified. Furthermore, far-reaching practical implications for life and ministry flow from what we believe are the answers to these questions. Earnest discussion is both appropriate and desirable if it helps us get at the truth.

The widespread doctrinal indifference of our times is in part a failure to recognize the important role of argument and even controversy in the life of the church. Of course, some arguments are fruitless and hinder the work of the gospel. This will always be the case when love is absent and neither side sincerely attempts to determine the truth and obey it. But when the truth concerning matters of great importance is at stake, indifference is hard to understand and defend. In view of this, the Baptists are to be commended for their doctrinal seriousness and their passion for being faithful to the truth of the gospel. Those who look down their noses with an air of urbane superiority on the Baptists (and on those who engage in doctrinal disputes) are the ones who are misguided here.

Accordingly, we will engage these matters forthrightly and with conviction appropriate to what is at issue. However, we need more than conviction and passion to engage these questions insightfully. These disputes have occupied many of the best minds in the church, and we cannot even understand the issues involved, let alone take an informed position, without patient inquiry and careful thought. Unfortunately, sometimes both sides of this debate give the impression that what is at issue is quite simple and easy to decide. For instance, Mohler claims that "Calvinism is nothing more and nothing less than the simple assertion that salvation is all of grace, from the beginning to the end."[12] Such a statement, however, is highly misleading, however effective it may be as a sound bite, for Calvinism is considerably more than that. We would certainly agree that salvation is by grace from start to finish, but that does not make us Calvinists. The really interesting questions are how grace is bestowed and how it effects our salvation.

These are multifaceted questions, and we acknowledge that to engage them seriously requires both informed interpretation of Scripture and careful conceptual analysis. In other words, the issues involved are exegetical (matters of biblical interpretation) as well as theological and philosophical. Both sides not only defend their views biblically but also make judgments that are philosophical in nature. Unfortunately, it is sometimes asserted that Calvinists base their views on Scripture while Arminians make their case primarily from reason and philosophy. This serious misunderstanding unfairly slants the issue in favor of Calvinism before the discussion has even started.

The reality is that Calvinists no less than Arminians rely on controversial philosophical judgments and assumptions. When this is not understood, contested philosophical judgments are sometimes passed off as simple biblical truth. But the less aware we are of our philosophical assumptions, the more they control our thinking. We need to be aware of the philosophical issues as well as the biblical issues, and sorting them out from each other requires our careful effort.

We want to stress emphatically that these are *not* matters only for experts to address. Indeed, this book is written for a popular audience. Too much is at stake in the life and ministry of the church to confine intelligent discussion of these matters to the relatively small circles of the professional theologians. Accordingly, in this book we have interacted both with pop-

---

[12]R. Albert Mohler Jr., "The Reformation of Doctrine and the Renewal of the Church: A Response to Dr. William R. Estep," <www.founders.org/FJ29/article2.html>.

ular Calvinist authors as well as with more scholarly and classical sources. We have attempted to write clearly and accessibly, while also providing enough detail to represent the issues fairly.

One of us is a biblical scholar, and one of us is a philosopher. There is some overlap in our discussions, and some issues, such as the nature of sovereignty, are so central that both of us deal with them. Of course, we do so from somewhat different angles since we work in different disciplines, but we arrive at conclusions that dovetail quite nicely.

It is our goal to do justice to the full range of questions involved in order to help readers make an informed decision on these crucial matters. But again, doing so requires a measure of patience, thoughtful inquiry and plain-old hard thinking. (This is not the sort of issue one can discuss in the batter's box while waiting for a fastball down the middle!) Understanding and insight can be achieved, but they will not come cheaply or easily.

So strap your boots on. It is time to get serious.

1

APPROACHING
THE BIBLE

᮫

We can expect that when evangelicals need to define or clarify any matter of doctrine or practice, they will instinctively turn to the Bible for divine instruction. Whether they fly the flags of Calvinism or Arminianism, whether they call themselves charismatics or dispensationalists, whether they are found in mainline churches or in small denominations, evangelicals resonate deeply with the underlying conviction of Billy Graham, that whatever "the Bible says" settles it. In a book such as this, it should come as no surprise that what "the Bible says" should therefore be given first and controlling attention.

This lofty estimation of the Bible far surpasses a respect for religious literature in general or an appreciation for the Bible's place in Western culture. Rather, we hold that the Bible *stands beneath* us, giving a foundation to our understanding; that it *encircles* us, marking boundaries for our speculation; that it *resides within* us, granting and confirming the true understanding of God and of ourselves; and that it ultimately *stands over* us, judging according to the very mind of God. The Bible for us, then, is not merely one religious resource among many, but an unrivaled touchstone for shaping all Christian belief and practice.

But despite our superlative declarations about the stature of the Bible, we evangelicals find ourselves in the slightly embarrassing position of acknowledging that we do not agree on just what the Bible teaches. Too often we assume that a high view of Scripture somehow ensures that our interpretations will be faithful to the intentions of the divine Author and edifying to the people of God. But as Robert K. Johnston has observed, several religious groups who clearly fail the basic tests of orthodoxy (The Way International and the Jehovah's Witnesses) were all inerrantists, holding to a strict, high view of Scripture.[1] It is apparent that strong affirmations about the authority and truthfulness of Scripture do not guarantee a sound interpretation of it.

DIVERSITY AMONG US

Even within the evangelical fold, where classical orthodoxy and a high view of Scripture are prized, the flock is divided into dozens of interpretive camps. Even though most evangelicals agree that the Bible is the inspired and inerrant (or infallible, as variously defined and delimited) Word of God, sometimes groups among them arrive at contradictory doctrinal conclusions. If it were all a matter of differing over how many animals entered Noah's ark or over what exact day and year Jesus began his public ministry, then I suppose we could sweep such differences under the carpet and move on.

But the differences among evangelicals are not trivial, and we doubt the judgment of Carl Henry when he suggested that our differences amount to "disagreement . . . over a limited number of passages."[2] We can point to numerous issues, spanning the entire scope of Scripture, that spark fervent debate and often separate us into distinct colonies of worship, ministry and witness. Consider these issues, for example:

- the eligibility of women for ordination in pastoral and teaching ministries without restriction, as well as the nature of a wife's submission to her husband

---

[1]Robert K. Johnston, ed., *The Use of the Bible in Theology* (Atlanta: John Knox Press, 1983), p. 10.
[2]Carl F. H. Henry, *God, Revelation and Authority* (Waco, Tex.: Word, 1979), 6:252.

- the relationship between church and state, and the viability of a specifically Christian legislative agenda for a (largely secular) modern democracy
- the moral status of state-sponsored violence, whether in the form of declared war, restricted peacekeeping military action or capital punishment
- the intersection between modern science and the Bible, with focus on the relationship between the creation accounts (Gen 1—2) and the prevailing theories of the big bang and biological evolution
- the fate of those who have never heard the gospel and of those who have heard or seen only a distorted presentation or modeling of it
- the theology of the sacraments, especially baptism—its proper mode (immersion only?), its proper subjects (infants or believers?) and the sense in which it imparts grace[3]

We can add to these the interests of this book—the questions that have defined the Calvinist-Arminian debate for centuries:

- Does God determine, solely according to his own unilaterally established will, exactly who will be saved and who will be lost?
- Did the atonement of Jesus make provision to save only the elect, or has actual provision been made for the salvation of the whole race of humankind?

---

[3]To these matters we could add *the appropriateness of divorce and remarriage,* with respect to the church's blessing and to (added) restrictions laid on ministers; *the scope and function of spiritual gifts* in this present "dispensation," with special reference to speaking in tongues, words of wisdom and healing; *the degree of corrective discipline* that ought to be administered by a congregation to its spiritually wayward members; *the normative spiritual profile of the Christian life,* with regard to the possibility of real moral transformation, victory over sin and genuine Christlikeness; *the viability of a clergy-laity distinction* and the role of ordination in creating and maintaining this distinction; *God's end-time program* (signs, rapture, tribulation, millennium, multiple judgments and final state) along with the definition and function of Israel in the total plan; *the role of Satan and the demonic* as personal, intentional, and particular forces of evil in the experience of believers; *the nature and scope of exorcism and spiritual warfare* as valued practices within the church; and *the nature of eternal punishment for the wicked.*

- Are human beings so fallen that they must be saved exclusively through the unilateral and unconditional action of God?
- Is it possible for human beings to resist (successfully) the saving approaches of God's grace?
- Does God enable all persons to respond positively to the available light?
- Can any who were once truly redeemed through faith in Christ fail to receive final salvation?

When considered together, the content and scope of these divides should be sobering. They range in their focus from the nature of God to the nature of human beings, from the time before creation to time beyond the final judgment, from the boundaries of salvation to those of damnation, from the contemplation of perplexing abstractions to the gritty business of daily life. If we admit that we haven't been able to reach a consensus among ourselves on matters of such importance, just how meaningful is it for us to continue affirming with glowing terms the authority of the Bible? How useful is it to confess that the Bible "has the last word," when we haven't determined among ourselves just what that last word says? How much disagreement can we experience before we must admit that the Bible, like uninterpreted glossolalia, is a "trumpet [that] does not sound a clear call" (1 Cor 14:8)?

THE QUESTION OF CLARITY

In effect, we are inquiring about the *perspicuity* (clarity) of Scripture. Does the Bible speak clearly about all things, most things or only a few? Should we expect clear resolution when we bring to the Bible our questions about how we should live, to say nothing of the flurry of questions surrounding the Arminian and Calvinist debate? What should we say about the communicative effectiveness of Scripture, and how should we speak to each other whenever consensus over its teaching continues to elude us?

Most of us hesitate to admit that the Bible is not perfectly clear on all counts. Many of us worry that any hedging along these lines may weaken our witness in the world and open up floodgates of doubt for the weak, or that disagreement may tempt some of us to excuse sinful behavior by blaming an imagined defect in Scripture. These are worthy fears, but they can be effectively countered. And the mere presence of these fears is not sufficient ground for ignoring the troubling realities of diverse and incongruent interpretation.

Some may resist the direction of our discussion simply by declaring, "The Bible is plenty clear to me! How could the 'days' of Genesis 1 be anything other than twenty-four-hour solar days, since each has an evening and a morning?" Or "Obviously the temple (which was destroyed in A.D. 70) will soon be rebuilt, since we know that it must be destroyed in the coming tribulation" (see Mk 13). Or "It's perfectly clear that the Bible considers any remarried person whose spouse is still living an adulterer" (see Rom 7:1-3).

But this confuses a subjective sense of clarity with the sort of clarity that might be externally demonstrated. Consider the scenario of a sinking ship, with the captain and a new crew trapped together in a low-lying compartment. Being unfamiliar with the layout of the ship, the crewmates are dependent on the captain's instructions for finding their way around the maze of damaged bulkheads to the open air above. Seriously wounded and unable to lead his crew out, the captain describes the one pathway that will lead them to safety. As soon as he finishes his verbal instructions, the crewmates scramble for their lives—each in a different direction!

We can imagine that each crewmate was absolutely certain that he or she understood the captain clearly. But the *internal* certainty of each crewmate failed to match the instructions of the captain. It is possible that the one crewmate who felt *most* certain that she understood the captain was indeed the one who found her way out. But we can also imagine that the one crewmate who felt *least* certain was the one who succeeded. He may have strained to hear the captain's voice, realizing that he missed a few words here and there. He may have been stunned to see his mates scattering in different directions and may have moved hesitantly in the direction his best sense of the captain's words indicated.

What are we suggesting? That in matters of biblical interpretation our own sense of certainty about what the Bible says on a given matter can't determine whether our particular understanding of the Bible is viable. If we think you may be perfectly certain *and* perfectly wrong at the same time, we must admit that the same is possible for us. These interpretive differences suggest that at least *some* of our cherished interpretations must be misguided, however certain we are of them, and no matter how clearly we believe the Bible teaches them.

PROTESTANT INSTINCTS AND HISTORY

Don't our Protestant instincts tell us that this discussion is moving in the wrong direction? Weren't two Reformation keynotes that the Bible can be understood by the common person and that the individual was free from the infallible and authoritative interpretation of Scripture as supplied by the Roman Catholic Church? If we surrender a robust confidence in the Bible's clarity, does the door slam shut on the entire Protestant project?

The specific terms of the classic debate on this matter are worth recalling in some detail. The principle players were Martin Luther, the great Reformer, and Erasmus, reputedly the greatest Christian scholar of his day. The two men struggled through a tortured and confusing relationship, but they were not the truculent enemies Protestant memory suggests.[4] Erasmus himself was a reformer, pouring enormous energies into the spiritual and moral renewal of the Roman Catholic Church, making not a few enemies among its leadership. He spoke positively about Luther and his aims and was perceived by many to be a friend of the Protestant movement. For his part, Luther sought Erasmus's public endorsement, believing that the reputation of the great scholar would

---

[4]For a convenient summary of these matters, see Philip S. Watson, ed. and trans., *Luther's Works* (Philadelphia: Fortress, 1972), 33:5-13.

add precious momentum to his own efforts of reform. Wishing to ride above the fray, Erasmus refused both Lutheran and Roman entreaties to break his neutrality longer than anyone thought possible.

Eventually Erasmus published *De Libero Arbitrio* (1524) to offer correction to Luther's belief in absolute determinism and to his blunt reform tactics. Within this irenic discourse, Erasmus collected and commented on various passages of Scripture that had bearing on the question of the freedom and bondage of the human will. As he labored to discern the sense of each text and to weigh its effect on the matter, he allowed that some biblical passages might be "secret places . . . into which God has not wished us to penetrate more deeply."[5]

Luther replied with the mighty force of his argumentative skill. (We will put aside his treatment of the primary issue of human freedom to focus on his reaction to Erasmus's claim that parts of Scripture might be obscure.) In a "take no prisoners" mode, Luther charged the great scholar with dishonoring the Bible itself:

> But that in Scripture there are some things abstruse, and everything is not plain—this is an idea put about by the ungodly Sophists, with those lips you also speak here, Erasmus; but they have never produced, nor can they produce, a *single article* to prove this mad notion of theirs. . . . Let miserable men, therefore, stop imputing with blasphemous perversity the darkness and obscurity of their own hearts to the wholly clear Scriptures of God.[6]
>
> In short, if Scripture is obscure or ambiguous, what point was there in God's giving it to us? Are we not obscure and ambiguous enough without having our obscurity, ambiguity, and darkness augmented for us from Heaven? . . . I say with respect to the *whole* Scripture, I will not have *any part* of it called obscure. . . . Those

---

[5]Charles E. Trinkaus, ed., *Controversies*, trans. Peter MacArdle and Clarence H. Miller, vol. 76 of *The Collected Works of Erasmus* (Toronto: University of Toronto Press, 1999), pp. 8-9.

[6]Watson, *Luther's Works,* 33:25, 27 (emphasis added).

who deny the *perfect clarity and plainness* of the Scriptures leave us *nothing but darkness.*[7]

Throughout his argument, Luther insisted that no middle ground could be found between confessing the Bible to be a blazing sun without shadows and conceding the Bible to be a hopelessly uncertain and thereby useless guide for believers. We must choose, Luther seemed to demand, between these stark alternatives and the train of theological conclusions that follow our choice.

Erasmus had hit a nerve, for Luther's vigorous protest in defense of the clarity of the Bible no doubt had less to do with the specific point being debated than with the threat Luther sensed to the entire Reform movement. If the truths of the Bible were not accessible to common believers, if the Bible had to be interpreted according to the theological framework established by the authority of the church, and if the clergy and specialized scholars were required to make sense of God's Word, then no one could ever deliver correction to the church and its accumulated traditions from an independent reading of Scripture. The rallying cry of *sola scriptura* would be meaningless apart from an accompanying declaration of *clara scriptura*.

While Luther supplied strong theological arguments for advocating the clarity of Scripture, various philosophical and political currents converged throughout the following centuries to further strengthen this stream of Protestant conviction. The rising tide of scientific inquiry infused Western culture with confidence in the scientific method. As commonly understood, the method promised that any rational human being who desired to discover truth could collect evidence, dispassionately evaluate that evidence and objectively infer right answers. It is no accident, then, that we commonly describe our own strategies for interpreting the Bible with scientific terminology (e.g., *evidence, inference, objectivity, method, procedure*) and deploy those strategies in machinelike fashion.

---

[7]Ibid., 33:93-94.

The parallel current of Scottish common-sense realism asserted that all persons possess "pre-rational intuition for distinguishing right from wrong, truth from falsehood, and facts from illusion."[8] Supposedly, personal observations would yield a direct and reliable knowledge of reality, meaning that all persons share a sizable tract of common ground from which to operate. The effects of common-sense realism permeated the layers of the Protestant education, further reinforcing the conviction that Christians, employing their common sense, could read the Bible for all it was worth.

Finally, by the beginning of the eighteenth century, political activists like Benjamin Austin Jr. of Boston were directly linking the political freedom of humans with their right to interpret Scripture for themselves apart from the oppressive control of the clergy and other social elites.[9] Radical Jeffersonians insisted that true political reform, which would resurrect "the spirit of 1776," must involve a reform of religion and its hierarchical structure. But these radicals were merely expressing the popular and pervasive orthodoxy of the right of "private interpretation" of Scripture.[10] The belief that all people had such a right fueled confidence in the Bible's clarity.

This bold Protestant confidence in the understandability of the Bible is still strongly affirmed today, especially in the United States. Informal Bible studies abound in which participants of all ages, backgrounds and educational levels gather with the assurance that a reverent, attentive reading of the Bible itself will reliably yield truth. Bibles without any running commentary to guide the reader in making right sense of the text are distributed by the millions to hospitals, prisons, schools, armies and hotels. Carl F. H. Henry, the aforementioned evangelical luminary, expresses well the conviction underlying these behaviors of ours: "The New Testament, significantly, was written in Koine, that is, popular mar-

---

[8]Nathan O. Hatch and Mark A. Noll, eds., *The Bible in America* (New York: Oxford University Press, 1982), p. 115.
[9]Ibid., pp. 64-66.
[10]Ibid., p. 64.

ketplace Greek, and it is intended for the masses. . . . The Bible was and is still addressed to the multitudes, to masses of the poor, uneducated, and even enslaved."[11] If ever a book was written to be read and understood by all, the Protestant believes, the Bible is it.

So it's easy to see why evangelicals struggle in the face of internal theological debate. If our deepest religious instincts tell us that the Bible is clear and open even to the simplest of readers, then our options are radically limited when we try to account for Calvinist or Arminian interpretations of the Bible. "He must be intellectually incompetent," we conclude, or "she must be morally perverse" (i.e., she understands what the Bible says but stubbornly refuses to yield to its truth).

While we grant that a few intellectually incompetent and morally perverse people have participated in the Calvinist-Arminian debate, we can surely agree that both sides of the debate are well represented by competently trained scholars whose hearts are humbly surrendered to God. Neither moral nor intellectual slander should characterize our theological dialogue.

MEANS OF ACCOUNTING FOR DIVERSITY

So how do we account for deeply diverse interpretations of a "clear" Bible? Those familiar with Luther's treatise *On the Bondage of the Will* have already recognized that our above quotations are selective and that Luther's understanding of Scripture's clarity was not quite so simple as we have portrayed it. Yes, many of his claims were cast in absolute language which seemed to eliminate any possibility of nuance. But alongside those extreme claims, Luther qualified his position, making his claims somewhat more realistic.

First, he distinguished the clarity of the biblical text itself from our imperfect understanding of its vocabulary and grammar. Whether or not such a distinction is helpful in the long run, it signals the importance Luther attached to a detailed knowledge of biblical languages and the

---

[11]Henry, *God, Revelation and Authority*, 6:252, 283.

linguistic worlds in which they functioned. Furthermore, it implies that there are better or worse interpretations of Scripture, corresponding to a reader's ability to handle the original languages; therefore the Bible will be clearer to some and less clear to others.

Second, Luther admitted that some Scripture passages might be obscure, but he insisted that interpretation could be helped by coupling these passages with clearer texts elsewhere in the Bible.[12] In theory such a procedure sounds helpful, but in practice it is fraught with difficulty. For example, do the texts make it clear that God wills all human beings to be saved, or that God wills to save only some humans? Whichever set of texts is judged *at the outset* to be the clearer will end up controlling our interpretation of those passages we have already classified as ambiguous. Luther's proposal, then, cannot adjudicate between persons who disagree over which passages should exercise interpretive control over other passages. Luther and Erasmus themselves were unable to agree on which set of passages was clearer in the matter of free will and determinism. Their impasse demonstrates that Luther's principle often fails precisely when needed most.

Third, Luther acknowledged scriptural ambiguity in the precise terms he used to affirm the Bible's clarity:

> I admit . . . that there are many texts in the Scriptures that are obscure and abstruse. . . . But these texts in no way hinder a knowledge of all the *subject matter* of the Scripture. . . . Namely that Christ the Son of God has been made man, that God is three and one, that Christ has suffered for us and is to reign eternally. . . . The *subject matter* of the Scriptures, therefore, is all quite accessible, even though some texts are still obscure.[13]

It is difficult to exaggerate the significance of this shift in Luther's emphasis. For instead of claiming that biblical *texts* were clear, Luther

---

[12]Watson, *Luther's Works*, 33:26.
[13]Ibid. (emphasis added).

attributed clarity to the *subject matter* of the Bible, to its *essential message*. Though a humble reader of the Bible may fumble through this or that text, he could *not* miss the Bible's core truth. In this simple shift—from defending the clarity of the Bible's *words* to defending the clarity of the Bible's *essential message*—Luther essentially conceded huge territory to Erasmus but opened up possibilities for understanding what it means to espouse the clarity of Scripture.

Just how condensed Luther considered this "subject matter" to be can be discerned from the summary of it he made for Erasmus: the incarnation, the Trinity, the atonement and the eternal messianic kingdom.[14] For Luther, these truths constituted the core knowledge necessary for trusting God for salvation through Christ. God's guarantee to the reader is not that any given word, verse or passage of the Bible will be clear, nor that any given doctrine taught in the Bible will be understood,[15] but that a small circle of truth, the *essential* subject matter of the Bible, the minimal understanding necessary for salvation, will clearly shine forth.

While the blustery Luther, with his categorical denials of any ambiguity in the Bible, stands as the champion of the humble reader, the reasoning Luther stands within the stream of creeds and scholarship that defines more soberly and narrowly the scope and nature of the Bible's clarity. Such care and reflection can be seen, for example, in the reserved language of the Westminster Confession: "All things in Scripture are not alike plain in themselves, nor alike clear unto all; yet *those things which are necessary . . . for salvation* are so clearly propounded . . . that not only the learned, but also the unlearned . . . may attain unto a *sufficient* understanding of them."[16]

In similar fashion, Calvinist theologian Louis Berkhof reduces the assured clarity of the Bible to its saving function: "*The knowledge necessary*

---

[14]Ibid.

[15]Donald G. Bloesch, *Holy Scripture* (Downers Grove, Ill.: InterVarsity Press, 1994), p. 192.

[16]John H. Leith, ed., *Creeds of the Churches*, rev. ed. (Atlanta: John Knox Press, 1973), p. 196 (emphasis added).

unto salvation, though not equally clear on every page of the Bible, is yet conveyed to man throughout the Bible in such a simple and comprehensible form that one who is *earnestly seeking salvation* can . . . easily obtain for himself the *necessary knowledge.*"[17]

But the tone of these limited affirmations is not one of embarrassment or despair. Even in so radically reducing the scope and sense of the Bible's clarity, Protestants can confidently confess that the Holy Spirit moves powerfully through Scripture to bring us to a saving knowledge of God. As Robert McAfee Brown expressed half a century ago,

> We do not see everything . . . but we see Jesus. . . . We may see darkly, but we do see. We see enough to walk with confidence, we see enough to commit our lives to God, we see enough to trust God, we see enough to believe that God can meet our deepest need. We see enough light shed on the mystery of Christ to know that he is the clue to the meaning of life.[18]

This balanced and cautious accounting of the Bible's clarity creates space for meaningful discussion about Christian doctrine. Since Protestant theology makes no claim that the Bible is crystal clear beyond that minimal knowledge necessary for salvation, it implicitly acknowledges that Christians may differ without having to accuse each other of intellectual weakness or moral corruption. Rather, those who insist that their entire theological program flows straight from the Bible—that it is biblically provable in every detail, that it stands as the inescapable interpretation for every rational and moral Christian—violate the caution, the restraint and the modesty of the classic Protestant view of Scripture. We want to be part of a vigorous discussion about what the Bible teaches, but we want to speak with a humility fitting for limited human beings who stand beneath the Word of God.

---

[17]Louis Berkhof, *Systematic Theology,* rev. and enl. ed. (Grand Rapids, Mich.: Eerdmans, 1996), p. 167 (emphasis added).

[18]Robert McAfee Brown, *The Bible Speaks to You* (Philadelphia: Westminster Press, 1955), pp. 307-8.

AN ESCAPE FROM THEOLOGICAL INQUIRY AND DEBATE?

Have we now undercut the entire project of this book? After all, if we are claiming that the Bible might not be as clear as we might have hoped, even about those issues directly related to the Calvinist-Arminian debate, why should we invest any time at all in the swamps and quagmires of this longstanding theological debate?

This question is neither meaningless nor trivial. If our labors will not eliminate doctrinal or ethical uncertainties but instead only deepen divisions within the body of Christ, then it is no wonder that many Christians consider biblical and theological study to be a waste of time and a dangerous diversion from the real work of the church. And if we all agree that the Bible *does* communicate a *saving* knowledge of God quite apart from technical study and theological argument, why should we press into uncertain territory?

Whether at a conscious or subconscious level, many evangelicals much prefer this pathway of minimal theology. They wistfully ask, "Why can't we all just get along, loving Jesus and sharing the gospel?"

Without wishing to dampen any zeal for evangelism or communal love, we insist that theological minimalism fails to measure up to biblical portraits of discipleship. Parachurch organizations with narrowly defined missions (e.g., famine relief, medical assistance, legal advocacy for the poor) may indeed function well with minimal theology, but only because they are not attempting to provide the full range of "body life" necessary for Christian discipleship. When we accept Jesus' vision of discipleship as including both *evangelism* and *instruction* in the full range of Christian truth (Mt 28:19-20) and the scope of Paul's ministry vision (Col 1:28), then we realize that Christian discipleship must engage the whole of Christian truth, not a slice of it. Followers of Jesus are commanded to "leave the elementary teachings . . . and go on to maturity" (Heb 6:1).

Even if we lay aside the force of these biblical mandates, we can still observe that theological minimalism is unworkable. If we consider the simplest form of evangelism, that of responding to those who inquire about the Christian faith, the theological minimalist is already at a loss to follow the advice of 1 Peter 3:15, "Always be prepared to give an answer to everyone who asks you to give the reason for the hope that you have." Reasons, after all, involve some degree of rational assessment: weighing causes and effects, making distinctions between valid and invalid conclusions, and anticipating how the inquirer might judge the strength of our response. This leads us deeper into the fabric of biblical revelation and requires careful reading and reflection.

Examining even the simplest form of evangelistic preaching, we find that our language reveals our theological assumptions about the nature of conversion, the possibility of faith, the scope of election, the inner working of atonement, the degree of certainty about our salvation, the relationship between faith and obedience, the role of the Holy Spirit and of rationality in faith, and so on. The strategies we use, our expectations of their success, the guarantees we offer, the tone of our appeal, the measure of "persuasive responsibility" we feel—all of these features of the evangelistic project are the expressions of our underlying theological commitments, *whether we acknowledge them or not.* Charles G. Finney's theology led him to invite public response to his evangelistic preaching, just as D. Martyn Lloyd-Jones's theology led him to discourage public response to his evangelistic preaching. Far from being theologically neutral territory, the "conversion zone" may be the most highly charged of all theological turf; there we receive an assessment of our past, a new identity and a vision of our placement in God's eternal purposes.

Not even the simplest moral instruction in the Christian life can be offered in a theological vacuum. One prominent feature of Promise Keepers is the call to sexual purity. Simple enough. Or is it? Even if we agree completely on what sorts of behavior constitute sexual impurity, the question of how one lives a pure life immediately arises.

Some would offer strategies for spiritual warfare against Satan and his demons. Others would suggest we seek out spiritually sensitive counseling or an explicit program of spiritual formation and accountability. Still others would point to a need for a particular "experience" of baptism in the Holy Spirit for power or for inward cleansing by the Holy Spirit. None of these recommendations is neutral, but rather each flows out of a particular matrix of biblical interpretation and theological constructions. It should be clear that any organization like Promise Keepers, which emphasizes its nondenominational character, will find it impossible to recommend *any* pathway to holy living without diving headlong into the swirl of biblical and theological interpretation.

Nor can Christian discipleship thrive with a cafeteria approach to theology, offering all theological options and leaving the "buyer" to choose according to personal taste. Consider the questions church leaders face daily, such as how we comfort the grieving or how we discipline the fallen minister. Doing theology, after all, can hardly be a matter of individual preferences, for it necessarily entails *community* decisions about how we live *together* to honor God and to bear witness for the gospel in a broken world.

So where have we arrived in our discussion? We have accepted what creeds, scholars and our own experiences have taught us: that the Bible does communicate in a sufficiently clear way what is necessary for salvation, but that it does not *guarantee* to the people of God an accurate understanding of the larger body of Christian truth. Even so, we are under mandate, from both biblical commands and practical necessity, to go beyond the minimal—to embrace the whole counsel of God and construct theology that enables faithful Christian living. We have been called to embark on a journey involving risks and requiring humility, a journey from which we cannot turn away.

THE TOOLS OF EXEGESIS

Are there tools that might help us judge the likelihood of a given interpretation? Yes. One tool prized by many evangelicals is *exegesis*, the formal study of the biblical text in it original languages, enriched by engagement with the literary, historical and cultural contexts of the Bible. My (Joe's) own romance with exegesis began in my sophomore year of college, when I was overcome with an insatiable passion to study the Greek New Testament. I lined my shelf with the best grammars, lexicons and concordances available. After a year of beginning instruction, I plunged into the book of Romans with all my might, and I continued my development by filling the remainder of my college and seminary years with original-language exegesis courses. Eventually, I became a seminary professor devoted to teaching effective biblical interpretation.

At the outset I was fueled by the hope that my mastery of Greek grammar and word-study methods would bring me to theological nirvana. Armed with this knowledge and these skills, I hoped to be able to resolve with perfect objectivity any theological issue at hand. But such a vision does not accord with the nature of language, the tone of divine revelation or the character of interpretation. I came to see the inherent openness of every interpretive process. Grammatical rules function more like the rules of a game: they form the boundaries within which subtle judgments and close decisions take place. But within the boundaries, players can still express individual judgment, boldness and creativity.

As we work our way through any scriptural passage, we will encounter interpretive questions that can be answered differently within the linguistic rules. While exegetical methods prescribe helpful procedures and point out pitfalls to avoid,[19] they don't form an algorithm that mechanically processes a text and neatly generates indisputable answers. At many points along the way, discernment, more than deduction, will be the necessary gift of the exegete.

Therefore, whenever we hear the claim that a single verse of Scripture "absolutely proves" a given theological position, we must conclude that the speaker either is unaware of the nature of the interpretive enterprise or has engaged in rhetorical flourish, and neither alternative holds promise for advancing fruitful dialogue. Conversely,

---

[19]D. A. Carson, *Exegetical Fallacies* (Grand Rapids, Mich.: Baker, 1984). The entire book catalogs a helpful list of "sins" that interpreters of Scripture should avoid.

though we disagree with his conclusions, we commend the tone modeled by Wayne Grudem in his study of Hebrews 6:4-6. In addressing this passage, Grudem admits that the Arminian interpretation (i.e., that some true Christians may fall forever from grace) is well-founded on the cumulative force of the words and grammar of that passage. He then suggests that "a different interpretation . . . is possible" and goes on to show why he judges his Calvinist proposal to be a better accounting of the textual data.[20] Grudem demonstrates throughout his study that the practice of interpretation involves weighing carefully the nearly balanced options, discerning probabilities hinted at by the surrounding literary context and using one's best powers of reason. Given the degree of play possible within each of these parameters, we should all speak with a measure of care and reserve when delivering our interpretive conclusions.

THE TOOLS OF REASON, INTUITION AND EXPERIENCE

It should be clear from all of this that interpreters play an active role in making sense of biblical texts and that our use of reason leads the way in much of our interpretive work. But here, as with exegetical method, we must guard against a naive optimism that promises too much and reflects too little. Sometimes we imagine that a short course in logic can inoculate us against all of the known logical fallacies, thereby guaranteeing the validity of our biblical interpretations. But we will still find that the *application* of these principles spawns fervent debate and fails to deliver the certainty we had hoped to attain. In other words, the use of rational principles takes place within the larger arena of the interpreter's wisdom, judgment and spiritual sensitivity—matters not easily quantified or reduced to objective standards.

This underlying arena of wisdom, judgment and sensitivity includes whatever we each consider to be axiomatic truths, that is, mat-

---

[20]Wayne Grudem, "Perseverance of the Saints: A Case Study from the Warning Passages in Hebrews," in *Still Sovereign*, ed. Thomas R. Schreiner and Bruce A. Ware (Grand Rapids, Mich.: Baker, 2000), pp. 133-82, esp. p. 139.

ters we consider true even if we cannot prove them to be true. Many Arminians consider it axiomatic that human beings make decisions (even eternal ones) by free will, that such choices have not been caused by any force outside themselves and that other real choices could have been made. Such an understanding of human behavior, they aver, is so obvious from our 'sensation of free choice that it is "practically unquestionable." Furthermore, they note, a great many biblical passages harmonize quite nicely with the perception that we act as free agents.

Calvinists are quick to point out the weakness of such a means of establishing truth, since what is "practically unquestionable" varies from person to person, from culture to culture and from age to age. Even the slightest awareness of the progress in science and technology will show that the common sense of one generation has repeatedly been shattered by the next's in stunning fashion. And if we add to this the biblical teaching that human thinking itself has been distorted by sin and is limited by its creatureliness, then we have every reason to tread lightly when constructing a worldview on what anyone imagines to be unquestionably obvious.

And yet many Calvinists surely suffer from variations of this same disease; repeatedly, assertions about what it must mean for God to be sovereign slip to the level of an axiomatic claim. In other words, many Calvinists simply can't imagine that a "real God" doesn't minutely and omnipotently control every detail of the created world. Subtract this minute determination from the activity of God, and you eliminate, from their point of view, the very core of God's "god-ness."[21] The axiomatic nature of this conviction for many is illustrated by the tone of Luther's charge that "natural reason itself is forced to admit that the living and true God *must* be one who by his freedom imposes necessity on us, since *obviously* he would be a *ridiculous* God . . . if he could not *and did not* do

---

[21]R. K. McGregor Wright, *No Place for Sovereignty* (Downers Grove, Ill.: InterVarsity Press, 1996), p. 220.

everything, or if anything took place without him."[22] We fear that large pieces of Luther's theology were hammered out inversely on the anvil of the "unimaginable" and that he then shoehorned biblical texts into serving his unexamined conviction.

Our point here is not to parade Luther as an oddity but rather to use him as an illustration of the challenge that we all face, Calvinists and Arminians alike. None of us can ever approach a theological question or a biblical text from a sanitized, neutral position. We all have personal histories and locations within our traditions that we cannot simply wish away.[23] Whoever she is and wherever she stands, the interpreter necessarily brings *her whole self* (both good and bad) into the equation. Our expectations, fears and motivations are with us as we read the sacred text, and they shape the ways we judge and discern, weigh and value, reason and decide.

Our experiential history can, of course, deliver valuable insight as we read the Bible. But our individual experiences will also limit and distort our reading of the Bible, even as we fervently seek to honor all of the grammatical, linguistic and logical rules at our disposal. Unless individual readings are tested against the experiences and interpretations of others, we will likely fail to arrive at a "faithful" reading of Scripture.

THE VALUE OF COMMUNITY

Fruitful Bible reading should take on the character of a community project shared by those who fear individualistic interpretation and long for partnership among God's people in learning and living the gospel. As Moisés Silva notes, "Modern Evangelicalism, fearing the abuse of church authority, has not always appreciated the need of Christians to submit their understanding of Scripture to the judgment of the established church." Yet in recent years, observes Silva, "there appears to be a new sensitivity to the significance of corporate authority in the church,"

---

[22]Watson, *Luther's Works*, 33:189 (emphasis added).
[23]See Wright's critique of Antony Flew in *No Place*, p. 198.

which should not be viewed as an alien intrusion, since "the Reformers' emphasis on the right of private interpretation was balanced by a recognition that no man was an island."[24]

But the determination to read the Bible within Christian community and against the backdrop of the whole of Christian history will set into motion even more questions and options than we had at the start. Of the many and varied Christian communities of interpretation, which one should we privilege? And at what point in its own evolutionary development should we privilege that community? How ought we to measure the likelihood that this community or that one has found a better reading? Does its greater success in evangelism and missions point to its greater faithfulness or rather to its dilution of the gospel with corrosive cultural values?

How do we weigh the luminaries who represent competing communities? As R. C. Sproul wisely observes, one can set a Philipp Melanchthon against a Martin Luther, a John Wesley against a John Calvin, a Charles Finney against a Jonathan Edwards, and a Billy Graham against a Philip Hughes to demonstrate the impossibility of proving the more valid biblical interpretation.[25] And while all of us may be tempted from time to time to evaluate theological positions according to the supposed successes or failures, the weaknesses or strengths, and the growths or contractions of the various communities of faith espousing them, this is surely a precarious venture complicated by a host of unknown factors.[26] In the end, we suggest that appealing to the larger Christian community, not only in its present latitude but also in its historical longitude, can res-

---

[24]Moisés Silva, *Has the Church Misread the Bible?* (Grand Rapids, Mich.: Zondervan, 1987), pp. 79-80.

[25]R. C. Sproul, *Chosen by God* (Wheaton, Ill.: Tyndale House, 1986), p. 16.

[26]Norman Geisler claims that Augustine was the first Christian luminary to argue against an operative moral free will in humans and that not until Luther was this perspective again endorsed. If true, such an assessment may stand as a mark against the Augustinian view, but it does not overthrow it entirely. It is possible that the people of God can come to see truth in Scripture in ways not fully grasped by previous generations. Norman Geisler, *Chosen but Free* (Minneapolis: Bethany House, 1999), pp. 145-54.

cue us from a narrow-minded, individualistic reading of Scripture. But the breadth of interpretive options often increases when we reach out beyond our personal boundaries, with no reliable strategy available for judging by external means which communities have stronger or weaker interpretations of Scripture.

A HOPEFUL OUTLOOK

How should we approach the Bible, and what expectations should we bring for understanding it? Our survey indicates that none of the resources available to us can definitively resolve the challenges we face in interpreting the Bible. We acknowledge the limitations of all tools and strategies and the difficulty of always employing them wisely. Furthermore, we realize that we all stand within the currents of the very realities we are trying to understand; there is no "dry ground" of pure objectivity from which to survey the whole. Biblical interpretation cannot be reduced to a technology.

Even more daunting is the realization that we are touching on the awesome reality of a transcendent God whose ways and thoughts are higher than ours. At many points in our exploration the trail will undoubtedly become impassable for human understanding, and we must then drop to our knees and adore the One who made us. Indeed, "The secret things belong to the LORD our God" (Deut 29:29). Yet this same verse continues, "but the things revealed belong to us and to our children forever, that we may follow all the words of this law." The self-revelation of God, both in Scripture and in the incarnate Son, invites us to search out the truth of God and gives us the hope of finding its contours as we seek, ask and knock (Mt 7:7).

Therefore we offer our work blended with realism and optimism. We will employ all of the exegetical and rational tools available to us, while fully acknowledging their limits and ours. We will invoke the reputations of reliable scholars and theological traditions, while admitting that neither can provide absolute closure to debate. We firmly believe that the interpretations we offer are stronger than those of our debate partners, but we also fully realize that they think just the opposite.[27] We offer our work in the confidence that all of us ultimately are depending on God to guide us into all truth through the ministry of the Spirit (Jn 16:13). Therefore we offer our work to the people of God as another installment in the larger conversation across the centuries that has sought to enable us all more fully to love, serve and glorify God.

---

[27]We have found the insights of Telford Work to be helpful in winning a place within the life of the church for healthy theological debate. In large part he depends on the insights of Alasdair MacIntyre: "MacIntyre envisions traditions as ongoing arguments over the realities they seek to comprehend. Rational inquiry . . . is itself inextricably embodied in a tradition of enquiry. When a church enquires into the Bible's meaning, it inevitably does so as a church. And a church, like any human community, inevitably features internal and external differences, conflicts, and incommensurabilities, which make it a living tradition of inquiry. A tradition is a kind of interminable argument over the nature of the tradition itself. Yet interminability does not mean futility. . . . In the church's language, the communal practice of discernment guides the Church into God's truth. As it seeks it finds." Telford Work, *Living and Active* (Grand Rapids, Mich.: Eerdmans, 2002), p. 238.

2

ENGAGING THE BIBLE

◈

Calvinists commonly charge that the sweeping transformation of American Protestant Christianity from being mostly Calvinist during the founding stages of our nation's history to being mostly Arminian during the present era has been caused by a turning away from the hard, clear teaching of Scripture toward the smooth and easy heresy of humanism. While the Reformers and their true offspring recovered a gloriously God-centered universe with a God-centered story of salvation, Arminians and their allies have steadily diluted the scriptural message with their feel-good theology and have thereby produced a tasty but deadly mixture.

According to the Calvinist analysis, Arminianized Christianity has pushed God to the edge of the stage and has shoved the human being to the center. In this revolution, human beings have now assumed the role of judging truth by their own reason, conscience or personal taste. Humans have assumed the power of determining their own destinies by making autonomous choices, and they have thereby assumed the right of overriding God's will by rejecting God's salvation plan. The marginalized God can now only hope for the best resolution to the drama of redemption; he occasionally negotiates or intervenes in the play but is unable to overcome the foundational principle of all reality—human autonomy![1]

---

[1]R. K. McGregor Wright, *No Place for Sovereignty* (Downers Grove, Ill.: InterVarsity Press, 1996), pp. 215-32.

We acknowledge that Arminianism can be associated with theological trends that tend to be controversial, occasionally unfortunate or perhaps completely contrary to biblical teaching. Liberal Protestantism, more akin to Arminianism than to Calvinism, is often indistinguishable from full-blown secular humanism. The God-language encountered there can sound like empty echoes from an earlier era, a time when people actually believed God was working dramatically and effectively on earth. The vertical pillars of a sounder theology have been melted down and recast as horizontal beams: religion has been flattened completely into social ethics. Concurrently, the Bible has been sharply demoted, serving as one source among many others for ordering theology and life.

American evangelicalism, also fairly characterized as Arminian, has earned the well-deserved reputation of being theologically shallow and easily blended with alien aspects of folk or civil religion. Many American Christians speak of Jesus and the Bible in the highest terms imaginable, but they seem unable to offer thoughtful reflections about or explanations of either. This theological vacuum draws in any number of beliefs hostile to the gospel and harmful to Christian living.

On another front, the Canadian theologian Clark Pinnock has spearheaded a scholarly challenge to Calvinism under the banner of Open Theism. Pinnock, who had once earned a scholarly reputation as a Calvinist, now stands as the most prominent and notorious convert to an Arminian perspective. We say notorious because his Open Theism actually moves beyond classic Arminianism toward process theology. It has drawn close scrutiny and even the condemnation by some as heresy. Though Pinnock has drawn a line in the sand between himself and process theology, his denial that God infallibly knows the future has caused many to conclude that Pinnock now stands outside the pale of orthodoxy on this matter and that Open Theism should more accurately be termed "finite godism."[2]

---

[2]Ibid. Though I (Joe) disagree with Open Theism at key points, I hesitate to label it as heretical, especially since Pinnock has taken pains to distinguish Open Theism from process theology. Actually, we (Joe and Jerry) do not completely agree with one another on the question of divine foreknowledge.

If from this survey we must conclude that Arminianism by definition is a humanistic, shallow or heretical venture or that it necessarily leads to any of these sad destinations, then we now urge all readers to discard anything that carries the Arminian scent. Conversely, if returning to biblical and theological integrity and to a muscular embrace of the true gospel must consist essentially of raising the Calvinist banner, then let us all rally around that flag at once and with enthusiasm.

But two considerations call such conclusions into question and open the door for us to offer a biblically oriented critique of Calvinism. First, while we all may agree that humanism stands as an enemy to the gospel, it is risky to enthrone Calvinism merely because it stands as the (conceptual) polar opposite to humanism; it is also risky to discredit Arminianism merely because it dwells in some proximity to humanism. To build Christian theology through a process of inversion (i.e., by identifying a given heresy and then generating Christian doctrine by creating polar opposites to each aspect of that heresy) ironically puts heresy in the driver's seat, allowing it to shape Christian theology according to its own (inverse) image. We should not, for example, combat pantheism by denying the very presence of God in the world, or avert polytheism by denying the Trinity, or preserve divine transcendence by denying the incarnation. If the battle against humanism is the primary issue at hand and theology by inversion is the best strategy to employ, then Islam should win the prize as humanism's ablest opponent.

Standing at the opposite end of the spectrum from antinomianism is legalism, but legalism is not thereby established as Christian truth. And though the doctrine of salvation by grace has been perverted by many into a gospel of moral license, none of us would argue that this proximity should bring the slightest disrepute on the doctrine of salvation by grace. As the wisdom of the ages has taught, the most pernicious errors are often those *closest* to the truth. Where Calvinism and Arminianism may lie on a map in relation to this or that heresy generates an interesting discussion but little illumination. Of far greater importance are their proximities to the bar of divine revelation, especially as secured for us in Scripture.

Our second reason for questioning Calvinism lies within in the very point we have just offered: scores of Arminians have declined to embrace Calvinism because they judge it to be at odds with the message of the Bible itself. They find that Calvinist theology, though exhaustively keyed to biblical texts and terminology, seems to do violence to the whole message of Scripture. They conclude that too many biblical passages must undergo heavy modification according to Calvinist precepts before they can be understood in Calvinist ways. This is not to say that Arminians find no difficulties of their own in trying to track the ways of God through the biblical story or that they never come to a theological knot that seems to elude explanation. Rather, they have reached the verdict that reading the Bible from a Calvinist viewpoint requires such a degree of adjusting, disrupting or undervaluing biblical passages that the Calvinist system itself must be defective. They have concluded that a more faithful reading of Scripture leads away from Calvinism toward some variety of Arminianism. The Bible itself, they aver, stands as the primary objector to the distinctive claims of Calvinism.

Here we engage what we judge to be the three strongest scriptural arguments for Calvinist theology: the sovereign nature of God, the gracious nature of salvation and the reality of divine election. We offer an accounting for each of these in ways we find more faithful to the contexts of individual biblical passages and more harmonious with the whole counsel of Scripture. Readers are invited to pray along with us that the words and thoughts of this presentation will honor God and prove edifying to the people of God.

THE SOVEREIGNTY OF GOD (CALVINIST PERSPECTIVES)

Calvinists believe that Arminians can cling to their theology only by diminishing or denying the sovereignty of God in order to accommodate certain understandings of human freedom. Such distortion at the very foundation of Christian theology, Calvinists warn, must not only twist every other Christian doctrine but also threaten to strip the very "godness" from God, since a god who is not sovereign *of all* fails to be god *at all*.

Calvinists point to an impressive collection of biblical passages for grounding their understanding of divine sovereignty. In the opening chapter of Genesis the range of divine commands extends throughout every region of the cosmos. Conspicuously absent is any hint of resistance or struggle, any hint of delay or partial fulfillment. No rival deities are present to aid or to hinder, and no human wisdom advises the Creator in the task. God is the supreme actor whose will is executed in complete and unchallenged triumph.

Similar themes of creation are developed in God's chastisement of Job, where all forces of nature respond to the Creator in perfect obedience (Job 38—42). It is easy to find similar passages throughout the Bible extolling God's absolute control over nature.

But divine power is not restricted to the realm of nature and its beasts, the Calvinist reminds us. This range of divine engagement comes to expression beautifully in the life of Jeremiah, who was personally known by God and assigned a mission prior to his fetal development: "Before I formed you in the womb I knew you, before you were born I set you apart; I appointed you as a prophet to the nations" (Jer 1:5). On the larger scale, Jeremiah's mission involved declaring the divine word on the international stage, a word empowered "to uproot and tear down, to destroy and overthrow, to build and to plant" the nations and kingdoms of the world (Jer 1:10). The God of Israel who shaped the tiny embryo buried within the body of Jeremiah's mother would also determine the destinies of mighty nations.

Perhaps no portion of the Bible can match Isaiah's depiction of God's utter supremacy in the realms of nature and of human affairs. "He sits enthroned above the circle of the earth, and its people are like grasshoppers. He stretches out the heavens like a canopy, and spreads them out like a tent to live in. He brings princes to naught and reduces the rulers of this world to nothing" (Is 40:22-23). Furthermore, the God of Israel unfailingly succeeds in accomplishing his will: "My purpose will stand, and I will do all that I please. . . . What I have said, that will I bring about; what I have planned, that will I do" (Is 46:10-11). "From ancient days I am he. No one can deliver out of my hand. When I act, who can reverse it?" (Is 43:13). Note that the very godness of God is demonstrated by his irrepressible power.

So completely does God wield authority and power over the whole creation that God's rule can be likened to the unanswerable mastery a potter has over a lump of clay: "Woe to him who quarrels with his Maker, to him who is but a potsherd among the potsherds on the ground. Does the clay say to the potter, 'What are you making?' Does your work say, 'He has no hands'?" (Is 45:9). In Romans 9:19-23, Paul appeals to this very image in asserting that the divine potter enjoys full authority to shape vessels as determined solely by the divine will.

Most Calvinists believe that God does *not* exercise this sovereign rule by coercing human beings to act against their wills.[3] While God may on rare occasions compel humans to act against their wills, Calvinists believe that God routinely acts *on* the will with the result that the humans desire to act as God has predetermined (Prov 21:1). Even as God's enemies imagine themselves to be resisting God's will, God has already moved their hearts to create those very desires and intentions: "I will harden Pharaoh's heart, and he will pursue them. But I will gain glory for myself through Pharaoh and all his army" (Ex 14:4). God's unhindered access to the very seat of human desire explains just how effortlessly God shapes the flow of human actions. So skillfully does God play on the human heart that human subjects need sense no coercion even as they perfectly execute the predetermined divine plan.

Calvinists also believe that these biblical descriptions of God's unqualified power should drive us to the conclusion that God never adjusts his will, never adapts his purposes to changing circumstances, never modifies his plans in response to human actions. The logic involved in reaching this conclusion is not difficult to grasp: God's will would need to be adjusted only if God were to encounter *effective resistance* to his plan. But since the Bible has already established that nothing can successfully resist God, it naturally follows that the divine will never meets

---

[3]We will discuss Calvinist understandings of human free will more fully in later chapters.

any occasion requiring its adjustment. Furthermore, a modified or evolving plan, perhaps by definition, cannot be a perfect plan, since any changes to perfection involve settling for second best.

In the language of the Westminster Confession, "God from all eternity did . . . freely and unchangeably ordain whatever comes to pass."[4] In effect, God becomes (whether directly or indirectly) the primary acting agent throughout the universe, since God acts upon everything that is not God.[5] By affirming this comprehensive divine causation, the very godness of God is preserved, as is the perfection of God's power and will. Reduced to simple language, God gets exactly what God wants in every detail of reality, period! That's what it means to be God![6]

THE SOVEREIGNTY OF GOD (AN ARMINIAN RESPONSE)

This Calvinist understanding of divine sovereignty necessarily generates a set of doctrinal conclusions denying human free will (in the sense of the power of contrary choice), asserting God's grace as perfectly triumphant and restricting God's saving intentions to a subset of humanity. We believe these conclusions create such turbulence in reading the Bible that one should be driven to reexamine the Calvinist understanding of divine sovereignty.

Restricted love? One stream of turbulence results from restricting God's

---

[4]John H. Leith, ed., *Creeds of the Churches,* rev. ed. (Atlanta: John Knox Press, 1973), p. 198.
[5]Jack W. Cottrell, "The Nature of the Divine Sovereignty," in *The Grace of God and the Will of Man: A Case for Arminianism,* ed. Clark H. Pinnock (Grand Rapids, Mich.: Zondervan, 1989), p. 105. While Calvinists are quick to insist that God effects his will through secondary causes (including human agents), they struggle to explain just how these secondary causes do not flow ultimately from divine causation. See chapter three, "Calvinism and the Nature of Human Freedom."
[6]Many Calvinists insist that God desires to save all sinners, though this desire is obviously not fulfilled. Partly to preserve their understanding of God's irresistible power, Calvinists see a deeper, controlling will of God that has unconditionally determined to save only a subset of the human race. From the vantage point of this deeper will, God gets exactly what he wants through the unconditional election of precisely those whom he chooses to save. We view such a view of divine will to be antithetical to the biblical teaching that God genuinely desires to save all persons, to be unnecessary for preserving divine sovereignty and to be unconvincing as an interpretation of the biblical doctrine of election.

saving intention to a subset of humanity, the elect. Just how wide are God's saving intentions? If "God so loved the *world* that he gave his one and only Son" (Jn 3:16, emphasis added), then it would seem that the loving heart of the Father embraced the whole world as he set in motion the saving mission of the Son. We read that Jesus "is the atoning sacrifice for our sins, and not only for ours but also *for the sins of the whole world*" (1 Jn 2:2, emphasis added). The same writer elaborates on this ministry of expiation by connecting it to the love of God: "God is love. This is how God showed his love among us: He sent his one and only Son into the world . . . as an atoning sacrifice for our sins" (1 Jn 4:8-10). It appears that God's universal love energizes God's worldwide mission of redemption.

Note also how Paul wheels the argument of Romans 1—11 to a climactic conclusion: "For God has bound *all* men over to disobedience so that he may have mercy on them *all*" (Rom 11:32, emphasis added). Here the scope of God's intention to have mercy matches the scope of human sinfulness, as indicated by the repeated *all*. If Paul has already established in Romans 1—3 that all human beings *without exception* have been consigned to disobedience, then the symmetry of Paul's expression in Romans 11:32 strongly implies that God intends to have mercy in a similar scope: on all human beings *without exception*. Even if we allow that Paul may here be referring to Jews and Gentiles as people groups, we must not imagine that God's desire to show mercy fails to apply to every individual within each group. After all, Paul establishes that all humans are under sin by arguing that both Gentiles (Rom 1:18-32) and Jews (Rom 2:1—3:20) *as people groups* are under sin. If we accept Paul's strategy of indicting every individual through indictment of the group, then consistency requires that we allow the same extension to hold with regard to God's mercy, as Romans 11:32 seems to say.

The Pastoral Epistles abound with passages pointing toward God's universal saving intentions: "God our Savior, who wants all men to be saved and to come to a knowledge of the truth" (1 Tim 2:3-4); "Christ Jesus, who gave himself as a ransom for all" (1 Tim 2:5-6); "We have put our hope in the living God, who is the Savior of all men, and especially of those who believe" (1 Tim 4:10); "For the grace of God that brings salvation has appeared to all" (Tit 2:11). Given the unqualified use of *all* in these passages to identify those whom God desires to save, the burden of proving otherwise is on those who hold that biblical writers assumed a limitation on those who would be saved.[7]

Of course Calvinists have offered their own accountings of these passages. Some argue, for example, that the "world" loved by God in John 3:16 must refer only to "the elect within the world."[8] Similarly, they read the unqualified *all* in restricted senses (e.g., "all types of people" or "all the elect"). Accordingly, the scriptural claim that Jesus died not only for our sins but also for the sins of the whole world means that Jesus died not only for the sins of (some) Jews but also for the sins of (some) Gentiles. But D. A. Carson, certainly no Arminian sympathizer, considers such moves to be clever but unconvincing exegetical ploys that feebly attempt to overcome "simply too many texts on the other side of the issue."[9] These restrictive interpretations of *all* require such textual gymnastics that they condemn themselves as invalid.

Yet some will insist that the rich and eloquent stream of scriptural passages celebrating God's special love for his own children teaches (by implication) that God reserves his love for the elect alone. Indeed we read that the Lord set his affection *on the nation of Israel,* setting them apart from all other nations (Deut 4:37-38; 7:7-8; 10:14-15). Furthermore, we read that *those who fear and obey the Lord* are assured of God's abiding compassion (Ex 20:6; Ps 103:8, 13). New Testament writers habitually refer to the objects of God's love in the first person, no doubt having Christian believers in view (Gal 2:20; Eph 2:4).

But these assertions of God's love for one group of persons do not

---

[7]For a helpful treatment of such terms as *all* and *every* in the Pastoral Epistles, see I. Howard Marshall, "Universal Grace and Atonement in the Pastoral Epistles," in *The Grace of God and the Will of Man: A Case for Arminianism,* ed. Clark H. Pinnock (Grand Rapids, Mich.: Zondervan, 1989), pp. 57-63.

[8]See D. A. Carson's characterization of this point of view in *The Difficult Doctrine of the Love of God* (Wheaton, Ill.: Crossway, 2000), p. 17.

[9]Ibid., p. 75.

prove that God doesn't love others. A strict application of this negative principle is actually impossible to carry out, since Paul's claim that the Son of God loved "me" (Gal 2:20) must then be heard as a denial that God loves anyone else in the universe. From the Bible itself we know that God's special love for Israel stood at the center of God's plan to bless the *entire* world (Gen 12:1-2). God's special love for Israel marked it as the divinely chosen agent in mediating redemption to all nations.[10] Furthermore, our own experiences as parents teach us that expressing love, even special love, for one child in no way implies an absence of love for another, even a difficult child.[11] However painfully the latter may have rejected us, we persist in loving that child with all of our strength and resources. It is precarious to read biblical affirmations of God's love for Israel or for the redeemed as simple proofs that God restricts his love to them alone.[12]

Several leading Calvinists have pressed for a shift in rhetoric and emphasis, taking pains to affirm that God loves the entire world, including the non-elect. Carson, for example, declares that God "displays a loving, yearning, salvific stance toward the whole world" and that he "presents himself as the God who invites and commands all human beings to repent."[13]

Yet while these Calvinists affirm that God loves all and passionately wishes all to be saved (as they agree Scripture clearly teaches), they nevertheless deny that God has made salvation *possible* for all. Arminians unaccustomed to reading Calvinist explanations can easily miss the subtlety of their language. Carson's declaration seems indistinguishable from typical Arminian formulation—until we realize that describing a God who *displays a salvific stance* toward all persons, is markedly different from af-

---

[10]See Isaiah 61—66 for a vision of Israel's universal role of redemption among the nations.
[11]Compare favorably here with Carson, *Difficult Doctrine,* p. 20.
[12]J. I. Packer, "The Love of God: Universal and Particular," in *The Grace of God, the Bondage of the Will,* ed. Thomas R. Schreiner and Bruce A. Ware (Grand Rapids, Mich.: Baker, 1995), 2:283.
[13]Carson, *Difficult Doctrine,* pp. 76, 17.

firming a God who *establishes a real salvific possibility* for all persons. While Carson affirms God's *wish* that all be saved, he believes that God's *will* has already decided to distribute saving grace selectively. God's love, in Carson's view, compels God to issue an earnest invitation for all to repent and believe, but it does not provide to all the ability to respond appropriately.

Imagine this scenario: Parents from around the world send their children to a rustic camp set in the midst of Kentucky's Bluegrass Region for the summer. All one hundred children become infected with a deadly virus during the first week of camp and have but one month to live. Fortunately, a specialist who has seen a similar outbreak in New Mexico knows of a treatment: the Yucca cactus, when ground to a pulp, blended with vinegar and ingested over the period of three weeks, will completely counteract the virus and return the children to full health.

Unfortunately, every single child finds the smell of the concoction so utterly repulsive that no amount of coaxing by even the best of counselors succeeds in getting anyone to eat any of it. To make matters worse, the virus somehow drives the children mad, prompting them to lash out in foul language at those trying to help them and to accuse their counselors of gross misconduct. Luckily, yet another specialist develops a serum that, when injected hypodermically, creates within the child an insatiable passion for eating the Yucca mash.

Now imagine that news of the virus reaches the alarmed parents. The camp director immediately sends a letter reassuring them that he *loves* all their children, that he is offering to *all* their children the life-saving Yucca mash in *liberal quantities,* that he will supply this expensive preparation *without charge* and that all children will be brought to the cafeteria three times a day and *strongly urged* to eat.

Three months later, the parents arrive in the Bluegrass to retrieve their children. But at the campsite, they are stunned to discover that seventy-five children have died from the virus. Interrogating the director, they discover that the life-saving food could not work its wonders unless the child was injected with the appetite stimulant. On further questioning they discover that the director had chosen to inject only twenty-five children with the serum, though he had an unlimited supply at his disposal. To say nothing about their anger and grief, the parents are utterly perplexed!

In chorus they immediately challenge the claim made by the camp director in the letter they had received, asking, "How can you claim to have *loved* the seventy-five dead children if you could have saved them but didn't?" We can imagine just how unconvincing some of the director's answers might be: "But I offered the Yucca mash liberally, freely and passionately." Yes, but all this talk about the merits of the mixture misses the issue of the serum! "But the children are to blame, since they ate exactly what they wanted and violently rejected my help!" Yes, but you fully controlled exactly what each child wanted! "But note how much attention I lavished on these children in the last weeks of their lives." And you call this love—to provide the most exciting camp activities to a child as she dies, while you withhold the very serum of life?

The director's claim to love all children rings hollow at best, deceptive at worst. If love will not employ all available means to rescue someone from ultimate loss, it is hard to hear the announcement of universal love as good news. Indeed, it is hard to hear it as love at all. In our judgment, it becomes meaningless to claim that God wishes to save all while also insisting that God refrains from making the salvation of all possible.[14] What are we to make of a God whose walk does not match his talk?

Irresistible grace? Calvinists do not deny that the Bible contains many reports of people successfully rejecting divine commands and invitations.

---

[14]John Piper argues that the Calvinist view of God's dual will (that all be saved but that only some be chosen to be saved) is really no more troublesome than the Arminian view of God's will (that all be saved but that only those who freely believe will be saved). But this structural similarity obscures the obvious and significant difference between Calvinism and Arminianism. In Calvinism, the precise limits of salvation are unconditionally determined by God, whereas in Arminianism the limits of salvation are conditionally limited by God and based fundamentally on human responses. In latter chapters we will unpack these distinctions more fully. John Piper, "Are There Two Wills in God? Divine Election and God's Desire for All to Be Saved," in *The Grace of God, the Bondage of the Will*, ed. Thomas R. Schreiner and Bruce A. Ware (Grand Rapids, Mich.: Baker, 1995), 1:107-31.

Nor do Calvinists object when Arminians flood the record with a host of passages, from Genesis to Revelation, mirroring the lament of Hosea 11:1-2: "When Israel was a child, I loved him, and out of Egypt I called my son. But *the more I called Israel, the further they went from me. They sacrificed to the Baals and they burned incense to images*" (emphasis added). In other words, Calvinists believe in irresistible grace without ignoring the biblical data of successful human rebellion against God's invitations.

Their explanation runs as follows: When one resists God's call, it is simply because God has chosen not to move the human will to respond appropriately. Furthermore, no human being can respond appropriately to any divine invitation or command unless God's unilateral, transforming action accompanies it. In other words, when one successfully rejects God's commands, one has not successfully resisted God's power, since God's power was never exerted in this case. Similarly, if a toddler successfully pinned her father to the carpet in a wrestling hold, we would all instinctively judge that the father was withholding his real strength and was only *simulating* a genuine struggle.

We face yet again the troubling prospect of a God whose action (or inaction) contradicts his words.[15] While his words may seem like a warm invitation or command to repent and seem to indicate that God desires an appropriate human response, God's choice to withhold his transforming power reveals his deeper desire not to create in humans the appropriate response. Returning to the story of the children at camp, God may tenderly entreat us to eat the healing paste, but he has withheld the crucial serum that would make it possible for us to do just that!

Pressing this understanding through the whole of Scripture seems to us a prohibitively costly project, since at every turn, the words of Scrip-

---

[15]In Isaiah 6, where the prophet is called to preach to those whose hearts have been hardened, it is important to note that this hardening is secondary to their own long-term stubborn resistance to God's invitations. This ministry of Isaiah is characterized as unusual and temporary and as part of God's specific punishment of rebellious Israel. For these reasons it is precarious to build from the template of Isaiah's mission a picture of God's general pattern of dealing with all human beings.

ture must then be read in ways most readers would never imagine. Take, for example, the word of God through Jeremiah to Judah:

> Hear and pay attention, do not be arrogant, for the LORD has spoken. Give glory to the LORD your God before he brings the darkness. . . . But if you do not listen, I will weep in secret because of your pride; my eyes will weep bitterly, overflowing with tears, because the LORD's flock will be taken captive. (Jer 13:15-17)

Knowing that Judah did not turn and listen, the Calvinist concludes that God had already chosen to withhold his transforming grace from them, though he could easily have granted it. So while the text appears to identify Judah's pride as the root cause of punishment, the Calvinist instead concludes that Judah's ability to repent depends on God's eternally fixed plan. Again, although the text seems to identify salvation as God's deepest desire, the Calvinist must conclude that at a deeper level God never intended to bestow transforming grace on Jeremiah's hearers. In other words, *the true intentions of God cannot be discerned from his words.*

Somewhere along the way, the burden of reading myriad passages throughout the Bible in such a counterintuitive fashion should anxiously bring us to this sort of question: since the Calvinist view of divine sovereignty routinely requires such an awkward "decoding" of biblical texts, should not we reexamine the Calvinist view of divine sovereignty itself?[16]

Divine perfection and sovereignty. Some Calvinists appear to ground their view of God's sovereignty on their understanding of God's

---

[16]We won't argue at this point the question of the perseverance of saints, though we believe it to be an important issue. Since many Arminians subscribe to a "once saved, always saved" position and base that conviction not on Calvinist logic (which they have by and large rejected) but on direct appeal to Scripture, an argument over this doctrine itself will not always distinguish between Calvinist and Arminian positions. See Norman Geisler, *Chosen but Free* (Minneapolis: Bethany House, 1999), pp. 115-30.

perfection,[17] and their views of perfection in turn eliminate the possibility of human freedom. For if human beings actually possessed a will undetermined by God, then human history would become a messy, unruly stream of events hardly corresponding to God's plan and only partly responsive to his power. Under such conditions, Calvinists reason, it would seem impossible to describe God as perfect, since God's will and God's power over the world would fail to qualify as perfectly enacted or effective.

But such theological reasoning reminds us of what Thomas Morris calls "perfect-being theology," an approach seeking to build theology out of the initial description of God as perfect. From that secure starting point, it is believed that many other features of God's character and activity can be logically deduced with certainty.[18] We suspect that Calvinists (whether knowingly or otherwise) move across the steppingstones from "God is perfect" to "God must be in perfect control" to "perfect control requires determining every detail of reality." In similar fashion, we might step from "God's will is perfect" to "God's will can never change" to "God will never adjust his actions in light of human behaviors." Each step feels right, since each lies but a short logical step from the next. In other words, a perfect-being approach to creating Christian theology can easily generate a view of sovereignty that eliminates at the outset any possibility of human free agents.

While perfect-being theology is attractive, we must not ignore its dangers. Long ago, Plato unwittingly demonstrated just how easily the notion of divine perfection can lead to a portrayal of God utterly alien to biblical revelation. Since Plato reasoned that any change in a perfect God

---

[17]Note Packer's strong dependence on his understanding of divine perfection: "God's sovereignty, in which the perfection of his powers operates to express the perfection of his moral character, straddles this classification, for it is essentially personal action on an altogether transcendent plane" ("Love of God," p. 279). The question we pose to Packer and others is whether (or to what degree) their understanding of divine perfection is defined philosophically rather than by appeal to the biblical record of God's actual self-revelation throughout the history of his interaction with his people.

[18]Thomas V. Morris, *Our Idea of God* (Notre Dame, Ind.: University of Notre Dame Press, 1991), pp. 7-9.

would make God imperfect, he concluded that divine incarnation and earthly visitation would be impossible. Since perfection should also entail perfect self-sufficiency, Plato concluded that God does not love, since love implies a lack of perfect self-satisfaction. God's inner perfection, furthermore, can experience neither joy nor sorrow, since these involve change and imperfection.[19] While some may protest that Plato has erred in each of these deductions, it is difficult to expose these errors by reason alone and to determine by independent analysis just what perfection should entail. Given only the abstract principle of perfection, we can reasonably deliver a God quite unlike the loving and redeeming Father revealed by the incarnate Son.[20] In other words, building theology deductively from an abstract principle is a risky venture.

Scripture warns against building theology primarily by logical deduction. If we were to set an abstractly defined perfection as the cornerstone and grant it those characteristics commonly associated with it (e.g., uniformity, symmetry, completeness, efficiency, unimprovability), we should puzzle over God's dealings with Israel. God chose an insignificant clan to achieve a worldwide mission, he labored with it through all of its tortuous turnings, he revealed himself at various times and places in different ways, he committed his truth to the limitations of human language, he allowed the presence of false prophets and evil leaders to ravage the chosen people, and he let this chosen nation suffer the ignominy of military defeat and captivity—choices that hardly reflect an abstractly defined perfection. The Christmas story shatters human expectations of what the perfect incarnation of a perfect God would look like. But the ultimate challenge to a deductive theology is the cross, where something utterly unthinkable took place. Richard Bauckham remarks:

---

[19]Here we are dependent on John Sanders, "Historical Considerations," in *The Openness of God*, ed. Clark Pinnock et al. (Downers Grove, Ill.: InterVarsity Press, 1994), pp. 62-64.

[20]Morris attempts to generate conclusions about the nature and character of God from the premise of divine perfection. We hesitate to follow him in this endeavor, partly because we think he overestimates the reliability of human reason in these matters while undervaluing the contribution of Scripture. See Morris, "Perfect-Being Theology," in *Our Idea of God*, pp. 35-45.

Here God is seen to be God in his radical self-giving, descending to the most abject human condition, and in that human obedience, humiliation, suffering and death, being no less truly God than he is in his cosmic rule and glory on the heavenly throne. It is not that God is manifest in heavenly glory and hidden in the human degradation of the cross. . . . The divine identity is known in the radical contrast and conjunction of exaltation and humiliation—as the God who is Creator of all things, and no less truly God in the human life of Jesus . . . as the God of transcendent majesty who is no less truly God in the abject humiliation of the cross.[21]

In other words, when we confess the perfection and sovereignty of God, we must radically surrender ourselves to the whole story of God's self-revelation in order to discern just what God's perfection might actually involve. We must guard against fencing God into a paddock defined by our own notions of divine perfection.

Divine foreknowledge and determinism. Many Calvinists have reasoned that God's knowledge of the future, since it is absolutely complete and infallible, locks every detail of the future into place and eliminates the possibility of human free will (as power to choose otherwise). If God knows that I will fly to Boston next Monday afternoon, then I have no power to do otherwise, since in no case can God's knowledge of the future be proven wrong.[22]

---

[21]Richard Bauckham, *God Crucified* (Grand Rapids, Mich.: Eerdmans, 1998), p. 68.

[22]For over a decade, proponents of Open Theism have argued that while God knows everything that can be known, God does not know the future. Since the future will involve decisions made by genuinely free creatures, knowledge of the future is said to be impossible by definition. Just as no one considers God's power to be defective if God cannot perform deeds that are by definition impossible (e.g., to create a rock too heavy to lift, to create an uncreated being, to be both God and not-God), so also we ought not consider God's knowledge to be defective if God cannot know the future choices of genuinely free creatures. Open Theists readily admit that they deny divine foreknowledge in order to escape the absolute determinism they imagine it requires. As Pinnock explains, "I knew the Calvinist argument that exhaustive foreknowledge was tantamount to predestination because it implies the fixity of all things from 'eternity past,' and I could not shake off its logical

But from our vantage point, it is not entirely clear that God's knowledge of the future must determine the future. Do we know that it isn't possible for God to know something without causing it? Do we know that God can't know what free agents will decide without causing or fixing those decisions? Why isn't it possible for God's knowledge of the future to be flawless and yet no more determine the future than our knowledge of the past determines the past?

A sizeable difficulty Arminians face in this matter is explaining just how God can know future choices of truly free creatures. If God can perfectly predict their actions, aren't they functioning according to some discernible principle? Three factors ought to lessen the problem. First, our inability to explain just how God created the world from nothing, or how he made Mt. Sinai tremble and smoke, or how he raised Jesus from the dead, doesn't prevent us from believing with good reason that God acted in these ways. Similarly, our inability to explain how God might know the future choices of free agents shouldn't immediately render such a belief illegitimate if the Bible attributes such knowledge to God.[23]

Second, it is possible that God knows the future not by peering forward but by knowing the future directly as already present. If God's presence dwells in all *places* (*spatially* omnipresent), then perhaps we can speak of God as dwelling in all *times:* past, present and future (*temporally* omnipresent). And third, the collapse of the traditional Newtonian view of space and time should make us all slow to declare what can or cannot happen regarding time and space, especially for

---

force. I feared that, if we view God as timeless and omniscient, we will land back in the camp of theological determinism where these notions naturally belong. It makes no sense to espouse conditionality and then threaten it by other assumptions that we make." In other words, Pinnock agrees with his Calvinist opponents in tightly connecting absolute divine foreknowledge with absolute divine control, so that (for Pinnock) human freedom can be won only by surrendering divine foreknowledge. Clark Pinnock, "From Augustine to Arminius: A Pilgrimage in Theology," in *The Grace of God and the Will of Man: A Case for Arminianism,* ed. Clark H. Pinnock (Grand Rapids, Mich.: Zondervan, 1989), p. 25.

[23]Alvin Plantinga, "Divine Knowledge," in *Christian Perspectives on Religious Knowledge,* ed. C. Stephen Evans and Merold Westphal (Grand Rapids, Mich.: Eerdmans, 1993), pp. 40-65.

God.[24] In other words, we must avoid restricting God's abilities with conceptual limitations of our own making.

Divine sovereignty in the biblical record. The Calvinist understanding of sovereignty conflicts with the biblical teaching of God's love for all people and threatens to cheapen God's word of invitation by teaching that God does not enable everyone to respond to it. Neither God's knowledge of the future nor God's perfection (if described biblically) requires that the world be minutely and exhaustively determined by divine will. But what can we say positively about the mighty power of God at work in the world and in human hearts?

When we read the Bible we are impressed with God's power not only to create a world but also to bring about mighty natural events within it. In the story of Jonah, we find God causing a fearsome storm to rise, preparing a fish to swallow Jonah, causing a vine to grow, providing a worm to eat the vine and raising a scorching wind to sear the prophet. But the report of these events as divine acts suggests that they represent unusual interventions of God into the otherwise normal course of nature and that the normal weather patterns on sea and land might not have turned out as they did were it not for God's intervening hand. In other words, could it be that God has created a natural order with its own room to operate apart from specific commands continually issued by God? Could it be that God sustains the world by upholding its principles of operation without at the same time determining its every motion—without regulating the duration and location of every storm or every wind that blows? If the Bible teaches that every natural event is directly and specifically willed by God, then the language in Jonah is strangely redundant when it claims that *this* storm and *this* wind and *this* vine were divinely caused. In other words, to de-

---

[24]I want to thank my friends and colleagues Dr. Lawrence W. Wood and Dr. Charles E. Gutenson for their instruction and insight, particularly regarding the issue of God and time. The language of God's being "temporally omnipresent" belongs to Gutenson. Both Wood and Gutenson generally follow Wolfhart Pannenberg's treatment of the issue. For fuller explication see Wolfhart Pannenberg, *Systematic Theology*, trans. Geoffrey W. Bromiley (Grand Rapids, Mich.: Eerdmans, 1991), 1:401-10.

scribe certain events as divinely caused encourages us to view the created order as significantly differentiated from God by his own choice, even while it is fully dependent on him and fully open to his actions within it.

In reading the Bible, then, we think it is important to refrain from immediately converting reports of God's specific actions into universal principles. We propose that God's sovereignty guarantees his freedom to act or not to act, if indeed he has chosen to create a world containing motions he has not specifically willed or caused.

The same caution in reading about God's actions in the realm of nature should hold in reading about God's influence on human beings. Without question, God enjoys full access to the inner sanctum of the human heart. Indeed, "The king's heart is in the hand of the LORD; he directs it like a watercourse wherever he pleases" (Prov 21:1). But it is unwarranted to transform this verse into the claim that God has actually chosen to control not only every decision of the king but also every decision made by every human being ever born. It is also unwarranted to extend the focus of this verse from its assurance to God's people that their leader is shaped by divine will, to a claim that the rise of saving faith in any individual heart has been unconditionally caused by God. Furthermore, this verse and others like it (e.g., Ps 135:6) can be parlayed into total determinism only by presuming that God's will itself contains divine preferences for the movement of every molecule, for every electrical impulse, for every rustling leaf, for every human thought. Conclusions of these sorts can be reached only by importing convictions and beliefs into these texts.

In our judgment, the Bible strongly warrants seeing the world with its human story as yielding to the large-scale plan and purpose of God, but not as being minutely controlled or determined by God. The Bible reports that God made humankind in his image, positing a fundamental likeness between God and human beings (Gen 1:27).[25] Scholars note the

---

[25]See Stanley J. Grenz's fine survey of the debate over this image in *The Social God and the Relational Self* (Louisville, Ky.: Westminster John Knox, 2001).

close connection between human likeness to God and the divine mandate that human beings rule over the created order (Gen 1:26-28). Somehow, humanity's likeness to God qualifies us to exercise dominion as vice regents over creation and points to the glory and honor with which God crowned the human race in this role (Ps 8).[26]

One could claim that the human vice regent would merely serve as the conduit for God's commands, as an intermediate link in the chain of divine causation. But we see telling proof to the contrary, for God "brought [all living creatures] to the man to see what he would name them; and whatever the man called each living creature, that was its name" (Gen 2:19). Here we learn vital truths about who God is and who we are; we find Adam invited to contribute from his own (divinely created) abilities without specific divine instruction. Not only was human rule inaugurated through the act of naming, but also a space for human freedom and creativity was demonstrated when God invited Adam to express himself.

But divinely created human freedom rests on deeper bedrock still. Up until this point in our discussion, we have referred to God without distinction, scarcely mentioning the Father, the Son and the Holy Spirit. According to Colin Gunton, this tendency to obscure the Trinity forms a blemish on the otherwise marvelous contribution of the Reformation. In their dependence on Augustine (who verged on viewing the persons of the Trinity as functionally indistinguishable), the Reformers forwarded a theological tendency to reduce God to a singularity, which in turn furthers the tendency to view the role of God toward the world largely in terms of causation.[27] Thus a vision of the rich beauty of eternal relational life among the Father, Son and Spirit is lost. As Gunton explains, Father, Son and Spirit are related to each other in a way that assures their "otherness" from each other: "Otherness is an essential feature of Trinitarian freedom, because

---

[26]D. J. A. Clines, "Image of God," in *Dictionary of Paul and His Letters*, ed. Gerald F. Hawthorne and Ralph Martin (Downers Grove, Ill.: InterVarsity Press, 1993), pp. 426-28.

[27]Colin Gunton, *The Promise of Trinitarian Theology* (Edinburgh: T & T Clark, 1991), pp. 130-34.

without otherness the distinctness, particularity, of a person is lost. . . . We would say, then, that the essence *of* the being in relation that is the Trinity is the *personal space* that is received and conferred."[28]

The presence of such personal space within trinitarian life offers the key to understanding the relationship between God and the created world. Whereas unitarian understandings of God move toward pantheism because no distance can be maintained between God and the world, the doctrine of the Trinity

> allows us to conceive of the world as other than, while yet in relation to, God. It thus generates a conception of contingency, in both senses of the word: the contingency of the world on God, and its contingent, non-necessary reality: a kind of ordered freedom which in turn becomes the basis for . . . human freedom.[29]

In trying to read the Bible cautiously and on its own terms, we see a sovereign God who has freely chosen to create a world fully dependent on him yet different from him, a world open to divine causation but not comprehensively determined by its divine Sustainer, a world inhabited by God but not utterly overwhelmed by divine presence. We are not seeking to establish human freedom at the expense of divine sovereignty; rather we are seeking to *affirm God's freedom to create whatever kind of world he desired,* even a world whose every movement is not to be traced back ultimately to specific divine determination. *If God has in fact chosen to create this kind of world, we neither glorify him nor magnify his sovereignty by insisting that he has created a world of a different sort.*

THE GRACIOUS NATURE OF SALVATION
(CALVINIST PERSPECTIVES)

Some Calvinists would agree in large measure with the critique we have offered above and have abandoned traditional Calvinist teaching about

---

[28]Ibid., p. 128 (emphasis in original).
[29]Ibid., pp. 129-30.

God ordaining all things in particular.[30] They narrow their claims about God's sovereign action to the matter of salvation, allowing that most ordinary human affairs unfold under the influence of human free will. They have no intention, however, of moving any further toward Arminian thought, since they believe Arminians have underestimated the effects of Adam's Fall and overestimated the present moral abilities of fallen human beings.

Indeed, biblical descriptions of the sinful condition leave little room to expect that the unredeemed would or could ever respond favorably to the gospel invitation. Famously, Ephesians 2:1-3 portrays sinners as both "dead" and following "the ruler of the kingdom of the air." Romans 6 employs the imagery of slavery to depict sin's binding force. John 9, with its story of the man born blind, brings into view the frightful reality of spiritual blindness. First Corinthians 2 makes it clear that those without the Spirit consider God's truth to be utter foolishness. This simple collection of passages clearly teaches that sinners will not on their own accord respond with repentance and faith to the gospel. We might as well preach to a corpse in a casket. Given these circumstances, Calvinists conclude that saving faith, whenever it does arise within the human heart, must have been caused directly and completely by God.

By viewing faith as God's doing, Calvinists believe that the gracious character of salvation is preserved. If we have repented and believed out of our own resources, then we have essentially saved ourselves. If we have contributed in any way to our salvation or if our cooperation was required, then salvation is no longer entirely by God's grace, and we have robbed God of his full glory: We have "become children of God—children born not of natural descent, nor of human decision or a husband's will, but born of God" (Jn 1:12-13).

---

[30]Richard A. Muller, "Grace, Election and Contingent Choice: Arminius' Gambit and the Reformed Response," in *The Grace of God, the Bondage of the Will,* ed. Thomas R. Schreiner and Bruce A. Ware (Grand Rapids, Mich.: Baker, 1995), 2:270.

THE GRACIOUS NATURE OF SALVATION
(AN ARMINIAN RESPONSE)

Perhaps the most serious weakness of contemporary Arminianism is its view of sin. Far too frequently, Arminians narrow the problem of sin to the matter of guilt, largely understood (merely) as liability to future judgment. Arminian evangelism, therefore, often focuses solely on the offer of forgiveness to avert this threat, presenting its invitation with the presumption that the audience enjoys freedom of will, relatively sound judgment and an openness to consider fairly the gospel message. Accordingly, the most significant factor in determining the rate of success in evangelism is the power of the evangelist, whether in logic, persuasion or personal winsomeness.

Such a view widely misses the fuller range of sin's destruction, the depth of human helplessness and the degree of human hostility to God. Calvinists surely have the clearer view, with a full arsenal of scriptural passages to prove that sin perverts the very mechanisms of insight and judgment, of desire and will, and of the fundamental moral disposition. The gospel call to deny oneself and to take up one's cross and follow Jesus (Mt 16:24; Mk 8:34; Lk 9:23) directly challenges every instinct for human self-preservation and self-rule and exposes human rebellion against God.

Robert Chiles has shown that contemporary Arminians' underestimation of sin represents a shocking erosion from classical Arminian convictions, especially as taught by John Wesley.[31] For his part, Wesley affirmed the dreadful effects of the Fall in the strongest terms, agreeing fervently with his Calvinist contemporaries that sinners, left to themselves, stand utterly hopeless and helpless before God. Yet in the generations succeeding Wesley, and especially in American Methodism, the pendulum swung from Wesley's emphasis on free grace to an emphasis on free will, with an accompanying tendency to consider free will a natural human possession fully capable in its own right of assessing and ac-

---

[31]Robert E. Chiles, "Methodist Apostasy from Free Grace to Free Will," *Religion in Life* 27, no. 3 (1958): 438-49.

cepting divine truth. While this innovation may resonate nicely with contemporary culture, it fails to account for biblical teaching about the fallen human condition. In the past, Arminians have agreed with Calvinists that salvation can only occur if God radically, powerfully and graciously invades the human heart. Given the human condition, this invasion will take place without human invitation and prior to any human interest in God or inclination toward the good. Only as God opens blind eyes, stirs the desire and loosens the grip of sin can saving faith follow.[32]

However closely Calvinists and (Wesleyan) Arminians should agree on this point, we do part ways over the nature of God's rescue operation. A three-way comparison should make the matter clear. The contemporary Arminian addresses the sinner as a convicted criminal standing at the gate of the penitentiary. Standing under a legal obligation to enter into eternal imprisonment, the prisoner will be escorted into inescapable confinement and punishment upon death. There at the front gate, an evangelist offers release from the coming horror and urges the convict to accept the gift of total pardon.

In contrast, Calvinists and classical Arminians see the sinner as already imprisoned in the deepest corner of a terrorist camp. Bound, gagged, blindfolded and drugged, the prisoner is weak and delusional. Calvinists and classical Arminians know that the preacher at the gate cannot reach the prisoner through the layers of confinement and sensory distortion. The prisoner can't even begin to plead for help or plan an escape. In fact, the prisoner feels at home in the dank squalor of the cell; she has come to identify with her captors and will try to fight off any attempted rescue. Only a divine invasion will succeed.

---

[32]Traditionally, Wesleyans have spoken of this dimension of God's grace as *prevenient grace,* grace that comes before conversion. It is understood to be universal in its scope and salvific in its intention, meaning that God pursues, invites and makes salvation possible for everyone. Calvinists speak of *common grace,* grace that operates among all persons and that allows even the non-elect to enjoy life, create benevolent governments, contribute positively to every dimension of culture, and so on. But common grace (as Calvinists define it) has no saving direction and purpose in it, whereas a Wesleyan views all of God's gracious work among humanity as having saving direction and intention.

The Calvinist view of divine invasion is simple. God invades the camp, carries the prisoner out, strips the prisoner of her shackles and blinders, and injects "faith" into the prisoner's veins. The former prisoner, having already been rescued from prison and positioned outside its walls, now trusts the Deliverer because of the potency of the administered faith serum. God has been the lone actor throughout, in the sense that the human response of faith is directly and irresistibly caused by God. Whether this saving action of God takes place over a longer or shorter period of time, faith is the inevitable result of divine illumination.

The classical Arminian believes that God steals into the prison and makes it to the bedside of the victim. God injects a serum that begins to clear the prisoner's mind of delusions and quell her hostile reactions. God removes the gag from the prisoner's mouth and shines a flashlight around the pitch-black room. The prisoner remains mute as the Rescuer's voice whispers, "Do you know where you are? Let me tell you! Do you know who you are? Let me show you!" And as the wooing begins, divine truth begins to dawn on the prisoner's heart and mind; the Savior holds up a small mirror to show the prisoner her sunken eyes and frail body. "Do you see what they've done to you, and do you see how you've given yourself to them?" Even in the dim light, the prisoner's weakened eyes are beginning to focus. The Rescuer continues, "Do you know who I am, and that I want you for myself?" Perhaps the prisoner makes no obvious advance but does not turn away. The questions keep coming: "Can I show you pictures of who you once were and the wondrous plans I have for you in the years to come?" The prisoner's heartbeat quickens as the Savior presses on: "I know that part of you suspects that I have come to harm you. But let me show you something—my hands, they're a bit bloody. I crawled through an awful tangle of barbed wire to get to you." Now here in this newly created sacred space, in this moment of new possibility, the Savior whispers, "I want to carry you out of here right now! Give me your heart! Trust me!"

This scenario, we believe, captures the richness of the Bible's message: the glory of God's original creation, the devastation of sin, God's loving pursuit of helpless sinners and the nature of love as the free assent of persons.

Here also is room for tragedy, for the inexplicable (but possible) rejection of God's tender invitation by those who really know better and who might have done otherwise. Sin shows up in its boldest colors when it recapitulates the rebellion of Eden and freely chooses to go its own way in the face of divine love and full provision. The tragedy of such rejection is the risk God took in making possible shared love between creature and Creator, the very love shared between the Father and his eternal Son (Jn 17:23-26).

As we see it, the prisoner's trust in the Rescuer was not caused by God, though God caused every circumstance that made it possible. God did all the illuminating, all the clarifying and all the truth telling. The prisoner's trust possessed no power of its own, for it didn't remove one shackle or take one step on the way to freedom. God alone shatters all bonds and lifts the emaciated body on his own shoulders. The prisoner's trust had no monetary value for enriching the Rescuer or compensating him for his wounds. Since God bore all the cost, took all the initiative and exercised all the power required for the saving event, God owns exclusive rights to all praise and glory for the miracle of redemption.

Though it includes repeated invitations to and commands for faith, the Bible does not consider faith to be a work that merits anything in return. Had God not already chosen to respond to our faith, our believing would have no consequence at all. Paul explicitly teaches that faith *by its nature* is the inverse of works: any benefit we receive from work is an obligatory payment for services rendered, whereas any benefit we receive as a consequence of faith is simply a gift, graciously credited to our account (see Rom 4:4-6). Works consist of exertion with the hope of earning something from God; faith is the abandonment of every hope of establishing ourselves before God or coercing divine favor. The prisoner did not will herself out of captivity with a grand display of grit and determination (Jn 1:13) but surrendered her will to a saving God. Throughout Scripture, faith is the supreme condition for salvation, and it never obscures to the slightest degree the grace of God or dilutes his role as the only Savior.

While unbelief must work to resist the good overtures of the Spirit and ward off the entreaties of a loving God, faith gives up the resistance and yields to God's will. In other words, belief and unbelief are not equal expressions of human effort or exertion. Sometimes Calvinists claim that Arminians fail to think consistently about the sin of unbelief. If Christ has died for all the sins of all persons as Arminians claim, then certainly Christ has died for their sins of unbelief. And if Christ has died for all sins of unbelief, then all will be saved. But this Calvinist objection misunderstands what Arminians believe about the atonement. We understand that the death of Jesus *makes provision* for the forgiveness of all sins, but it doesn't enact that forgiveness until sinners surrender in faith to God.[33] This makes it entirely reasonable to state that Christ died for all types of sins, including the sin of unbelief, but that those who persist in unbelief have not received the pardon that is yet possible for them.[34]

---

[33]Often it is charged that we who see the atonement as establishing the potential of salvation for all have created a theological system in which it might have been possible for no one to have believed and, therefore, for God to have utterly failed. Let us respond to this charge. First, it is a scenario that hasn't materialized. By the witness of Scripture itself, many scores of souls have believed and have received full salvation (e.g., Heb 11). Second, even if we were to grant a scenario (solely for the sake of argument) in which no human being ever responded in faith to God, we would insist that God's perfect love, mercy and justice would have been fully vindicated and that God's glory and reputation would in nowise be tarnished.

[34]This discussion includes the obviously complex questions of the atonement, such as which atonement theory best captures the biblical message. Calvinists typically subscribe to the *penal satisfaction* theory, which views the death of Christ as having fully paid, right there at Calvary and in fairly precise fashion, the penalties of all the sins of all who would be saved. In emphasizing the objective dimension of atonement (that it has been fully accomplished by Christ at Calvary), Calvinists tend to balk at any talk of the atonement as offering the possibility of forgiveness or the potential of salvation for any given individual.

In his helpful discussion of atonement theory, Donald Bloesch offers an account of the atonement that seeks to hold together its objective and subjective dimensions: "The situation of man has been objectively and radically changed [because of Calvary]. . . . Yet the new reality of Christ's redemption must penetrate and transform the inner being of man if he is to be included in the body of Christ. Christ suffered and atoned for all vicariously, but man remains bound to the powers of sin and corruption until he is brought by the Spirit into personal contact with the saving work of Christ. . . . All people have been redeemed objectively and de jure, but only the believer is redeemed in toto and de facto, since only he has personally appropriated the reality of Christ's salvation." And again, "God's . . . forgiveness is realized only in the decision of repentance and faith. In contrast to both Calvinistic and Arminian rationalism, we recognize that we are dealing with a rationally insurmountable mystery wherein the universality of God's electing love is held together with the particularity of realized salvation." Donald G. Bloesch, *Essentials of Evangelical Theology* (San Francisco: HarperCollins, 1978), 1:163-64, 167.

God's love for everyone guarantees that the Holy Spirit pursues everyone in every age, creating space for surrender and the possibility of final salvation. Since the conviction brought by the Holy Spirit includes an initial degree of illumination and enabling, we might even say that God unilaterally begins the process of salvation for everyone and presses to extend that process toward full salvation. The Spirit no doubt works in and through the varied experiences of life, creating greater or lesser windows of opportunity and seasons of greater or lesser conviction. Obviously, the Spirit has worked in cultures and contexts where truth has been limited and where the name of Jesus is not yet known. But God has not left them without a witness to basic truth (Acts 14:17), assuring that all can perceive the reality of a Creator and the necessity of surrendering in thankfulness to him (Rom 1). The sacrificial death of Jesus underwrites all of God's saving activity and assures that all the redeemed explicitly confess him as Lord, whether in this life or on that great day when they first see and recognize him.

But we must round out the story of the liberated prisoner in a way that leaves no ambiguity. Once rescued from captivity, the prisoner is not released to the outside world to do whatever she pleases. The Bible makes it clear that human freedom must choose between two masters— sin, which leads to death, or obedience to God, which leads to life (Rom 6:15-23). There is no third option. One cannot sit on the fence. To detach ourselves from God and pursue our private agendas is the essence of sin, and it detaches us from the very source of all life. Humans, created and sustained in freedom by God, ultimately face a simple fork in the road that they are not free to adjust or modify: "Choose for yourselves this day whom you will serve" (Josh 24:15).

PREDESTINATION (CALVINIST PERSPECTIVES AND AN ARMINIAN RESPONSE)

It is not uncommon for us to encounter folks who are convinced that the message of the Bible overwhelmingly affirms what we have proposed above:

- God has created a world distinct from himself with room for action and choice.
- God loves the whole world, fallen though it has become.
- Sin has exacted a terrible toll, rendering human beings unable and unwilling to receive the gospel.
- But God pursues every human being with inviting love and makes it possible for each person to respond positively to available light.
- The new life of liberty involves nothing less than full surrender to the Lord of life.

Yet many of these same folks are troubled, and rightly so, by those biblical passages that seem to teach an unconditional, individual predestination—that God unilaterally and unconditionally decides which individuals will be saved. We won't address here all the passages related to the Calvinist-Arminian debate, only those that have figured most prominently in discussions over the years.[35] Fresh assessment of these passages, studied in the light of their contexts, can lead to the view of redemption we are proposing.

John 6:37, 39, 44

All that the Father gives me will come to me, and whoever comes to me I will never drive away. . . . And this is the will of him who sent me, that I shall lose none of all that he has given me, but raise them up at the last day. . . . No one can come to me unless the Father who sent me draws him.

Calvinists detect in these words support for the belief that God has already selected those particular individuals he wishes to save. It will be these, and only these, whom God will draw to Jesus for salvation. All others will not be drawn and will therefore have no ability to see who Jesus really is or to believe in him. Many contemporary Arminians may

---

[35]For a wider response to a great many verses, see Geisler, *Chosen but Free*, pp. 55-114. See also the older but serviceable volume by Robert Lee Shank, *Life in the Son,* 2nd ed. (Springfield, Mo.: Westcott, 1960).

puzzle a bit over these verses, since their view of fallen humanity doesn't necessitate God's gracious work to make faith possible. Classical Arminians strenuously affirm the necessity of God's drawing grace but insist that such grace is universally and dynamically active in the Spirit's work among all peoples.

We have already explained why we find the contemporary Arminian view unacceptable, since it underestimates the binding and blinding power of sin. But neither of the other explanations accounts for the larger context of these verses. Against the classical Arminian explanation, it must be noted that Jesus was addressing hostile Jewish leaders who were in fact rejecting the teaching of Jesus. We must conclude, then, that Jesus' claim (that the Father *must* draw any who would come to Jesus) stands as the precise explanation for why these very hearers had rejected Jesus: the Father had not drawn them! It will not do, therefore, to imagine that the *drawing* Jesus has in mind here is a universal drawing of all persons toward salvation.

But the Calvinist reading likewise fails to account fully for the context. Jesus is locked in strenuous debate with religious leaders who claim special knowledge of and standing with God. From this privileged position, they seek to discredit Jesus completely. Their implied charge essentially involves an attempt *to sever Jesus from God, affirming the latter while rejecting the former.* In doing this, they wish to establish the right to claim, "We know God intimately, but you are utterly alien to us! We stand in right relationship to God, but we completely reject you."

Jesus' countercharge strikes directly at the root of their authority: the presumption that they knew God in the first place! "You have never heard his voice nor seen his form, nor does his word dwell in you" (Jn 5:37-38). Far from knowing God, then, Jesus' opponents had already rejected not only the testimony of John the Baptist but also of Moses: "If you believed Moses, you would believe me, for he wrote about me. But since you do not believe what he wrote, how are you going to believe what I say?" (Jn 5:46). In this question posed by Jesus we discover the key principle: rejecting God's first offerings of truth will utterly block further illumination. God will not offer more truth or manifest his full glory (the eternal Son) while light at hand is being spurned. In other words, we can't actively reject the Father and at the same time have any chance of accepting the Son. Since the Father and Son are one in nature, character and mission, the rejection of one necessarily involves the rejection of the other. The fundamental issue of this passage is not that of predestination but of Christology and the unity of the Father and Son.

The Jewish opponents' inability to come to Jesus did not lie, then, in the hidden, eternal plan of God but in their own track record of trampling prior light, of having already denied God himself and spurned God's corrective punishment. Had they received Moses fully, thereby coming to know the Father to the degree possible at that time, they would already have belonged to the Father's flock, and the Father would have drawn them to the Son. But in rejecting Jesus, they demonstrated that *they had never surrendered to God in the first place,* that they had set their faces like flint against all of his continued overtures. Since they did not belong to the Father's own flock, they wouldn't be part of the transfer of sheep already trusting the Father into the fold of the Son (Jn 6:37, 39). Their spiritual vanity came to full light when they imagined themselves as being qualified to pass judgment on Jesus, the very embodiment of all truth, while persistently spurning God's lesser lights (e.g., Moses and John the Baptist). Were they willing to drop their pretensions and surrender to God's teaching, they would have been taught by God and led on to the Lord of life, since Jesus promised that "everyone who listens to the Father and learns from him comes to me" (Jn 6:45).

Ephesians 1:4-5; 2:8

For he chose us in him before the creation of the world to be holy and blameless in his sight. In love he predestined us to be adopted as his sons through Jesus Christ, in accordance with his pleasure and will. . . . For it is by grace you have been saved, through faith—and this not from yourselves, it is the gift of God.

The most conspicuous feature of Ephesians 1:3—2:10 is the phrase "in

Christ" (or a similar expression), which occurs twelve times in Ephesians 1:3-14 alone. This unusual linguistic feature serves to fix our attention on Jesus as the source of all spiritual blessing, especially of redemption in all of its dimensions.

But have we said enough in saying this? The thrust of the language here in Ephesians is not simply that spiritual blessings come to us *through* Christ, as if he were merely their conduit, but that these rich treasures are found *in* Jesus. Since we have been baptized *into* Jesus (Rom 6:3) and have been united *with* him (Rom 6:5-8), we who have been redeemed have a new location, a new cosmic address. Now that we have been incorporated into Christ, we have entered into the drama of his own story. His death has become our death, his resurrection has become our resurrection (Eph 2:5), and his position of privilege at the Father's right hand brings us an immeasurable wealth of grace (Eph 2:6-7). Only by being *in him* can we share in the blessings he provides.

The reality of our incorporation into Christ saturates Paul's thinking and helps us grasp the idea of divine choice and predestination as taught in this passage. It is in him that we have been chosen and predestined (Eph 1:4-5), just as it is in him that we have been seated in heavenly places (Eph 2:6-7). This means that Jesus Christ himself is the chosen one, the predestined one. Whenever one is incorporated into him by grace through faith, one comes to share in Jesus' special status as chosen of God. As Markus Barth expresses it, "Election in Christ must be understood as the election of God's people. Only as members of that community do individuals share in the benefits of God's gracious choice."[36] This view of election most fully accounts for the corporate nature of salvation, the decisive role of faith and the overarching reliability of God's bringing his people to their destined end.[37]

But how do individuals enter (and remain in) the redeemed commu-

---

[36]Markus Barth, *Ephesians* (Garden City, N.Y.: Doubleday, 1974), p. 108.

[37]One of the most forceful voices from within the Reformed tradition advocating a corporate (as opposed to an individualistic) election is Herman Ridderbos, *Paul: An Outline of His Theology*, trans. John Richard de Witt (Grand Rapids: Eerdmans, 1975), pp. 350-54.

nity of God's people? We enter by faith: "For it is by grace you have been saved, through faith" (Eph 2:8). All agree that God's salvation requires a believing human response to God's gift of grace. But not all agree on the nature of this faith, especially on how faith itself arises. Calvinists are quick to point to other verses where an exact description of faith's origin appears to be provided: "through *faith*—and *this* not from yourselves, *it* is the gift of God" (Eph 2:8, emphasis added).

If faith is not our doing but God's gift, then the well-known features of Calvinism fall into place. Those who "have faith" have been given faith by God, and those who don't have faith have not been given faith by God. By this view, faith becomes a function of divine causation operating according to the individual electing will of God.

But the terms *(faith, this, it)* that seem so clearly linked in English are not so neatly connected in Greek. The English ear depends largely on word order for making sense of language, and so automatically presumes that *this* (which "is not from yourselves") must obviously refer back to *faith,* since *faith* immediately precedes *this* in the word order of the text. But Greek, being an inflected language, actually depends on "tags" that are attached to words for guiding the reader. If our writer had desired readers to connect *faith* directly to *this,* these two words should have matched each other as grammatically feminine. We find, however, that *this,* being neuter in gender, likely points us back several words earlier— to the idea of salvation expressed by the verb. Accordingly, we should read the text with a different line of connections as follows: "For it is by grace you have been *saved,* through faith—and *this [salvation is]* not from yourselves, *[this salvation]* is the gift of God."

Many Calvinists fear that any retreat from the conviction that God causes faith will make salvation a human accomplishment. If faith is something *we* do, then salvation rests on our deeds and no longer on God's grace. If faith is viewed as *our part* in the process of salvation, then salvation must be viewed as a cooperative affair, and we should then describe ourselves as *self-saviors* in part.

But the flaw in this Calvinist fear lies in its improper understanding of the nature of faith itself. The Bible itself does not describe faith as a work that accomplishes a task, or as a deed that establishes merit, or as a lever that forces God to act. Instead, we find that genuine faith is something quite different. As Paul's treatment of Abraham shows, the patriarch's faith had no power over God, earned no merit before God and stood as the polar opposite to honorific deeds. Abraham believed God, and righteousness was "credited" to him, not paid to him. God alone justified Abraham freely on the basis of Abraham's faith (Rom 4:1-6). Since *by its very nature* faith confesses the complete lack of human merit and human power, it subtracts nothing from the Savior's grace or glory. By its very nature, faith points away from all human status and looks to God alone for rescue and restoration.[38]

In an earlier discussion we explained that faith cannot arise unless God graciously clears the way for it by illuminating blind eyes, by enabling the will to yield to God's wooing and by instilling yearnings for God's love. Every believer is rightly grateful to God for his blazing a trail for faith through an impossible jungle of confusion and rebellion. Were God not to soften hearts and bring truth into focus, no one could or would believe at all.

Whenever humans begin yielding themselves in faith to God's saving work, their response in no way detracts from God, whose grace and power alone bring salvation. Imagine a horribly wounded victim lying helpless in an emergency room. The attending physician flies into action without waiting to obtain the victim's permission. She must establish a pulse, she must begin a blood transfusion, she must inject stimulants and seal the victim's wounds. Likewise, the process of salvation has been set into mo-

---

[38]We are aware that Calvinists will reject this analysis of faith. They insist on analyzing faith either as something caused by God (and therefore adding to God's glory) or as something caused by man (and therefore adding to man's glory). There is a simplicity and attractiveness to these alternatives, but we judge them inadequate for explaining faith as biblically portrayed—as something made possible by God and enacted by man, but not adding to man's glory. Again, the depiction of Abraham's faith (in Rom 4) points us in this direction, for it neither names God as the cause of Abraham's faith nor names Abraham as the one deserving praise.

tion long before the victim has any awareness of any need for help.

As the victim slowly emerges from unconsciousness, the physician begins engaging the patient and revealing both the somber realities of the moment as well as the long road ahead to recovery. "You are not yet free from the clutches of death, and even then you face many more surgeries. I want to rescue you and transform you! Will you let me?" If the patient says yes, this much is clear: all credit for the rescue belongs to the physician's caring initiative and skill. Months later, the restored patient will rightly insist that there is only one hero to thank and praise. Genuine human faith travels hand in hand with God's grace, as we see in the life of Abraham. Salvation is God's gracious gift granted to sinners on the condition of faith.[39]

Romans 8:29-30

For those God foreknew he also predestined to be conformed to the likeness of his Son, that he might be the firstborn among many brothers. And those he predestined, he also called; those he called, he also justified; those he justified, he also glorified.

Calvinists often speak of these verses as "the golden chain," an unbreakable sequence of steps in God's sovereign plan leading from unconditional, individual election to final glorification. The elect can find great comfort in the assurance that *all* those who begin the process (by God's election) *will* make it through to glorification. All those who know for certain that they have been justified possess an ironclad guarantee of their final salvation and glorification.

Our first hesitation in accepting this interpretation stems from the warning Paul issued to his Roman readers only sixteen verses earlier: "If you live according to the sinful nature, you will die; but if by the Spirit you put to death the misdeeds of the body, you will live" (Rom 8:13).

---

[39]The powerlessness of faith in itself can be seen if we imagine a different accident victim pinned under a car on a remote road. Hundreds or even thousands of signed permission slips will accomplish nothing in the absence of a doctor who desires to rescue the victim. It is God's gracious will both to make faith possible and to respond to human faith when it arises.

Paul makes it clear that glorification depends on a Christian's continued connection to Jesus: "If we are children, then we are heirs—heirs of God and co-heirs with Christ, if *indeed we share in his sufferings*" (Rom 8:17, emphasis added). Later we find Paul again warning his Gentile Christian readers that those who veer away from God's grace face fearful prospects: "If God did not spare the natural branches, he will not spare you either. Consider therefore the kindness and sternness of God: sternness to those who fell, but kindness to you, provided that you continue in his kindness. Otherwise, you also will be cut off" (Rom 11:21-22). Why would such warning ever be uttered if the "golden chain" of Romans 8:29-30 functions as an absolute guarantee for individuals?

Likewise, in Galatians, Paul identified the two lifestyles and their consequences: "Do not be deceived: God cannot be mocked. A man reaps what he sows. The one who sows to please his sinful nature, from that nature will reap destruction; the one who sows to please the Spirit, from the Spirit will reap eternal life" (Gal 6:7-8). This warning itself reemphasizes what Paul had declared to the Galatian believers earlier: "I warn you, as I did before, that those who live like this will not inherit the kingdom of God" (Gal 5:21).

It has often been suggested that these warnings expose no eternal danger to real Christians. We are told either that Paul was not addressing genuine Christians at all or that he was envisioning purely temporal dangers, such as illness or premature (physical) death.[40] But neither of these explanations can account for the specific content of these passages. At other times we are asked to imagine that Paul was engaging in rhetorical overstatement to spur his readers on to good behavior. This suggestion is both psychologically and morally troublesome, reminding us of parents who use empty threats to manipulate their unruly children (e.g., "Put that toy down now and come with me, or Mommy's going to leave the store without you"). If Paul believes that the elect are absolutely

---

[40]This does appear to be the case in 1 Corinthians 5:5; 11:30 and James 5:15-16. It would seem that sin can and sometimes does have an effect on health and lifespan.

guaranteed ultimate salvation and that this guarantee forms the very bedrock of Christian confidence in the face of suffering and trial, then it is puzzling to find him undercutting this very guarantee with warnings to the contrary. But if these stern warnings teach that the journey from election to glory is *not* inevitable, then we doubt that Paul was attempting to establish just the opposite in Romans 8:29-30.

If there is good reason to question the Calvinist interpretation of Romans 8:29-30, what other viable understandings might the text suggest? One direction relates to the verb tenses found in the fivefold sequence of God's actions: he foreknew, he predestined, he called, he justified, he glorified. Many point out that Paul expresses the last step in the past tense (*glorified*) even though for Paul and all Christians to date, glorification lies in the future. Less often realized is that the third and fourth steps (*called* and *justified*) are likewise presented as past events, though God has been and continues to be about the business of calling and justifying people down through the ages. This may show us that Paul is viewing the entire series not from a vantage point within human history but from the end of human history, after God has brought to completion the whole redemptive plan. Seen from the end of history, Paul observes that *all* Christians who have been glorified have of course been foreknown, predestined, called and justified. As James Dunn suggests:

> Paul is not inviting reflection on the classic problems of determinism and free will, or thinking in terms of a decree which excludes as well as one which includes. . . . His thought is simply that from the perspective of the end, it will be evident that history has been the stage for the unfolding of God's purpose, the purpose of the Creator fulfilling his original intentions in creating.[41]

A second (non-Calvinist) understanding of Romans 8:29-30 takes its cue from Paul's teaching in Romans 5 and 6 that sinners who once lived in Adam's lineage may (through faith) be incorporated "into Christ" through

---

[41]James D. G. Dunn, *Romans 1—8* (Dallas: Word, 1988), p. 486.

baptism (Rom 5:12-17; 6:3-4). Those now residing "in Christ" live in a new reality and benefit from the mighty events of death and resurrection that Jesus himself experienced. The apostle can therefore address believers themselves (all of whom are "in Christ") as those who have been buried with Jesus, or as those who have died with him, or as those who walk in newness of life, or as those who will experience resurrection "with him" (Rom 6:4, 8). Since Jesus is the primary character in the events of God's redemptive drama, we experience these events only indirectly, by being "in" the lead player. It is difficult to overstate just how significant for the whole of Pauline theology is this corporate vision of the church finding its identity, its salvation, its wealth and its security "in him."

Here we are back to the same ground already covered regarding Ephesians 1:4-5, where believers are described as having been chosen and predestined "in him." This only encourages us all the more to read Romans 8:29-30 as referring not to a specific, set number of persons who individually progress through the five "steps" without mathematical gain or loss, but to the whole body of Christ, without particular focus on the individuality of its members. The people of God as a whole, having been incorporated into Christ, are most certainly destined to arrive at the goal God has established from the beginning. Each of us is assured of participating in that most certain end, provided we *remain among* this people and *remain in* his kindness (Rom 11:22).

We can hardly improve on the way Herman Ridderbos, a Dutch Reformed scholar, has addressed the whole matter:

> [The certainty of salvation] does not rest on the fact that the church belongs to a certain "number," but that it belongs to Christ, from before the foundation of the world. Fixity does not lie in a hidden *decretum*, therefore, but in the corporate unity of the Church with Christ, whom it has come to know in the gospel and has learned to embrace in faith.[42]

---

[42]Herman Ridderbos, *Paul: An Outline of His Theology,* trans. John Richard de Witt (Grand Rapids: Eerdmans, 1975), pp. 350-51.

A third (non-Calvinist) understanding of Romans 8:29-30 asserts that the fivefold "chain," while certainly stressing divine action, must not be read as teaching that human actions play no role within the "chain." As all would agree, justification (element four in the chain) is explicitly conditioned throughout Romans upon human faith (e.g., Rom 5:1), and glorification (element five in the chain) is explicitly conditioned upon faithful suffering (Rom 8:17; compare with Phil 3:10-11). John Murray is even willing to permit, for the sake of argument, that God's loving choice of the elect (element one in the chain) is conditioned upon God seeing ahead of time who would believe. But before anyone imagines that Murray has inexplicably fallen into the Arminian camp, Murray hastens to explain that (in his view) acts of faith themselves cannot be defined as human activity, since God himself creates faith.[43] In other words, Murray allows that faith operates inside and between various elements of the chain but denies that faith is a genuinely free human act. In this way, Murray ends up defending a thoroughgoing monergism in which "God alone is active in those events which are mentioned and no activity of men supplies any ingredient of their definition or contributes to their efficacy."[44]

Our point here shall be modest. Murray's treatment undercuts the claim many Calvinists have made regarding Romans 8:29-30: that it stands as an immovable rock of Gibralter smashing all attempts to disprove Calvinism. In our judgment, Murray and others must already have in hand specific convictions about the nature of faith, along with particular beliefs about the necessity of "divine monergism," to guarantee an interpretation of Romans 8:29-30 that supports Calvinist views of predestination, etc. Arminian readings that understand (along with Dunn, for example) the chain as viewed by Paul from the end of time, or that understand (along with Ridderbos, for example) the entire chain as contained within the election and glorification of Christ,

---

[43]John Murray, *The Epistle to the Romans: The English Text with Introduction, Exposition and Notes*, one-volume ed. (Grand Rapids: Eerdmans, 1968), pp. 316 and 321 n. 62.
[44]Ibid., p. 321.

or that understand (in more traditional Arminian fashion) the chain as assuming—though not stressing—the conditions of human faith throughout, deal no less cogently or reasonably with the text at hand. In this case as in others, what we (all) bring to the text tends to be more than we might imagine.

As a final matter, we note that Calvinists often decry Arminian interpretations of Romans 8:29-30 as failing to provide a sufficiently strong sense of comfort and security to the believer. But it is ironic to hear Calvinists reject these interpretations on these emotional grounds, since it is Calvinists who often charge others with interpreting Scripture so as to gratify human emotions and sensitivities. In the case of Romans 8:29-30, why can't we claim that the Arminian interpretations challenge the human demand for absolute certainty and comfortable security, while the Calvinist interpretation caves in to that demand? In any event, Arminian readings do provide a large measure of comfort and assurance by affirming that God's overall plan will certainly come to fulfillment for all who continue trusting in God. It is our judgment that *this kind* of assurance is what this passage affirms, however fervently one might prefer the "ironclad guarantee" proposed by Calvinist interpreters.

Romans 9:11-12, 16, 18, 21

[God commanded that Esau serve Jacob] before the twins were born or had done anything good or bad—in order that God's purpose in election might stand: not by works but by him who calls. . . . It does not, therefore, depend on man's desire or effort, but on God's mercy. . . . Therefore God has mercy on whom he wants to have mercy, and he hardens whom he wants to harden. . . . Does not the potter have the right to make out of the same lump of clay some pottery for noble purposes and some for common use?

These verses form the most contested territory of the Calvinist-Arminian dispute. They appear to support directly the Calvinist teaching of an individual, unconditional election to salvation (and to damnation). What could be clearer than these straightforward declarations that God has mercy on whomever he wills, that human beings are but clay in his hands, and that the individual fates of Jacob and Esau were divinely determined without any consideration of their future responses to God? Indeed R. C. Sproul, a prominent Calvinist, claims that the entire edifice of Arminian theology is destroyed by a single verse: "It does not, therefore, depend on man's desire or effort, but on God's mercy" (Rom 9:16).[45]

But the context in which these verses are planted helps us grasp their sense more clearly, that is, Romans 9—11, recognized by most scholars as *a single cohesive argument* forming the climax of Romans 1—11.[46] Romans 9:1-5 sets the tone for the remainder of chapters 9—11, as Paul reveals the anguish of his heart over his fellow Jews, who have in large measure turned away from the gospel. If we fail to see that Paul from the start identifies *Israel's* unbelief as the cause of his anguish and the issue he wishes to pursue, we will likely misread many statements throughout these chapters and mistakenly build a theology on a single verse.[47] These three chapters, properly read together, address not so much the question of how *individuals* are saved (see Rom 3—6 for a direct address of these matters), but rather what Christians should say about *Israel* in light of its current rejection of the gospel.

If many of Paul's fellow Jews resisted the gospel because God had (unconditionally) chosen to elect some individuals for salvation and others for damnation (as Rom 9:11 alone might be read), it is hard to understand why such a simple claim requires three chapters of explanation,

---

[45]R. C. Sproul, *Chosen by God* (Wheaton, Ill.: Tyndale House, 1986), p. 151.

[46]The single greatest weakness of John Piper's Calvinistic interpretation of Romans 9 is his failure to account adequately for the remainder of Paul's argument in Romans 10—11. In these chapters (esp. in the image of branches being broken off, perhaps being grafted in, perhaps being broken off again and then perhaps grafted in yet again) we see most vividly that Paul views unconditional election in a corporate sense and individual salvation conditioned not on a divine decree, but on the faith of individuals. Not once does Piper mention Romans 11:22-23, verses that directly challenge his interpretation of unconditional, individual divine election in Romans 9. John Piper, *The Justification of God* (Grand Rapids, Mich.: Baker, 1983), p. 306.

[47]For a readable treatment of the whole argument of Romans 9—11, we recommend Paul J. Achtemeier, *Romans* (Atlanta: John Knox Press, 1985), pp. 153-92, esp. pp. 161-65.

and why the warning against the clay's questioning the potter (Rom 9:19-20) should not immediately end the entire discussion. If it is God's sovereign will to unconditionally damn specific persons, then it is also difficult to account for Paul's anguish over their loss and for his zealous and hopeful efforts to *save* some of them (Rom 11:14). But Paul has much more to say beyond Romans 9:23, and his line of argument leads away from a deterministic interpretation of salvation.

Paul contends that Israel is still God's designated lineage of salvation and that faith in Christ remains God's designated avenue of salvation. Both elements of this claim must be preserved for Paul's gospel to stand. If Paul allows membership in Israel to determine salvation, then salvation by faith is no longer the sole avenue through which God redeems fallen creatures. But if Paul casts off the unique status of Israel in order to safeguard salvation by faith alone, then God's character and reliability are undercut and all is lost. The care Paul takes in establishing both of these seemingly irreconcilable claims signals just how essential their harmony is for bringing his whole argument (Rom 1—11) to a successful conclusion.

Paul is apparently worried that some Gentile Christians are all too ready to dispense entirely with Israel and its history (see Rom 11:18-21), perhaps reasoning that if God awards salvation by faith alone apart from national identity, and if most Jews have rejected God's call to this salvation, then the nation has sinned away its privileged position; its national identity has become irrelevant. But Paul emphatically halts such thinking. He asks, "Did God reject his people?" and immediately supplies an unequivocal answer, "By no means!" (Rom 11:1). Though some (if not most) Israelites have fallen, Paul insists that the nation still functions as God's chosen vessel, serving as God's instrument in extending his gospel to the world (Rom 11:11-12, 15). Furthermore, Gentiles who now believe in Jesus must realize that they, like wild olive branches, have been grafted into an ancient tree. Despite having lost many branches, the original tree remains the chosen tree—the vital trunk supplies God's life to all living branches, whether natural or engrafted ones (Rom 11:18, 24).

The ancient tree of Israel, planted by grace, remains the chosen tree, for "God's gifts and his call are irrevocable" (Rom 11:29).

Paul distinguishes the irrevocable call of the nation of Israel as a whole from the fate of individual Israelites. While the final destination of the people of God is absolutely certain, the future of any given individual is determined by his or her continued faith and trust in God. Gentiles who believe are grafted into the ancient tree, whereas Jews who fall into unbelief are broken off. Since faith is the sole condition for remaining engrafted, Paul issues both warning and hope. On the one hand, those Gentiles who have recently been grafted into the ancient tree through faith must humbly guard against falling into unbelief, since they too would then be severed from the tree. On the other hand, the natural branches lying on the ground can "be grafted into their own olive tree" if "they do not persist in unbelief" (Rom 11:23-24). In other words, the destiny of God's people as a whole is unchanged throughout the ages, though each individual branch participates in this salvation only if he or she remains engrafted by faith (cf. Jn 15:5-6). As Paul Achtemeier explains, Paul teaches destiny without teaching individual determinism.[48]

But we have yet to see the fullness of Paul's agony. For though God's faithfulness to Israel's lineage stands secure alongside the gospel of salvation by faith, Paul is painfully aware that most of his people have turned aside from the gospel, even showing a hardened resistance to it. Neutral observers could wonder whether God has properly proclaimed the gospel of Jesus to Israel or whether the large-scale rejection of the gospel among the people of Israel will ultimately derail God's larger plan.

In Romans 10 Paul asserts that Israel's failure to receive the gospel did not follow from simple ignorance. Instead, Israel refused to submit to God's provisions, stubbornly insisting on establishing its own righteousness (Rom 10:3). The gospel message has been spread so widely that Paul employs Psalm 19:4 to characterize its reach: "Their voice has gone out into all the earth, their words to the ends of the world." If Israel is

---

[48]Ibid., pp. 163-64.

ignorant of God's gift of righteousness by faith (Rom 10:3), this igno-rance is Israel's own creation, rooted in its refusal to listen to the message even now. God's lament over wayward Israel in Isaiah's day remains trag-ically accurate in Paul's day: "All day long I have held out my hands to a disobedient and obstinate people" (Rom 10:21; cf. Is 65:1-2).

But what then of the divine plan for Israel? Is it a success if in the end only a few original branches can be found on the ancient trunk? Here we reach Paul's remarkable vision of the future. Essentially, he envisions the reversal of an older prophetic expectation. Isaiah, for example, looked forward to the day when God's people would so thoroughly cast out evil and obey the Lord that they would become a beacon of truth to the world: "The nations will see your righteousness, and all kings your glory" (Is 62:2; see also Is 56:7-8; 60:1-22). Israel's restoration would lead to the gathering of the Gentiles in an "Israel first, then the Gentiles" sequence of redemption.

But in light of Israel's present rejection of the gospel, Paul announces that God will now work in the inverse sequence: it will be the Gentiles first, then Israel. Israel is in a hardened state, while multitudes of Gen-tiles are streaming to God and will continue to do so until the Gentile response reaches its fullness. At that point, Paul envisions that many Jews will turn in faith to Jesus, marking the completion of God's redemp-tive plan (Rom 11:12, 25-27). So unexpected is this reversed sequence that it constitutes a "mystery" only recently made known to the church (Rom 11:25; see also Acts 15:14-21).

Israel's present condition, though it grieves God and Paul alike, does not represent the end of Israel. Israel's hardness is temporary because this hardness may be reversed; it is conditional because it will last only so long as unbelief persists (Rom 11:23). Paul hopes to penetrate the Jews' hard hearts from time to time through proclamation of the gospel (Rom 11:14), showing that such hardness can scarcely be considered an unconditional and irreversible decree of God's eternal will.

But we must ask why God hardens hearts at all. What does he hope to accomplish? Pharaoh's story will help us clarify Paul's argument. With

Pharaoh, we see a man already shaking his fist in defiance even as Moses first issued God's command: "Who is the LORD, that I should obey him and let Israel go? I do not know the LORD and I will not let Israel go" (Ex 5:2). We see that Pharaoh was obstinate even before God began to harden his heart. It is apparent that God did not transform Pharaoh from a meek and mild gentleman to the fire-breathing dragon Moses met; rather God strengthened Pharaoh's heart in the perverse direction Pharaoh himself had already resolutely chosen.[49]

Why was such strengthening necessary? To enable Pharaoh to go more than one round with the omnipotent God, so that God could repeatedly display his overwhelming power through a series of plagues. But here is the key: God designed this impressive display of power to reveal the truth about himself to Pharaoh's people. God tells Moses, "The Egyptians will know that I am the LORD when I stretch out my hand against Egypt and bring the Israelites out of it" (Ex 7:5). We discern the positive aspects of this gift when we realize that God desired to also reveal himself to his own people: "[I shall bring about the fourth plague] so that you will know that I, the LORD, am in this land" (Ex 8:22). God strengthened Pharaoh's obstinacy in order to reveal himself more widely among all peoples of the earth as the one and only God (Ex 9:16; Rom 9:17).

Turning back to Paul's argument, we see that understanding Pharaoh's story helps us make sense of Israel's hardness. God did not create Pharaoh's initial hostility any more than he caused Israel's initial unbelief. Rather God reinforced their tendencies to bring about a greater proclamation of his truth around the world. While some might have wondered whether the unbelief of God's chosen people would thwart God's plan to redeem the world through Israel, Paul assures us that God will triumph even more spectacularly by using Israel's unbelief to serve his larger purpose. While Paul does not flesh out the dynamics involved, the book of Acts repeatedly shows that the Jews' hostile reaction to Christian preach-

---

[49]Here we agree with Sproul's assessment of the hardening of Pharaoh as "passive hardening." Sproul, *Chosen by God*, pp. 143-46.

ing actually propelled the gospel to ever-wider Gentile audiences.[50] Jewish resistance to the gospel formed, in effect, a bridge the apostles and evangelists crossed to evangelize the nations of the world. God transformed their resistance into opportunity.

But standing in the way of Paul's teaching were the strong presumptions of many Jews that Abraham's descendants were assured salvation and that any theology which allowed that an Israelite might be "lost" would render God's promise to Abraham a failure (see Rom 9:6). To counter this view, Paul shows that a genealogical approach to salvation has never been valid, even in Israel's own history. God chose Isaac but not Ishmael, though Abraham was the father of both. God chose Jacob over Esau, though they were both sons of Isaac. God's distinction between children within the genetic lineage of Abraham proves God's freedom to operate along lines other than genetic ties (Rom 9:6-13).

To make sense of Romans 9—11 as a whole, we must identify properly those most offended by Paul's claim that God may choose to be merciful to whomever God wishes (Rom 9:14). Calvinists typically understand the objectors to be the non-elect worldwide whom God has chosen to "hate." According to this interpretation, the non-elect accuse God of acting unfairly because he chooses some humans for salvation while passing over others for no discernible reason. Paul, according to the Calvinist view, defends God's right to act unconditionally in choosing to have mercy on or to harden whomever he wishes.

While this interpretation makes some sense within the confines of Romans 9:6-26 alone, it stands at odds with the rest of Romans 9—11, which emphasizes that faith is what distinguishes the redeemed from the lost. Furthermore, the focus of chapters 9 through 11 has not been on the world at large but on Israel—eternally chosen but still unbelieving (Rom 11:28). If Paul is claiming that God can be faithful to this nation as a whole while pouring out his wrath on many of its individual members, the chief objectors to Paul likely are Jews! Indeed, the presumption

---

[50]See Acts 8:1-4, 14; 11:19-23; 13:46-48; 17:1-15; 19:8-10; 23:1-11; 28:25-29.

of Paul's Jewish opponents in Romans 2:1—3:20 is that their membership in Abraham's genetic lineage and possession of the law should render them immune to God's final wrath (see esp. Rom 2:1-29).

To identify God's accusers in Romans 9:14 as Paul's Jewish opponents,
then, makes all the difference in interpreting the rest of this passage. The
justice Jews were demanding from God was not equal treatment of all
human beings (in the spirit of modern liberals or humanists who demand "fairness" from God on their own terms); rather, they were demanding the guarantee of salvation to every individual Israelite. In effect,
the accusers were demanding that God's mercy be given only to the descendants of Abraham and that Gentiles first transform themselves into
Jews before receiving salvation (cf. Gal 2:14).

When Paul asserts God's freedom to have mercy on whomever he
wishes, Paul is not forging a doctrine of unconditional individual election but establishing God's freedom to pour out his mercy beyond the
boundaries of Jewish ethnic identity. To those Jews who cherished a nar-
rower version of God's mercy, Paul repeated God's word to Moses: "I will
have mercy on whom I have mercy, and I will have compassion on whom
I have compassion" (Rom 9:15; cf. Ex 33:19). There is a wideness in
God's mercy!

Paradoxically then, God's selection of Isaac and Jacob over Ishmael
and Esau ultimately served to *broaden* the flow of mercy by dethroning
simple genetic connection to Abraham. Now the gates are open wide for
God's plan of universal mercy to come into play. The question that naturally arises at this point is, how wide is his mercy? The answer is explicitly announced in Romans 11:32: "For God has bound all men over to
disobedience so that he may have mercy on them all." In other words, as
wide as the *problem* of sin reaches (universally), so wide has God's mercy
spread in granting the *possibility* of salvation (universally). While Paul
himself does not draw these loose ends together, we may surmise that
even the descendants of Ishmael and Esau—whose lineages were ruled
out as carriers of the sonship, the covenants, the receiving of the law, the
temple worship and the promises—can enter into the stream of God's

mercy by faith, just as any other wild olive branch might.

We are now in a position to clarify two of the most challenging issues in chapter 9: the right of God to harden whomever he desires and the role (if any) of human faith in God's sovereign choice of Jacob over Esau. Our review of the whole drift of Romans 9—11 now provides crucial guidance in seeing the point Paul shapes in using the story of Pharaoh and the image of the potter. Since the present unbelief and possible future conversion of (presently) unbelieving Israel drives the whole of this three-chapter argument (Rom 9:1-5; 11:25-32), it is nearly certain that Paul's reference to two different vessels being crafted from the "same lump" (Rom 9:19-24) correspond to the two different subgroups making up the one nation of Israel: believing Jews and unbelieving Jews. God has the right, Paul explains, to harden and make use of this unbelieving portion of Israel *even though* these very folk are Abraham's physical descendants, those privileged to possess the sonship, the glory, the covenants, the law, the temple worship, the promises and the patriarchs (see Rom 9:3-5), and even though they are beloved for the sake of the fathers (Rom 11:28). In other words, their privileged position on these matters cannot shield them from God's punishment for their sin and faithlessness, or from God's choice to harden them in their sin in order to accomplish God's larger purposes. And it is clear from the way Paul wraps up his treatment of the whole matter in chapter 11 that the hardening of some Jews and their preparation (as vessels of wrath) for destruction (Rom 9:22-23) is *not* rooted in an irreversible, eternal, unconditional divine decree, since it is rooted in nothing other than their own unbelief (Rom 9:31-32; 10:1-4, 18-21; 11:20, 30-31), *which may one day yield to saving faith,* whether on a small scale (Rom 11:13-14) or on a larger scale (Rom 11:12, 15, 23-27). God has a sovereign right, insists Paul, to condition the salvation of individual Israelites upon their faith, however deeply this may offend their sense of entitlement based on their racial connection to Abraham (Rom 11:19-21).

Finally, we approach Paul's teaching that God chose Jacob over Esau "before the twins were born or had done anything good or bad—in order that God's purpose in election might stand: not by works but by him who calls" (Rom 9:11-12). Accordingly, "It does not, therefore, depend on man's desire or effort, but on God's mercy" (Rom 9:16). Now if these verses are stripped from their place within the whole argument of Romans 9—11, then they quite easily conform to the Calvinist doctrine of unconditional, individual election to salvation. But again the larger context and flow of the argument takes us in another direction. If Paul's focus all along has been upon that large body of unbelieving Jews who imagine that their physical connection to the people of Israel guarantees salvation, then it is quite likely that the "doing of good or bad" and "works" and human "desire or effort" have reference to what Paul has targeted again and again throughout Romans: *Jewish confidence that possessing and doing (specific features of) the Mosaic law will guarantee salvation* (e.g., Rom 2:17-29). Put differently, Paul is not sweeping every human response or choice or act of faith off the table as irrelevant in the matter of salvation. He is sweeping away the kind of narrow dedication to doing the law that Paul himself reported as part of his own pre-Christian past: "If anyone else thinks he has reasons to put confidence in the flesh, I have more: circumcised on the eighth day, of the people of Israel, of the tribe of Benjamin, a Hebrew of Hebrews; in regard to the law, a Pharisee; as for zeal, persecuting the church; as for legalistic righteousness, faultless" (Phil 3:4-6).

That precisely this kind of "doing" is in view here in Romans 9 is confirmed when Paul immediately turns to diagnose the problem of unbelieving Jews: "For I can testify about them that they are zealous for God, but their zeal is not based on knowledge. Since they did not know the righteousness that comes from God and sought to establish their own, they did not submit to God's righteousness. Christ is the end of the law so that there may be righteousness for everyone who believes" (Rom 10:2-4). Note that Paul does not condemn zeal in and of itself, but misdirected zeal. Nor does Paul sweep human choice and response away as irrelevant, but he urges submission and faith. In other words, God's choice of Jacob over Esau reinforces Paul's steady opposition to trust in the (Mosaic) law: God chose one lad over the other before either had a chance to engage the works of the law, making it clear that *by such works*, righteousness will not be attained.[51] Rather, salvation is found by submitting to and trusting in the gracious God of Israel.

In summary, Romans 9—11 tells the story of God's determination to extend his mercy beyond the confines of Abraham's genetic lineage, to preserve the special status of this nation as "gifted and called" despite the disobedience of many individual Israelites, and then to lavish them with an even grander measure of mercy when they abandon their unbelief (Rom 11:23-27). God, in his sovereign freedom, does extend mercy even to Gentiles while hardening some disobedient Jews, though this may offend Jewish sensitivities. Furthermore, God's unconditional selection of Jacob over Esau before they could do any good works shows that God's salvation will be granted *neither* as a birthright to Abraham's physical descendants *nor* as a reward to those privileged to possess (and perform in part) the Mosaic law. Rather, it is the sovereign God's will that all who believe, whether Jew or Gentile, be grafted into the holy tree of salvation. The beauty and majesty of God's plan for universal mercy stirs Paul to an outburst of praise: "Oh, the depth of the riches of the wisdom and knowledge of God! How unsearchable his judgments, and his paths beyond tracing out!" (Rom 11:33).

In this brief treatment of biblical material, we have defended a view of God's salvation that honors his decision to create a world of free creatures. It celebrates God's loving pursuit of all persons for salvation; it

---

[51]A similar case is made in James D. G. Dunn, *Romans 9—16*, Word Biblical Commentary (Dallas, Tex.: Word, 1988), p. 549. It is surprising that Moo rejects the possibility that performance of the Mosaic law (after a fashion) is in view in the case of Esau and Jacob (Douglas J. Moo, *The Epistle to the Romans* [Grand Rapids: Eerdmans, 1996], p. 582 n. 55). While it is true that Paul in Galatians insists that the law came centuries after the patriarchs (Gal 3:17), it is also true that here in Romans Paul argues that Abraham's faith preceded his *circumcision* (Rom 4:9-12). The point of identifying Abraham's circumcision no doubt relates to the strong place of circumcision in the Mosaic law, and the common Jewish belief (in Paul's day) that Abraham knew and obeyed the Mosaic law. See Joseph A. Fitzmyer, *Romans: A New Translation with Introduction and Commentary* (New York: Doubleday, 1992), pp. 372, 384.

finds human faith (uncaused by God) as the fundamental condition for receiving God's gracious salvation; and it views the divine election of Israel and Christ as that tree of redemption into which all persons can be incorporated by faith. We read in Scripture of sin's devastating power to cripple all dimensions of the human realm, but we also find clues that God lovingly pursues all persons by graciously creating room for their positive response to available light. We discourage any approach to Scripture that imagines a single verse can prove or disprove a given doctrine. Rather, we encourage the study of passages within their various contexts with literary and theological sensitivity.

3

CALVINISM
AND THE NATURE
OF HUMAN FREEDOM

உச

I (Jerry) encountered a full-blooded, serious Calvinist for the first time during my student years at Princeton Theological Seminary. Princeton is one of the great institutions in the Reformed tradition, and it was home to such giants of Reformed theology as Benjamin Warfield and Charles Hodge. By the time I was a student there, it had long since abandoned its founders' staunch confessional views in favor of tolerant diversity, and most of the students were mainline Presbyterians who were no more sympathetic toward the classic Calvinistic account of predestination than I was. If you wanted to debate matters such as unconditional election and irresistible grace, it was hard to find advocates with whom to argue.

There were, however, a few exceptions to the polite Presbyterian theology held by most students and faculty. I met one of these exceptions soon after my arrival at Princeton, and he quickly became one of my best friends. Bruce was a great friend to have if you enjoyed a good theological argument. Although he was a new student, as I was, he was finishing a Ph.D. in mathematics at Princeton University. Obviously very intelligent, he was also truly Reformed and was willing to defend even the more controversial aspects of Calvinism.

Although my undergraduate years had been split between Circleville Bible College and Houghton College, both Wesleyan institutions, I had been raised in a denomination that did not take sides between Calvin and Wesley. I had Wesleyan leanings by the time I enrolled in Princeton, though I was still far from committed on the matter. But Bruce was a convinced Calvinist, so I took the Wesleyan position for the sake of argument. And argue we did, for countless hours.

An argument, philosophically speaking, is nothing more or less than a reasoned presentation of ideas. Argument in this sense is not only one of the most valuable ways we have to learn, but it is also a way to clarify our own convictions. And these arguments were certainly very valuable for developing my understanding of the issues in this dispute. I was never persuaded to embrace Calvinism and, so far as I know, Bruce was never convinced that he should give it up.

I do not remember all the details of these debates, but I do recall my perplexity at what seemed to me to be obvious inconsistencies in Calvinism and the difficulty in pinning these down; my sense was that Calvinistic theology was deeply incoherent, but I was unable to identify exactly why this was so. For instance, according to Calvinism, it is entirely up to God who is and is not saved, and if one is not numbered among the elect, one cannot help but sin. And yet God blames sinners and punishes them for their unbelief even though they cannot act otherwise. Round and round Bruce and I went as we argued matters like this, but the debate always seemed to reach an impasse.

After graduating from Princeton, I went on to Yale Divinity School, where I spent another year studying philosophical theology and writing a master's thesis. It was during this research that I began to see for the first time why the difficulties I sensed in Calvinism are so elusive. What I discovered were some basic philosophical categories that shed new light on my numerous debates and on what I had read on the matter. Once enlightened, I saw that insightful discussion of this controversy could not proceed without an understanding of these categories.

In this book we certainly do not mean to give philosophy pride of place over Scripture. But we are saying that philosophical commitments, however modest or unformed they may be, are inevitable. Moreover, people who are least aware of their philosophical commitments are most bound and blinded by them. So we need to be aware of our philosophical commitments, constantly scrutinizing them for their faithfulness to Scripture and their coherence with our other convictions.

The categories we want to discuss pertain to different ways of understanding the nature of freedom, particularly human freedom. Philosophical analysis often only makes explicit and precise what is implicit and general. Scripture of course does not explicitly state these categories, but that should not count against them in any way. It is also the case that Scripture does not explicitly state the orthodox doctrines of the incarnation and the Trinity, but most evangelicals would readily assent to the historic creeds that make them explicit and defend them as crucially important statements of our faith. The classic doctrinal statements on the Trinity and the incarnation employ philosophical categories to make explicit what is only implicit in Scripture. Similarly, the philosophical categories we will discuss in relation to the nature of freedom will help us make explicit what is implicit in Scripture and help us to interpret it in a coherent fashion.

We will begin by simply naming the categories for readers who may be unfamiliar with these terms. They are as follows: "hard determinism," "libertarian freedom" and "soft determinism" (also called *compatibilism*).[1] These three terms represent three significantly different views of freedom in relation to determinism. So before we can define these terms properly, we need to define *determinism*.

DETERMINISM DEFINED

Determinism, simply put, is the view that every event must have hap-

---

[1]The discussion below follows standard definitions of these terms. See, e.g., Richard Taylor, *Metaphysics,* 4th ed. (Englewood Cliffs, N.J.: Prentice-Hall, 1992), pp. 35-53; and William Hasker, *Metaphysics* (Downers Grove, Ill.: InterVarsity Press, 1983), pp. 29-55.

pened exactly as it did because of prior conditions. Given these prior events and circumstances, the event could not have happened any other way. In philosophical language, these prior events and circumstances represent a *sufficient condition* for the event to occur. When such a condition is present, the event must occur exactly as it does.

A sufficient condition must be distinguished from a *necessary* one. Here is an illustration of the difference. A necessary condition for a match to ignite is the presence of oxygen. However, the presence of oxygen is not a sufficient condition for a match to ignite. There are lots of matches—wet ones for example—that do not ignite in the presence of oxygen. However, suppose that in addition to being in the presence of the necessary oxygen, the match is also dry and is properly struck or otherwise exposed to heat. In this case, we have a sufficient condition for the match to ignite. Given these circumstances, it not only will ignite but must ignite. Given these circumstances, it is a matter of causal necessity that the match will light.

To put it another way, determinism affirms what philosophers call the *principle of universal causality*. In essence this principle claims that all things that happen are caused by sufficient conditions in which nothing that happens could vary in even the slightest detail. Nothing lies outside the pale of universal causality. All events are part of an unbreakable causal chain that stretches back perhaps to infinity. Every link in the chain is strictly caused by the one that preceded it.

Let's consider another example to help us get a clear picture of the deterministic view of reality. Think about the motion of the moon as it revolves around the earth. We can predict with great precision the location of the moon two months from now. We can do so because we know both the moon's present position and state as well as the laws that govern the motion of such heavenly bodies. Given these circumstances, it follows as a matter of causal necessity that the moon will be in such and such a location two months from now.

The theory of determinism says that all events are determined just as surely as the motion of the moon and the planets are. Why? Because universal laws govern the rest of the physical world just as they do the motion of the planets. Everything from the largest planets down to the smallest particles of matter is determined to behave just as it does. Of course, we do not yet know all the relevant laws, but if we did, it would be possible in principle to know the future with complete certainty. In addition to knowing all the universal laws of nature, we would need to know the state and location of every piece of matter in the universe. Knowing all of this, it would be possible in principle for someone of extraordinary intelligence to have comprehensive knowledge of all future events in the physical universe.

This theory of determinism had its heyday in that era of modern science when laws of nature were being discovered with dizzying success and when it seemed that everything could be explained in terms of natural law. More recently, the deterministic view has been shaken by the discovery of fundamental indeterminacy at the quantum level of physics, not to mention chaos theory and the like. Whether this indeterminacy is a serious problem for determinism at the level of larger objects is not clear.

But the point is that the ambition of deterministic theory was to embrace everything under its purview, including human actions. After all, our bodies are physical objects and as such are constituent parts of the larger cosmos governed by natural law. In theory then, our actions are determined just as the motions of the heavenly bodies are, even if we have not yet discovered the relevant laws. Given prior conditions, none of our actions could ever be other than they are. Everything we do is causally necessary. The fact that the very words you are reading, and not others, were typed was necessitated by conditions and events that existed long before you were born. These events and conditions led to others in an unbreakable causal chain that eventually led to my typing and your reading these very words!

In contemporary deterministic theory, other factors besides natural law are often cited to account for why our choices must occur as they do. Advocates of determinism appeal, for instance, to psychological, social and cultural conditioning, along with genetic theory, in order to explain human behavior in deterministic terms. It is not necessary for our purposes to engage these different theories in detail because it does not matter how our choices are allegedly determined in order for us to distinguish the different views of freedom. The essential point is that according to determinism, prior conditions—however those conditions are specified or identified—causally determine all later events, including our choices.

Now we have the essential background information that we need to define the relevant categories of human freedom. Before formulating these three definitions, however, we want to describe a scenario involving morally significant choices in order to make vivid the differences between the three positions.

Consider Jonny, a teenage boy who, along with his friends Steven and Adam, has been involved in some minor acts of vandalism. As the young culprits engage in their nocturnal activity, they experience a range of emotions. On the one hand, they enjoy a certain thrill from doing what is forbidden, from the element of risk and secrecy. On the other hand, they realize that what they are doing is wrong, and they feel some sense of guilt; they also realize they could be punished if they are caught and would prefer to avoid this consequence.

As they negotiate these thoughts and feelings, the thrill and excitement they experience outweighs their sense of guilt and prudence. But one night, Jonny and his cohorts have second thoughts as they plan their business. They have heard that the local police may be onto them, and they admit to one another that they have certain reservations about continuing, although the reservations are not decisive. "Hey, we've made it so far. And we will be extra careful tonight," Adam remarks. Steven adds with a smile, "I don't think they will catch us. At least they won't catch me." After a moment's thought, Jonny brushes his reservations aside and replies, "Whatever. Let's go."

Still, their reservations persist, and they continue to debate in their own minds whether they should carry through with the night's escapade. Just before they reach the scene of their crime, they nearly back out. But they tell themselves that they will not get caught and that even if they do, their crime is a minor one. Holding on to these thoughts, the young vandals steal the hood ornaments from several cars. Unfortunately for them, their assessments were wrong. The police were onto them; they were apprehended and taken to the station for questioning.

HARD DETERMINISM

With this scenario in mind, let's define *hard determinism*. First, the fundamental assumption of hard determinism is the principle of universal causality: every event has a sufficient cause and is part of an unbreakable causal chain with a very long (perhaps infinite) history. Second, hard determinism has a distinctive understanding of a free act: namely, a free act is one that has no cause and thus no causal history.

It takes very little logical skill to see what follows from these two claims. If every event has a cause and a free act has no cause, then clearly there are no free acts. And this is exactly what hard determinists readily conclude. We are not free, they claim; and moreover, we are not responsible for our actions. Consequently, one deserves neither blame nor praise for one's actions, since all actions are the necessary result of natural law.

We can put the argument connecting freedom and moral responsibility more explicitly:

Premise 1: If we are morally responsible for our actions, then we must be free.
Premise 2: We are not free.
Conclusion A: Therefore, we are not morally responsible for our actions.

This is a valid argument. That is to say, the conclusion follows logically from the premises by way of the valid argument form *modus tollens.* If the premises are true, then the conclusion must be true as well. It is important to emphasize that the conclusion is true *if* the premises are true. If the premises are true and the argument form is a valid one, then the argument is sound. Note that all sound arguments are valid, but not all valid ones are sound. Hard determinists believe both premises to be true, so they take this argument to be both valid and sound.

In denying that we are free, the hard determinist does not mean to deny that all of us have a subjective sense of freedom—we feel we are free. So in the scenario described above, Jonny and his friends experience certain psychological states such as thoughts and feelings, including the feeling that they could have chosen not to vandalize the cars. But the sense of freedom and the feeling that the choices they made were up to them are illusory. In reality, all of their feelings and the resulting choices were determined by factors long before Jonny and his friends were born. Their actions are part of a causal chain that stretches back indefinitely into the past and unbreakably forward into the future. They could not have made any other choice than to steal the hood ornaments.

In view of this, the hard determinist will insist, the police chief has no rational grounds to blame them morally or to scold or punish them. Of course, the chief is also determined in his thoughts, feelings and actions, and it may be that the causal chain is so constituted that he inevitably will punish them. After all, if no one is free and responsible for his or her actions, then the chief is no freer to behave differently than are the young hoodlums he is determined to punish.

LIBERTARIAN FREEDOM

Now let's describe a second position, *libertarian freedom*. The essence of this view is that a free action is one that does not have a sufficient condition or cause prior to its occurrence; it also holds that some human actions are free in this sense. Defenders of libertarian freedom hold to this view for a number of reasons. First, the common experience of deliberation assumes that our choices are undetermined. When we deliberate, we not only *weigh* the various factors involved, we also *weight* them. That is, we decide how important different considerations are in relation to one another. These factors do not have a preassigned weight that everyone must accept. Part of deliberation is sifting through these factors and deciding how much they matter to us. All of this assumes that it really is up to us how we will decide.

Second, it seems intuitively and immediately evident that many of our actions are up to us in the sense that when faced with a decision, both (or more) options are within our power to choose. Of course, our feeling that we have this power could be illusory, as determinists claim. We have to decide between conflicting claims. As is often the case with philosophical judgments of this sort, we must decide which claim is more certain. Libertarians argue that our immediate sense of power to choose between alternative courses of action is more certain and trustworthy than any theory that denies we have this power.

Third, libertarians take very seriously the widespread judgment that we are morally responsible for our actions and that moral responsibility requires freedom. They would assent to the first premise of the argument spelled out above. However, they would deny the second premise and replace it with another one, and then draw a different conclusion, as follows:

Premise 1: If we are morally responsible for our actions, we must be free.
Premise 4: We are morally responsible for our actions.
Conclusion B: Therefore, we must be free.

This argument is also valid, but in this case the argument form is *modus ponens*.[2] So the issue debated between the hard determinist and the libertarian is which second premise is true. According to the libertarian, the deeply rooted human belief in moral responsibility is a strong indication that we are free.

Of course, premise 1 is crucial to the argument as well. While hard determinists and libertarians can agree on it, others would dispute it. For instance, Calvinist theologian R. K. McGregor Wright claims that no one has ever demonstrated that moral responsibility requires free will. He

---

[2]*Modus ponens* and *modus tollens* are, of course, two of the most basic and well-known valid argument forms and can be found in any standard logic text. *Modus ponens* follows this form: If *P* then *Q*; *P*; therefore *Q*. *Modus tollens* takes this form: If *P* then *Q*; *not Q*; therefore *not P*.

recognizes that this is a widely shared assumption, even among many Calvinists, but he believes it needs proof: "I will simply repeat here Gordon Clark's challenge to the Arminians to write out a proof that responsibility is in any way dependent upon, or can be derived from, their concept of free will."[3]

This is an interesting challenge, but I wonder what could count as proof in this case. In order to prove a claim, we must begin with other claims already known or justifiably believed, namely, the premises. By definition, premises must be more certain, at least initially, than the conclusion we are trying to prove. So the question is, what premises could we take to prove that moral responsibility depends on freedom? We are not sure what would qualify as premises here. We believe that libertarian freedom is intrinsic to the very notion of moral responsibility. That is, a person cannot be held morally responsible for an act unless he or she was free to perform that act and free to refrain from it. This is a basic moral intuition, and we do not believe there are any relevant moral convictions more basic than this one that could serve as premises to prove it.

Let us address again how we understand moral intuitions. We are not appealing to our moral judgments as a standard higher than God and to which he is accountable. Rather, our moral intuitions are an aspect of the image of God, so God himself is their author. One way to think about moral intuitions is in terms of *common grace,* a concept accepted by Arminians and Calvinists alike. Common grace is the grace God gives to humans to enable them to live together in civil society. One aspect of common grace is our legal system. It is noteworthy that in our legal system, one's degree of moral responsibility is thought to correspond with one's degree of freedom. The less freedom and deliberation involved in an action, the less responsible a person is judged to be.

At this point, Calvinists may agree that our legal system requires us to be free in the sense necessary for moral responsibility. They may object,

---

[3]R. K. McGregor Wright, *No Place for Sovereignty: What's Wrong with Freewill Theism* (Downers Grove, Ill.: InterVarsity Press, 1996), p. 55.

however, that the freedom involved need not be libertarian freedom and that it is begging the question to assume libertarian freedom in this context. I am not sure how this question could be settled without extensive legal research. So I will simply register my judgment that the common-sense view of freedom is libertarian freedom and that indeed this view is foundational to our legal system. One indication of this is that lawyers sometimes defend clients on the grounds that the accused could not have avoided his or her actions due to factors such as upbringing, emotional state and the like. Even if the defendants performed the actions willingly, they are sometimes considered less culpable if it is apparent that they could not have done otherwise. By contrast, when we are convinced that criminals could indeed have acted otherwise (the assumption of libertarian freedom), we have a clear sense of their moral responsibility and legal liability.

Consider another angle. What if someone challenged us to prove that it would be wrong to torture infants when they cry? It would be difficult to prove this to someone who doubted it. We might argue that it is wrong to punish anyone who is not a moral agent, but then the critic might ask us to prove that an infant couldn't be a moral agent. We might try to argue that an infant couldn't be a moral agent because infants lack both the understanding and freedom necessary to act differently than they do. But then, of course, the critic might challenge us to prove that such freedom is necessary for moral agency and responsibility, which is the very issue we started with. The fact that we can't prove this is not the slightest reason to concede the point. We believe it is as obviously true that responsibility requires libertarian freedom as it is wrong to torture infants when they cry.[4]

So here is a major parting of the ways, and Calvinists no less than Arminians rely on contested philosophical judgments at this point. The

---

[4]For more on moral intuitions and their role in this debate, see Jerry L. Walls, "Divine Commands, Predestination, and Moral Intuition," in *The Grace of God and the Will of Man: A Case for Arminianism,* ed. Clark H. Pinnock (Grand Rapids, Mich.: Zondervan, 1995), pp. 261-76.

conclusions reached by those who believe that people are morally responsible even if they are not free to do otherwise will be very different from the conclusions reached by those who are convinced that moral responsibility requires such freedom.

To bring this into focus, consider how libertarians would assess the case of Jonny and his friends. They would argue that the young criminals could have avoided their crimes and that punishment is appropriate because they freely declined to make better choices. For instance, they could have given greater weight to their sense of guilt than to their desire for thrills. Granted, their character influenced their choices, but more importantly, their choices shaped their character. For character isn't static; it is dynamic—formed and molded by the choices we freely make. We can and sometimes do act out of character, and when we do, our character is thereby altered to some degree. Each time Jonny and his friends hesitated and deliberated over their choices, they could have weighted things differently and thereby made a different choice. That they didn't do so when they could have gives moral force to the judgment of the police officer, namely, that they should have chosen not to vandalize the cars and are therefore blameworthy for their actions.

SOFT DETERMINISM (COMPATIBILISM)

Now let's turn to *soft determinism*. The driving motivation behind this view is twofold. First, this view accepts the principle of universal causality and therefore holds that all things are determined. Indeed, the soft determinist is no less committed to determinism than the hard determinist is. It's important to underscore this point because the term "soft determinism" can be misleading to readers unfamiliar with it. The term suggests to them a partial or halfhearted determinism, a sort of quasi-determinism. These impressions need to be put aside so the reader can clearly understand that all things are rigorously determined according to this view.

So what is the difference between soft and hard determinism? The difference is in the second motivation that drives soft determinism. In addition to affirming universal causality, soft determinists also believe that we are responsible for our actions, and they agree that we must be free in some sense if this is the case. In other words, soft determinists want to affirm both complete determinism and freedom. This position is also called *compatibilism* because it holds that freedom and determinism, contrary to what hard determinists and libertarians claim, can be compatible.

It is easy for the reader who has never encountered these concepts to get confused and to be misled. To avoid this confusion, the reader must realize that soft determinists define freedom differently than do both libertarians and hard determinists. Clearly, if a free act has no cause, as hard determinists claim, then we cannot coherently affirm both that there are free acts and that everything is causally determined. Just as clearly, if a free act has no sufficient cause prior to its occurrence, as libertarians say, then we cannot coherently hold both that there are such free acts and that all things are determined by prior causes and conditions.

Fortunately for soft determinists, they are guilty of no such incoherence. They offer a very different account of freedom, one that is carefully crafted to ensure that it is compatible with determinism. More specifically, they define an act as free if it meets three conditions:

- It is not compelled or caused by anything external to the agent who performs it.
- However, it is caused by something internal to the agent who performs it, namely, a psychological state such as a belief, a desire or, more precisely, a combination of these two.
- The agent performing it could have acted differently, if the agent had wanted to do so.

Although this definition seems rather straightforward, we will offer a few more words of explanation. First, to say an act is compelled or caused by something external to the agent is to say that the act was forced against his will. For instance, suppose someone picked you up, carried you into a voting booth and forced your hand to push a button indicating a vote for the notorious politician Mack E. Velley. This would not qualify as a free act because it would violate the first condition.

Second, an act is free if it has the right sort of immediate cause—in particular, a psychological state internal to the agent. Now given the thesis of determinism, these psychological states are themselves caused by prior conditions and states of affairs. Indeed, given those prior conditions, no other psychological states are even possible. Something external to the agent ultimately caused these internal psychological states, but at the time of the act, these thoughts, desires and so on are owned by the agent in such a way that she willingly acts on them. In other words, the agent is merely acting in character when she chooses as she does. Her character determines her choices, and she could not will or act otherwise, given her character. But it is still the case that she acts as she wishes, out of the beliefs and desires that she has been caused to have and the character that has accordingly formed.

Finally, we must keep these points in mind to understand the third condition for a free action in the soft determinists' definition, or else we may be misled by the condition concerning the agent's ability to have acted differently if she had wanted to do so. The crucial point to keep in mind is that the agent *could not want* to do otherwise than she in fact does. *If* the agent had wanted to do differently, she could have done so, but it was impossible for her to *want* to do differently, given the prior causes and conditions that strictly determined her psychological states and character.

Still, soft determinists have formulated a definition of freedom that is compatible with strict determinism. So they can't be fairly faulted on this score. The question is whether their view of freedom is an adequate one. Is it enough if the three conditions spelled out above are met?

Let's return to the scenario with Jonny and his friends and add a twist to the story. Suppose the police chief is a staunch law-and-order man who wants to demonstrate his no-nonsense approach to crime. However, there is little crime in the small town where Jonny and his friends live, so the police chief devises an ingenious plan to generate some illegal activity he calls "Project Character Formation." He targets Jonny and his friends when they are young boys, and through a series of skillfully executed incidents and training events coordinated by his subordinates, he manages to form in them over a few years characters that find criminal activity irresistible. Then he sits back and waits for the inevitable to happen. On the night of their most recent crime spree, he was in his office, anxious to bring a little law and order to his town.

Though this example is not very realistic, it serves to highlight the issues we are considering. So how would we assess this case? Given Project Character Formation, could Jonny and his cohorts rightly be blamed and held morally responsible for their actions by the police chief or anyone else for that matter? Using the soft determinists' definition of freedom, the actions of Jonny and his friends would in fact still qualify as free.

Notice in the first place that they were not compelled against their wills to steal the hood ornaments. Rather, the immediate causes of their actions were internal psychological states, flowing out of the character that had been formed in them. Moreover, they could have chosen differently if they had wanted to do so. But they could *not* have wanted to choose differently, given the character they actually had. But it is still true that they could have chosen differently *if* they had wanted to do so, that is, if they had been determined to have different desires, a different character and so on.

The point is that it does not matter what causes our character and the internal psychological states and beliefs involved. According to determinism, *everything* that happens is causally necessary. Given prior conditions, things could not happen any differently than they do. Causal chains are often complicated, and it makes no difference what links make up the chains that produce our character.

CALVINISM AND HUMAN FREEDOM

We have now defined the three distinct views of freedom in relation to determinism and illustrated the differences between them. The task at hand is to see how these categories can help us understand and assess Calvinism more insightfully. As noted in the beginning of this chapter, these categories helped me (Jerry) make sense of claims that were baffling and even utterly contradictory to me.

For an example, let's consider a classic Calvinistic document, namely, the Westminster Confession, a standard statement of faith for churches in the Reformed tradition. The chapter on God's eternal decree begins with the following words: "God from all eternity did by the most wise and holy counsel of his own will freely and unchangeably ordain whatsoever comes to pass." Now this is a rather strong claim of all-embracing determinism. Everything is ordained by God's unchangeable will from all eternity. This is not a matter of impersonal fate but rather of a determinism flowing out of the will of a personal being who is most holy and wise. But notice that everything is determined by the will of God according to the Westminster Confession.

Now consider what immediately follows in the Confession: "Yet so as thereby neither is God the author of sin, nor is violence offered to the will of the creatures, nor is the liberty or contingency of second causes taken away, but rather established" (art. 3.1). In other words, despite the fact that God ordains everything, he is not responsible for sin since he doesn't cause people to sin against their will. To the contrary, the freedom of "second causes" (namely, the freedom of humans) is still maintained. Humans are second causes only because they are caused to do as they do by God, who is the first cause. (Similarly, the moon secondarily reflects the light of the sun, the first cause.)

The difference between first and second causes is similar to the distinction between *remote* and *proximate* causes, a distinction often invoked by Calvinists when discussing sin and evil. Whereas God is the remote cause of evil, human beings and other agents are the proximate causes of evil. Although God causes all things, the responsibility for the evil rests with the creatures because they are the proximate causes who actually perform it.[5]

What should we make of these distinctions? Do they successfully place the blame for evil on creatures even if God is the cause of all things? Return to the second excerpt from the Westminster Confession, above.

---

[5]See Wright, *No Place*, pp. 199-200.

It is interesting that at first glance it seems to be inconsistent with the first excerpt in the previous paragraph. For if God has unchangeably determined all things, then it seems he must be the author of sin. And if he has ordained everything that comes to pass, then it seems that freedom would be eliminated. However, the Confession denies these two apparently obvious implications of the claim that everything is ordained by God's eternal decree. It insists, first, that God is not responsible for sin and, second, that human freedom remains intact.

Does this make coherent sense, or is it riddled with contradiction and inconsistency? *It depends altogether on how we define freedom.* If we define freedom as hard determinists or libertarians do, then it is incoherent. However, if we accept the soft determinist account of freedom, then the claims can be consistently held. What on first observation seems to be double talk and sleight of hand can in fact be read in a way that makes sense.

Think again of Jonny and his band of merry thieves. If we accept the teaching of the Westminster Confession, then God from all eternity determined that Jonny and his friends would steal hood ornaments from cars. However, Jonny and his friends, not God, bear full responsibility for their crimes. For God does not do violence to their wills or force them to do something they do not want to do. Rather, he ordains their thoughts and desires in such a way that they willingly engage in their petty theft. Because their acts flow from their own thoughts and feelings, their freedom and responsibility for their actions remain intact—even though their thoughts and feelings are determined by God.

Consider another passage in the Westminster Confession in the same light. This passage describes God's "effectual calling" of those who are elected for eternal salvation. The Confession makes it clear that only the elect can be saved. Moreover, elect people will be effectually called, which means that they will be called in such a way that they will surely respond favorably to the call. The grace of the effectual call is irresistible in this sense. Those who are fortunate enough to be chosen to receive this grace cannot do other than receive it. However, they aren't forced against their wills to receive this grace, as the following explains:

> All those whom God hath predestinated unto life, and those only, he is pleased, in his appointed and accepted time, effectually to call, by his Word and Spirit, out of that state of sin and death, in which they are by nature, to grace and salvation by Jesus Christ; enlightening their minds spiritually and savingly, to understand the things of God; taking away their heart of stone, and giving them an heart of flesh; renewing their wills, and by his almighty power *determining them to that which is good,* and effectually drawing them to Jesus Christ, *yet so as they come most freely, being made willing by his grace.* (art. 10.1, emphasis added)

Notice particularly the emphasized phrases. On the one hand, we are told that those who are effectually called are determined by God to that which is good. But on the other hand, and immediately following, we are informed that those who come to Christ come "most freely, being made willing by his grace."

Again, we have a strong claim of determinism joined with an insistence on freedom. And as before, the key to making sense of this is to read it as affirming soft determinism: those who come to Christ by irresistible grace are not forced against their will to come. Sometimes critics of Calvinism make this charge, but it betrays a serious misunderstanding of Calvinism. The preceding lines of the passage cited above elaborate on how God can determine people without coercing them. He does it by changing the elect internally. He enlightens their minds, renews their wills, gives them a new heart and so on. So they come "most freely" in the sense that they want to come to Christ once God has caused them to think differently and desire differently. Given these factors, they couldn't choose to reject Christ. Again, this doesn't mean that they want to reject Christ, but God won't let them do so. Rather, their desires have been so determined by God that they gladly come to Christ.

In identifying a soft determinist view of freedom in these passages of the Westminster Confession, we don't mean to imply that the authors were fully and consistently committed to this position or even were fully aware of it. Indeed, the distinctions between the different views of freedom we have identified were made fully explicit after the Confession was written, over several centuries of discussion and analysis. Even today, many persons who discuss these issues do so without an awareness of these categories. So the Westminster divines can hardly be faulted if they were not fully apprised of these distinctions.

Our speculation about how clearly the Westminster divines were committed to compatibilism is not crucial to our case. Indeed, little rides on it. What we do want to insist on, however, is that one can make coherent sense of the theology of the Westminster Confession only with a soft determinist view of freedom. The principle of charity in interpretation instructs us that we should always give a text a coherent reading if there is a plausible way to do so. The Westminster Confession can be read as broadly coherent if the references to freedom we have noted are understood in the compatibilist sense of the word.[6]

We also want to emphasize that we are not trying to saddle Calvinists with our judgment that, in order to be logically consistent, they must understand freedom in the compatibilist sense, which is contrary to their own judgments. Indeed, philosophically informed Calvinists typically agree with us on this matter. For instance, in a recent two-volume set of scholarly essays that set forth a contemporary articulation and defense of Calvinism, philosopher John Feinberg insists on this very point. While Feinberg acknowledges that both libertarian and compatibilist views of freedom are coherent in their own right, and therefore possibly true, he also recognizes that libertarian views are not consistent with Calvinism.

---

[6]While the Westminster Confession can be read in a way that is broadly coherent, we believe it is still inconsistent at a deeper lever because it also has strands of libertarian freedom running through it. For argument, see Jerry L. Walls, *Hell: The Logic of Damnation* (Notre Dame: University of Notre Dame Press, 1992), pp. 57-70. We will take this issue up in chapter five.

Consequently, he points out, "Calvinists as determinists must either reject freedom altogether or accept compatibilism."[7] Since he believes Scripture clearly teaches that human beings are free and responsible for their actions, he believes that Calvinists must opt for compatibilism.

We appreciate Feinberg's fairness in acknowledging that both views of freedom are at least possible. Some writers on both sides of this dispute try to avoid the debate by simply claiming that the view of freedom they reject is incoherent. We agree with Feinberg that this strategy does not further the discussion or resolve anything. While we reject compatibilism for what we believe are good biblical, theological and moral reasons, we don't want to claim that it is a view of freedom that is not even possibly true.

Although compatibilism is a popular position among Calvinists, particularly among the philosophically informed, we want to stress that not all Calvinists embrace it. Some Reformed theologians have argued for another option. These writers do not agree with Feinberg that a Calvinist must either give up freedom altogether or accept compatibilism. To the contrary, they hold that we are required by Scripture to accept both God's control of all things and human freedom, but they insist that it is not up to us to find a way to reconcile these truths. Popular evangelical author J. I. Packer is a proponent of this view. He endorses this position in his widely read book *Evangelism and the Sovereignty of God*.

As he notes, divine sovereignty and human responsibility are both clearly taught in Scripture. And he understands sovereignty in the Calvinistic sense that God unconditionally determines everything that happens. "Man is a responsible moral agent, though he is *also* divinely controlled; man is divinely controlled, though he is *also* a responsible moral agent."[8] Packer identifies this pair of claims as an "antinomy" because he

---

[7]John S. Feinberg, "God, Freedom and Evil in Calvinist Thinking," in *The Grace of God, the Bondage of the Will*, ed. Thomas R. Schreiner and Bruce A. Ware (Grand Rapids, Mich.: Baker, 1995), 2:465.

[8]J. I. Packer, *Evangelism and the Sovereignty of God* (Downers Grove, Ill.: InterVarsity Press, 1961), p. 23.

believes we cannot dispense with either one of them, nor can we understand how they are compatible. From the standpoint of finite human reason, it may seem contradictory to affirm both of these claims and therefore impossible to do so. Here is Packer's advice for dealing with such antinomies.

> Accept it for what it is, and learn to live with it. Refuse to regard the apparent inconsistency as real; put down the semblance of contradiction to the deficiency of your own understanding; think of the two principles as, not rival alternatives, but, in some way that at present you do not grasp, complementary to each other.[9]

Apparently Packer means to affirm that both determinism and freedom in the libertarian sense are true. It is the affirmation of both of these that produces antinomy. By contrast, the affirmation of determinism and the compatibilist account of freedom produces no such intellectual tension. The resolution of antinomy will need the perspective of eternity, but it is easy to see here and now how freedom and determinism can be held together if one accepts a compatibilist account of freedom.

Our reasons for rejecting this sort of approach—as well as for rejecting compatibilism—will be spelled out in later chapters, but before concluding this chapter it will be helpful to make a couple of preliminary points. First, it is crucial to this discussion to identify an aspect of compatibilism that has far-reaching implications: If freedom and determinism are compatible, then it is possible that God could determine all persons to freely do good at all times. This wouldn't involve God's forcing people to do what they didn't want to do. Rather, he could control everyone's thoughts and desires in such a way that everyone would willingly and gladly obey him, serve him, worship him and so on. Now if this is so, it raises profound questions about the problem of evil. (See chapter six.)

---

[9]Ibid., p. 21.

Second, we believe that there are large stretches of Scripture that are hard to make sense of if humans aren't free in the libertarian sense of the word. In chapter two we examined some of these, but now let us consider another one, namely, Jeremiah 7:1-29. In this passage God calls his people to repentance. God enumerates the sins of his people and reminds them that while they were doing such things, he spoke to them again and again (Jer 7:13). But instead of repenting, they persist in idolatry and other self-destructive behavior. God promises to punish them for their sin, but he again reiterates that he repeatedly sent his prophets to them to urge them to obedience (Jer 7:20-26).

This passage is hardly unusual. The book of Jeremiah contains several other similar passages, as do most of the Prophets as well as some other biblical texts. Now the question we want to raise is, What view of freedom is implied in such texts? Of course, as we have already noted, Scripture does not expressly define the nature of our freedom or draw philosophical distinctions for us. But it is still worth asking what sort of freedom is implied by various texts of Scripture.

We would argue that what we call libertarian freedom is assumed in many biblical texts. In the text just cited, it seems clear that God truly desired for his children to repent and turn from their self-destructive ways. That God sent prophets to them over and over suggests not only that he wanted them to repent but also that they were able to do so. The prophets themselves were a means of grace by which truth confronted Israel and made repentance possible. God's threatening to punish them for their refusal to repent implies that they were responsible precisely because they could have repented and yet freely chose not to do so.

Now consider how difficult it is to make sense of such passages if a compatibilist view of freedom is assumed. On this assumption God has determined his people to refuse to repent, for whatever people willingly do is what they have been determined to do. Moreover, God could, if he wanted to, cause his people to gladly turn from their sins and to joyously worship him. He could do this by causing them to have the appropriate desires so they would willingly repent and obey him. But if God has chosen not to do this, what do we make of his apparent desire that his people repent? What do we make of his sending his prophets over and over if the people can't really repent, given that God has determined them to remain hard-hearted and unwilling to repent? All of this is puzzling to say the very least.

Finally, we want to point out that those Calvinist writers who affirm compatibilism believe it is assumed or even taught in Scripture. Biblical scholar D. A. Carson, for instance, examines several passages that he interprets in support of this contention.[10] Obviously, this is another instance of how one can find competent exegetes on both sides of this issue, all of whom appeal to numerous texts that appear to substantiate their case. In chapter four, our chapter on sovereignty, we will examine one of the classic texts that, according to Calvinists, supports compatibilism. The issue remains: which view makes better sense of the large sweep of biblical teaching about divine sovereignty and human freedom? Our conviction is that if the categories we have discussed in this chapter are clearly understood and the implications of each are kept squarely in view, Calvinism loses much of its initial plausibility.

---

[10]D. A. Carson, *How Long O Lord? Reflections on Evil and Suffering* (Grand Rapids, Mich.: Baker, 1990), pp. 199-227. The texts Carson discusses are Gen 50:19-20; Lev 20:7-8; 1 Kings 8:46ff; 11:11-13, 29-39; 12:1-15; Is 10:5ff; Jn 6:37-40; Acts 4:23-31; 18:9-10; Phil 2:12-13.

4

CALVINISM AND
DIVINE SOVEREIGNTY

ల

R. C. Sproul tells of a time he was teaching a seminary course on the theology of the Westminster Confession and began a class by quoting the opening lines of article 3 of the Confession. This passage, which we have already considered, reads as follows: "God from all eternity did by the most wise and holy counsel of His own will freely and unchangeably ordain whatsoever comes to pass." Sproul had announced the week before that he would lecture on predestination, and a number of visitors were there that evening, expecting a little controversy. After reading the passage, he asked if anyone did not believe what it claimed. A number of hands went up, signaling dissent from Sproul's Calvinism. Sproul then asked if there were any atheists in the room. When no hands were raised, Sproul reports that he said something "outrageous," namely, "Everyone who raised his hand to the first question should also have raised his hand to the second question."[1] Not surprisingly, a number of groans rose from the audience.

The point Sproul wanted to drive home with this exchange was that belief in God's sovereignty is not distinctive to Calvinism. To protest against sovereignty is not to deny merely Calvinism but to deny theism itself. As Sproul later put the point, "That God in some sense foreordains

---

[1] R. C. Sproul, *Chosen by God* (Wheaton, Ill.: Tyndale House, 1986), p. 25.

whatever comes to pass is a necessary result of his sovereignty."[2]

The Westminster Confession is saying something much more pointed than that God "in some sense" foreordains whatever comes to pass. The claim of the Westminster divines is that everything is particularly and unchangeably foreordained, and not all orthodox Christians would agree with this. So Sproul is wrong on the details, but he is surely right that all orthodox theists, including Christians, would insist on divine sovereignty as essential to their faith.

To see what is at stake here, let us consider a specific event, one shared with us by a former student at Asbury Theological Seminary.[3] Several years ago, this student's beautiful sixteen-year-old sister, Suzi, missed a day of school and was home alone because she was ill. On that day, a man (let's call him Randy) burglarized the house in order to get money to buy drugs. When he unexpectedly found Suzi at home, his crime ended up being far more complicated and serious than he planned. Randy dragged her from the house, locked her in the trunk of his car, and later stabbed her to death and buried her in a shallow grave in a farmer's field.

Randy was later convicted of his crime and sentenced to death. In the years before his eventual execution, he repented and received Christ as his Savior. He accepted responsibility for his actions and even said he was prepared to greet Suzi in the afterlife.

Suzi's parents are Christians. Obviously, this incident raised hard questions for them. They admitted the difficulty of forgiving their daughter's murderer and acknowledged their doubts about the sincerity of his conversion. As Christians, some even more fundamental questions were inevitable: Where was God in all of this? And what does it mean to say that God is sovereign in a case like this? These questions are inevitable because sovereignty is all-embracing. As Sproul points out, any orthodox believer must say that in some sense *everything* is ordained by God.

---

[2]Ibid., p. 26.
[3]This incident was related to us by our student Brad Holliman.

Cases like Suzi's may make us uneasy with this claim. We may be tempted to make some exceptions to divine sovereignty and look for some escape clauses. But the hard truth is that Christians must continue to believe that God is sovereign, even in the face of tragedies such as this one. The issue lies in the details. In just what sense are events like this ordained by God?

The issue of sovereignty involves a number of closely related topics, some of which have been among the most carefully examined and hotly debated in recent theology and philosophy of religion. One of these topics concerns the extent of God's knowledge of the future, particularly his knowledge of the free actions of his creatures. Another closely related matter is the whole notion of divine providence. While we can distinguish *sovereignty* from *providence,* the two topics are tightly connected. In what follows, we will examine three different views of sovereignty, providence and foreknowledge, beginning with the Calvinist account. Next, we will consider Molinism and then conclude with a look at what may be broadly called the Openness view.

The three views vary considerably on the question of how precisely and particularly God exercises his providential control. *Note that the issue is not sovereignty. The issue is what kind of world God, in his sovereignty, chose to create.* Our discussion will proceed from the view that is the most meticulous in its account of providence and end with the view that is least so.

THE CALVINIST ACCOUNT

Let's begin our examination of Calvinism by turning again to the Westminster Confession. Here is what the Confession says about God's knowledge: "In his sight all things are open and manifest; his knowledge is infinite, infallible, and independent upon the creature, so as nothing is to him contingent or uncertain" (art. 2.2). Note first that God's knowledge, including everything about the future, is infallible. God knows all things, including the future, with infallible certainty. Second, note that God's knowledge is in no way dependent on any creature. Indeed, this is why his knowledge is not contingent in any way and is utterly certain.

In order to understand more clearly what this means, consider the Confession's explanation of how God knows the future, particularly with respect to the vital issue of who will be saved. Although the language here is a bit archaic, this is a classic statement that clarifies the Calvinist view on these issues.

> Although God knows whatsoever may or can come to pass upon all supposed conditions, yet hath he not decreed anything because he foresaw it as future, or as that which would come to pass upon such and such conditions.
>
> By the decree of God, for the manifestation of his glory, some men and angels are predestined unto everlasting life, and others foreordained to everlasting death.
>
> Those of mankind that are predestined unto life, God, before the foundation of the world was laid . . . hath chosen . . . without any foresight of faith or good works, or perseverance in either of them, or any other thing in the creature, as conditions, or causes moving him thereunto; and all to the praise of his glorious grace. (art 3.2-3, 5)

The first paragraph of this passage spells out what it means to say that God's knowledge of the future is in no way contingent on creatures: it does not in any way depend on what he knows creatures will do or will not do. Notice, God knows what can or may come to pass on given conditions, but this has no effect on his sovereign decrees.

Here is what the Westminster divines insisted on. God's sovereign decrees do not in any way hinge on his foreknowledge of what his creatures will do or of their choices. God's knowledge of the future is not logically prior to his sovereign decrees, nor are his decrees based on foreknowledge. Rather, it is the other way around. God knows the future because of his sovereign decrees. He knows what will happen because he has determined from all eternity what will happen and what choices we will make.

These points are brought into clear focus as the Confession elaborates on God's sovereign election of some to salvation and his choice not to save others. Again the authors emphasize that God's decrees are in no way contingent on anything we do. God did not foresee that some people would have faith and therefore elect to save them. He did not foreknow that some would persevere and on that basis determine that they will be saved. Rather, in his sovereignty he chose to determine some persons to believe and to persevere. He foreknew which persons would believe and persevere because from all eternity he chose the persons he determined to do so. As the authors of the Confession see it, all of this works to magnify God's glorious grace.

The advantage of the Calvinistic view of things is clear. It provides a readily intelligible account of how God can know the future, including our choices, with complete and infallible certainty. God knows the future because he has determined, from all eternity, everything that would ever happen. All he needs to know to have complete knowledge of the future is his own power and intentions. He can know everything he intends to happen and how he will execute his intentions. Some things he will cause directly and others he will cause by working through human actions or through natural forces. In the case of those things that he does not cause directly, he must arrange and structure things so that earlier events and choices cause later ones in a very specific fashion.

We can understand this by analogy with our own knowledge of our future. As I (Jerry) type these words, I know that I will shortly eat lunch at Solomon's Porch, a local sandwich shop. Knowing this requires no mysterious ability to peer into the future or gaze into a crystal ball. All I need to know are my own intentions and powers. I know I intend to eat at Solomon's Porch, and I know I have the ability to walk there, purchase a sandwich and so on.

Of course, my knowledge is fallible. For all I know, I might slip and fall on the way to lunch and injure myself and thus fail to reach my destination. Or I might decide to have a "Wesley Club" sandwich rather than a "Calvin" (or perhaps a "C. S. Lewis," another Arminian option on the menu). My knowledge of my powers and intentions is not utterly certain. But God's knowledge is, and he knows with complete certainty what he has determined to do, and he has the power to execute his intentions in every respect.

The advantage here is considerable if we assume that God has detailed and infallible knowledge of the future. The view that God has such knowledge is surely the majority position in traditional theology, and Calvinism provides a clear and cogent account of how such knowledge is possible. Without the sort of determinism Calvinism espouses, it would be hard to explain how God can know the future choices of his creatures. Indeed, it is a mystery how God could know in detail the choices of people who have not yet been born if those choices are undetermined. But if God determined who would be born as well as all the choices everyone would ever make, along with a blueprint specifying how these choices will be determined—there is no mystery as to how he can foreknow these choices.

In order to be consistent on this point, Calvinists need to be thoroughgoing determinists. One of the interesting things about Calvinism is the variety of opinions on this whole matter. Some Calvinist writers are at best ambivalent about identifying their position in these terms; others clearly wish to repudiate determinism as a hallmark of Reformed theology. Richard Muller, for instance, acknowledges that Calvin's doctrine of the divine decrees is deterministic, but he insists that later thinkers in the tradition balanced Calvin's views. Muller cites a number of Reformed theologians who appear to deny determinism and to maintain that we are free at least with respect to everyday actions. Presumably, these theologians believe that choices such as what we eat for breakfast are not determined. I can eat either oat bran or eggs.[4] The issue, Muller insists, is not philosophical determinism but humanity's inability to save itself. At this point, however, Muller acknowledges "a certain determin-

---

[4]Muller cites the Second Helvitic Confession, which says that man is free in such a way that "he may speak or keep silence, go out of his house or abide within." See Richard A. Muller, "Grace, Election and Contingent Choice: Arminius's Gambit and the Reformed Response," in The Grace of God, the Bondage of the Will, ed. Thomas R. Schreiner and Bruce A. Ware (Grand Rapids, Mich.: Baker, 1995), 2:270.

ism in the order of grace."[5] Because God chooses to save only some of those who cannot save themselves—the rest are inevitably damned—"a certain determinism" is unavoidable.

It's not clear what advantage Muller thinks is gained by insisting that everyday choices are not determined. That seems like a rather trivial matter so long as our eternal happiness or misery is determined. However, we would readily grant that there is nothing necessarily inconsistent in holding that some choices are determined and are free only in the compatibilist sense, while others are undetermined and presumably free in the libertarian sense.

Here are some questions for those who take this view, however: Does God foreknow our everyday choices? And if he does, how does he do so? Does he know what I will have for breakfast ten years from now? If such choices are not determined by God, how does he know them from all eternity? Does he simply peer into the future in some mysterious fashion that we can't begin to fathom? Is God outside of time in such a way that all moments are present to him, so that what is future to us is present to him?

One must acknowledge that the view of foreknowledge affirmed by the Westminster Confession is contradicted if one claims that God somehow foreknows things he does not cause. For if God knows, let's say, what my grandchildren, who do not yet exist, will have for breakfast on July 17, 2023, but he has not determined it, then his knowledge is contingent on their choice. That is, he somehow sees their choice, and his knowledge depends on what he sees they will choose. The Westminster Confession, of course, insists that God's knowledge is in no way dependent on creatures or their choices.

The same general point applies to Calvinists who hold that God *permits* or *allows* certain things. Now the language of *permission* is natural and makes perfect sense for the other two positions we will consider. But it does not sit well with serious Calvinism. Indeed John Calvin himself noted this and warned against any use of the term that might deny that

---

[5]Ibid., 2:277.

everything happens exactly as willed by God. This means that for Calvin everything that happens does so necessarily, so to speak of God's permitting things is misleading.[6]

Nevertheless, Calvinists often appeal to the notion of permission, particularly when they are attempting to account for evil. Consider the following from Sproul:

> We know that God is sovereign because we know that God is God. Therefore we must conclude that God foreordained sin. What else can we conclude? We must conclude that God's decision to *allow* sin to enter the world was a good decision. This is not to say that our sin is really a good thing, but merely that God's *allowing* us to do sin, which is evil, is a good thing. God's *allowing* evil is good, but the evil he *allows* is still evil. . . . The fact that God decided to *allow* us to sin does not absolve us from our responsibility for sin.[7]

It is remarkable that in the space of a relatively short paragraph, Sproul speaks five times of God's "allowing" sin and evil. Perhaps even more striking is that later in the same book, Sproul explains one of the most difficult passages in Scripture (the hardening of Pharaoh's heart) in the same terms. Ironically, in doing so, he follows not John Calvin but John Wesley, who offered a similar explanation of this text. Sproul contends that this hardening was only in the *passive* sense: that is, God removed the restraints he previously had placed on Pharaoh: "All God had to do to harden Pharaoh further was to remove his arm. The evil inclinations of Pharaoh did the rest."[8]

But if God only permits certain things without specifically causing them, it is hard to see how this would square with the Calvinist claim of

---

[6]John Calvin, *Institutes of the Christian Religion*, ed. John T. McNeil, trans. Ford Lewis Battles (Philadelphia: Westminster Press, 1960), 3.23.8.

[7]Sproul, *Chosen by God*, pp. 31-32 (emphasis added).

[8]Ibid., p. 146. See John Wesley's similar explanation in *Works* (1872; reprint, Grand Rapids, Mich.: Baker, 1979), 10:236. By contrast, Calvin rejects the idea that the hardening of Pharaoh was merely a matter of permission. See Calvin *Institutes* 1.18.2.

all-embracing determinism. Does this make his providential control dependent on our making the right choices—the choices God wishes to permit? It's not altogether clear what Sproul has in mind here.

Sproul is similarly vague elsewhere in stating his view of how God has infallible foreknowledge. Consider his following words: "[God's] knowledge extends down to the smallest details. . . . He doesn't have to wait to see which fork in the road we choose to know which fork we most certainly *will* choose. He knows the future precisely because He wills the future."[9] At first glance it appears that Sproul is affirming the view that God can know the future in infallible detail because he *determines* it. However, he makes the more indefinite claim that God knows the future because he *wills* it. This is, to say the least, compatible with saying that he foresees things that he does not determine but allows to happen. If this is what Sproul means, then God wills them only in the sense that he permits—but does not determine—them to occur.

At this point Calvinists may object that we have misrepresented their position. They may insist that it is a fundamental misunderstanding of their view to contrast God's permission with his determinism. To be sure, God determines all things, without exception. But he does not determine all things in the same way. Some things he determines by *causing* them to occur, but other things he determines by *permitting* or *allowing* them to occur. Everything happens exactly as God intends, the permitted no less than the directly caused.

CALVINIST PERMISSION?

A good deal hinges on whether the concept of permission is intelligible in Calvinist categories. So it is important to take the time to examine this more closely, since it is initially plausible and holds out hope of helping Calvinists deal with evil choices in a way that is morally acceptable. However, on closer inspection it poses more difficulties for Calvinism than it answers.

---

[9]R. C. Sproul, *The Invisible Hand: Do All Things Really Work for Good?* (Dallas: Word, 1997), p. 44 (emphasis in original).

This move does not begin to explain how God knows in the first place the things he permits or allows. If he does not cause these things, how does he know they will occur in order to permit them? Going with Sproul's example, how does he know which way I will choose at a fork in the road if he only wills my taking that way in the sense that he permits me to take it? Could I take the other way? If my choice is not *causally* determined, then presumably I could. If God only determines my choice in the sense that he permits it, then he must insure that at the fork in the road I take the way he intends if everything is to be determined by his will. But again, if my choice is not causally determined, there is no guarantee that I will choose as he intends.[10]

Next, this problem is magnified if we hold, as many Calvinists do, that all events from the beginning of time until the end are causally connected like links in a chain. For example, consider Sproul's interpretation of the Joseph story. He says God "governed all things that occurred in the life of Joseph," beginning with his "technicolored coat" through his being sold into slavery, and eventually to his ascension to prime minister of Egypt. But as Sproul sees it, these events are causally connected in a very tight way with much later events. Indeed, the chain of events beginning with Joseph's coat extends through the exodus and ultimately stretches to Jesus' death on the cross. As Sproul notes, we can ask *what*

---

[10]Terry Tiessen has suggested to us (in correspondence) that a Calvinist doctrine of providence relies on divine knowledge of counterfactuals of freedom, that is, what choices we would have made in different circumstances than obtain in the actual world. The notion of counterfactuals of freedom is usually associated with Molinism, the view we will consider next. Tiessen believes it is not possible for God to know such counterfactuals if we are free in the libertarian sense. Thus, he suggests a Calvinist version of Molinism based on a compatibilist view of freedom. Given a compatibilist view of freedom, God could know counterfactuals, Tiessen holds, and he thereby could bring about the circumstances in which we would freely (in the compatibilist sense) choose at the fork in the road the way that God intends. The difficulty with this suggestion is that the only way to make sense of God's knowing counterfactuals of compatibilist freedom is to assume that those choices are causally determined by God. That is, God's knowledge of such counterfactuals is his knowledge of what choices he would have causally determined in different circumstances. But the assumption of causal determinism undercuts any meaningful sense of permission. That is, if a choice is causally determined by God, it makes no sense to say that same choice is permitted by God.

if—what if Joseph had not received his coat in the beginning, and so on. As he sees it, this would have had drastic consequences. "If we telescope this collection of 'what ifs?' we conclude that if it were not for Joseph's technicolored coat there would have been no Christianity, and every chapter of human history would have a different ending."[11]

In Sproul's view, then, there is an unbroken chain of events from the colorful coat to the cross and beyond. Or to switch metaphors, the trail from the technicolored coat to the tree of Calvary followed one very specifically determined route. If at any fork in the road the persons involved had chosen differently, there would have been no Christianity. If one accepts this claim, then each choice would have to be meticulously determined to keep everything on track and moving in the right direction. Each event in the causal chain must lead precisely and surely to the next.

Some of Sproul's fellow Calvinists might think Sproul got a little carried away with his example about Joseph and would insist that surely there are other ways God could have directed history so that Jesus would have been crucified and Christianity founded. But if one is a determinist, each event must be understood in light of its connection with events that precede it as well as those that follow it. Even if we grant that God could have determined things in a very different way than he did, the fact remains that for a determinist—and this is the crucial point—no event can be seen in isolation from the events that cause it. When this is kept clearly in mind, it's hard to see how Calvinists can speak of any events or choices as being *permitted*. Seen as isolated choices this may seem plausible. But if God has arranged things in such a way that previous events and choices cause later ones in a deterministic fashion, then the persons involved could not possibly choose differently than they do precisely because of God's intentional activity.

To bring this into focus, consider a link that appears in the chain after Joseph, namely, Pharaoh. Recall Sproul's account of how God hardened his

---

[11]Sproul, *Invisible Hand,* p. 95. Sproul goes on to acknowledge that God could have worked out a different plan of salvation. But the point remains that in the actual world, everything depended on Joseph's coat.

heart. All God had to do, he said, was to "remove his arm. The evil inclinations of Pharaoh did the rest." Now this is a curious claim in light of
Sproul's description of the chain of events from Joseph to the cross and beyond. Presumably, in this view not one thing could have been different in
the chain of events leading up to Pharaoh and his dramatic confrontation
with God. What this means is that Pharaoh's character was not an isolated
fact or reality. Pharaoh did not become the person he was in a vacuum.
Rather, his character was formed by a long series of events and choices, all
of which were determined by God (according to Calvinism).

Now then, let's assume that things have been determined in such a
way that Pharaoh has an evil character. Is this enough to explain how
God can determine Pharaoh's actions merely by permitting him to act as
he will? We don't think so. Let's grant for the sake of discussion that Pharaoh is determined to act in line with his character. This is not nearly
enough to support the Calvinist account of God's all-determining control
because, although character may arguably determine a certain *type* of action, it alone is far from sufficient to explain *specific* actions. That is, an
evil character may determine that evil actions will be chosen, but far
more is needed to account for exactly which evil actions are chosen.

Consider another example. Suppose a man has a character that is given
to drunkenness. Imagine that he likes several types of alcohol and that he
is walking down a street where there are a number of different bars that he
has frequented in the past. Now it may be argued that his character determines that he will choose to get drunk at one of these bars. However, his
character alone does not explain which bar he will choose, what exactly
he will drink, who he will talk to, exactly when and how often he will go
to the restroom, when he will leave, and the like. Now according to Calvinism, not only does God foreknow all of these details, but he has also
determined them. In order to account for all this, God must determine
things much more precisely, either by causing them directly or by specifically arranging things so that only one choice is possible in each case.

Returning to Pharaoh's case, it is the Calvinist view that all of Pharaoh's
actions were specifically determined. Appealing to his evil character is

not nearly enough to account for how God could so precisely determine all his actions. So, on the Calvinist account, God must have causally determined things in a specific way not only to guarantee that Pharaoh formed a particular sort of character, but also to ensure that Pharaoh performed exactly the deeds he did, spoke the very words he did and so on.[12]

What sense, then, does it make to say that God permitted Pharaoh's actions, given this picture? What sense does it make to say that God further hardened Pharaoh's heart merely by "removing his arm" if Pharaoh was determined to have the character he did because of God's all-encompassing control of all events? Moreover, what sense does it make to say that God permitted Pharaoh's specific evil choices if God determined things so that he could not possibly have chosen other than he did? Sproul's description of how God hardened Pharaoh's heart suggests that Pharaoh formed his evil character quite independently of God and that God simply let Pharaoh's character have free reign in the choices he made.

In a normal case of permission, the person granting permission does not determine the choices of the one who is granted permission. Moreover, the person who grants permission usually also has the power to deny it and may even prefer that what is permitted not be done. For example, a mother may permit her child to make a purchase that she thinks is unwise. Perhaps she would prefer the child to purchase something less expensive or something less fragile, but she allows the child to make his purchase in hopes that the child will learn the consequences of financial decisions and grow in responsibility.

To Calvinists, permission is a very different matter. According to Sproul, God permits choices that are determined to happen precisely because of his own providential control. Since everything is determined by God, no

---

[12]Presumably many Calvinists would agree that God, in his sovereignty, could have determined Pharaoh to be a righteous man who freely worshiped God. Otherwise, the Calvinistic account of sovereignty is a rather hollow notion. But if God had chosen to do so, then we would see a significantly different chain of events from Joseph to Jesus. But given the chain of events God in fact determined, Pharaoh must have been determined to have just the character he did and to act just as he did.

choices are made that he does not prefer. He could prevent those decisions, but to do so would radically alter the course of history. God's permission, then, is simply his choice to allow things to unfold as he has already determined they will. This is an odd way to think of permission and a highly misleading way of speaking. Calvinists can insist on using the language of permission, but we think it's strained and unnatural, given their view that all things—including our choices—are determined by God.

This is another instance where Calvinists, no less then their opponents, make philosophical judgments. How they understand and make use of the notion of permission is highly controversial and depends on contested judgments of what is coherent and rationally intelligible.

Calvinists who use the concept of permission must make sure they employ this notion in a way that is consistent with their account of determinism and human freedom. They cannot properly use *permission* to suggest that we are free in the libertarian sense or that God permits some choices he has not determined. The notion of permission loses all significant meaning in a Calvinist framework. Therefore, it's not surprising that Calvin himself was suspicious of the idea and warned against using it.

Recall that part of what motivates the Calvinistic account of sovereignty is that it provides a readily intelligible understanding of how God knows our future choices. Therefore, Calvinists who allow that some of our choices are not determined must either say God cannot foreknow those choices or say that his knowledge of them is contingent on what his creatures, independent of his determinism, will choose to do. If they take this latter option, they no longer enjoy the advantage of having a readily intelligible account of how God can foreknow these choices.

This dilemma is part of what motivates many Calvinists to "bite the bullet" and embrace a thoroughgoing determinism. In volume 2 of *The Grace of God, the Bondage of the Will*, the volume in which Muller's essay appears, some of his Calvinist colleagues represent this option. One of these is John Feinberg; another is J. A. Crabtree, whose critique of the Molinist position we will consider in the next section. Crabtree, who identifies himself as a "Calvinistic divine determinist," defines that position as "one who believes that every aspect of everything that occurs in the whole of reality is ultimately caused and determined by God."[13] He acknowledges that one of the primary reasons he espouses determinism is because it makes sense of how God knows future choices. "Only on the assumption of divine determinism is the divine foreknowledge of free-will choices a rationally plausible doctrine."[14] This means, of course, that Crabtree believes freedom and determinism are compatible.

If the strength of Calvinistic determinism is its ability to provide a rationally plausible account of how God can know the future free choices of his creatures (free in the compatibilist sense), its weakness is readily apparent. Calvinism is hard-pressed to account for sin and evil in a way that is morally plausible. For if God determines everything that happens, then it is hard to see why there is so much sin and evil in the world and why God is not responsible for it.

Consider the murder of sixteen-year-old Suzi, described at the beginning of this chapter. If all events are caused and determined by God, then on the day Suzi was murdered, everything happened as planned and determined by God. God caused her to be sick that day, and he causally determined that Randy would choose her particular house to rob. He did so either directly or indirectly by determining previous events in such a way that things would unfold that day precisely as they did. That is, God determined Randy to choose to proceed with the actions that led to Suzi's brutal death and to choose to repent later in prison. Since God can determine things any way he chooses, there are presumably many other ways he could have caused Suzi's killer to repent, but since things happened this way, this was his exact plan.

Now this may be a bit hard to swallow, and it's not surprising that some Calvinists resort to language of permission when they deal with sin and evil. God ordained Suzi's death only in the sense that he permitted it to

---

[13]J. A. Crabtree, "Does Middle Knowledge Solve the Problem of Divine Sovereignty?" in *The Grace of God, the Bondage of the Will,* ed. Thomas R. Schreiner and Bruce A. Ware (Grand Rapids, Mich.: Baker, 1995), 2:429.

[14]Ibid., 2:447.

happen, they would say. It is easier for us to accept this idea than the more straightforward claim that God determined the murder to happen.

However, we cannot view the murder in isolation. Rather, it is one event in a series of connected events, each of which is determined by God. The murderer was formed into the person he was by a long series of events and choices all determined by God, just as surely as God's providential control determined that Suzi would be sick and at home the day Randy came calling. Language of permission should not distract us from keeping these points squarely in view.

THE MOLINIST ACCOUNT

Let's consider a second position, namely, Molinism, named after Luis de Molina, a Jesuit theologian and one of the main figures in a sixteenth-century controversy concerning the relationship between God's grace and human free will. Molina's original and carefully argued works have received considerable attention recently, particularly from philosophers of religion who are interested in the same issues debated in his day.

Molina is probably most famous for his view that God possesses what he called "middle knowledge." This notion is key to understanding Molina's views of foreknowledge, providence and sovereignty, so let us consider his definition of it. He characterizes it as that knowledge

> by which, in virtue of the most profound and inscrutable comprehension of each faculty of free choice, He saw in His own essence what each such faculty would do with its innate freedom were it to be placed in this or in that or, indeed, in infinitely many orders of things—even though it would really be able, if it so willed, to do the opposite.[15]

---

[15]Luis de Molina, *On Divine Foreknowledge: Part IV of the Concordia,* trans. Alfred J. Freddoso (Ithaca, N.Y.: Cornell University Press, 1988), qu. 14, art. 13, disp. 52, no. 9. For the definitive defense of Molinism see Thomas Flint, *Divine Providence: The Molinist Account* (Ithaca, N.Y.: Cornell University Press, 1998).

Why did Molina call this *middle* knowledge? Because this is knowledge "between" what he called God's *natural* knowledge and his *free* knowledge. God's natural knowledge is of truths that are necessary, that is, truths that could not be other than they are, such as mathematical and logical truths. Such necessary truths are obviously known to God prior to his decision to create the world and would have been known by him even if he had never created any world at all. God's free knowledge, by contrast, is his knowledge of contingent truths, that is, truths that could have been other than they are. In particular, these are truths known to God as a result of his decision to create. For instance, it is a part of his free knowledge that our solar system has nine planets. This knowledge is free because it depends on God's free choice to create our solar system with nine planets instead of seven or ten.

Middle knowledge is "between" natural knowledge and free knowledge in the sense that it shares a characteristic of each. On the one hand, it is similar to natural knowledge in that it is known by God prior to his decision to create and it does not depend on what he decides on that score. On the other hand, it is similar to free knowledge in the sense that it pertains to truths that are contingent rather than necessary.

So what are these truths? What is it that God knows by way of middle knowledge? The object of middle knowledge, broadly speaking, is what all possible created free wills would do in all possible circumstances or states of affairs. Middle knowledge thus embraces circumstances and situations that are not and never will be actual. For instance, in the actual world, Bobby Knight won three national championships as basketball coach of the Indiana Hoosiers. And in the actual world, before Knight took the coaching job at Indiana, he was interested in the Notre Dame job, which was soon to become open. As sports fans (one of whom is a graduate of Notre Dame), we have sometimes wondered how many championships Notre Dame would have won if Knight had gone there to coach. Unfortunately for us, all we can ever do, given the limits of our knowledge, is speculate about this fascinating but never realized possibility. According to Molina, however, God knows not only how Knight would have done had he coached at Notre Dame but also how he would have done as coach at Kentucky or Duke or Northwestern. (Might Northwestern be a hoops power today?!) He knows not only exactly how many games Knight would have won at each school but also exactly what the scores would have been, who would have played in each game and so on.

Moreover, middle knowledge pertains not just to unrealized circumstances but also to persons who will never exist in the real world. Think again about Bobby Knight. He exists as a unique person because, among other things, he has just the parents that he does. Suppose that his father had married another woman and that they had children together. In that case, Knight's father would have had different children than he had in the actual world. According to Molina's theory, God knows which children would have been born in this alternative marriage, and he also knows just what they would have done with their life. He knows whether any of them would have been basketball coaches, where they would have coached and so on. Indeed, he knows everything they would have done in all possible circumstances. Furthermore, he knows what their children and their grandchildren would have done and so on indefinitely.

The choices in question here are free in the libertarian sense of the word. That is, God knows what choices all of these persons would have made even though none of these choices are determined by God. Again, God has no control over what he knows by middle knowledge. Although the latter part of Molina's quote above can be read in such a way that compatibilists would affirm it, it is clear from Molina's larger discussion that he is committed to a libertarian understanding of freedom. His opponents in the sixteenth century were theological determinists, and this was one of the central issues dividing the participants in this noted controversy.

We are now in a position to state Molina's understanding of providence, predestination and sovereignty. The essence of his account of providence is that God arranges the world as he chooses based on his middle knowledge. God exercises sovereign control in the sense that he creates the persons he wishes to create and brings about the circumstances he wills, knowing just what choices all those persons will make in the circumstances he has brought about.

God is completely sovereign for Molina because everything that happens is either intended by God or at least permitted by him. All good choices are intended by God, whereas evil choices are permitted by him for the sake of some greater good. Now the language of permission makes perfect sense in a Molinist framework since God has no control over what he knows by way of middle knowledge. That is, God may know that certain evil choices will be made in the circumstances he chooses to create, but he may allow those choices because he knows that good will ultimately come out of them.

To see this, let us consider again Suzi's tragic murder. According to Molinism, God knew by middle knowledge, before the world was created, that if Randy were to rob Suzi's house while she was at home, he would freely choose to murder her, even though he could have done otherwise. Moreover, God knew that if Randy were later in prison for this crime, he would repent and accept Christ.

On the Molinist account, God ordained all of this in the sense that he created the world and the relevant states of affairs knowing that these events would unfold in just this fashion. Molinism is similar to Calvinism in holding that God knows precisely what will happen before it occurs. The difference for Molina is that God does not determine choices. Again, God has no control over what he knows by middle knowledge. He does not determine things in such a way that Randy cannot do other than murder Suzi. But given what he knows by middle knowledge, he knows that if Randy were to face that situation, he would surely do so. So God cannot create this very situation in which Randy is free without permitting the murder. Unlike the Calvinist determinist, the Molinist believes God's decrees are dependent on what he knows creatures would freely do in various circumstances.

Similarly, God predestined Randy to salvation only in the sense that he brought about or permitted the circumstances in which he knew Randy would freely repent and believe. God's choice to predestine Randy for salvation depends on God's prior knowledge that Randy would repent in the relevant circumstances. Again, for the Calvinist, God's election is not dependent on any such considerations. He can choose to save whomever he will and his choice to save a particular elect person is prior to his knowledge that the elect person will believe. Indeed, his knowledge that the person will believe logically follows his choice to determine the person to believe.

Molinism is an attractive position in many ways. It offers an account of providence that explains how God can have a highly particular degree of control over various circumstances without resorting to determinism of human choices. For those who are attracted to Calvinism's account of providence and sovereignty but are hesitant to embrace determinism, Molinism may seem like the perfect alternative. Indeed, more than once, when reading Calvinistic authors, we have suspected that something like Molinism was unconsciously being affirmed, especially when Calvinists shrink from determinism and appeal to divine permission to explain certain events. Molinism is close to Calvinism in many respects, and it is understandable that Calvinist authors might slide into it if they are not careful to stay consistent with their principles. It's also understandable that Molinism might be seen as a compromise between Calvinism and Arminianism.[16]

But at the end of the day, Molinism is not a compromise position that Calvinists can embrace; rather, it is a variation on Arminianism. As Muller has recognized, if Molinism were accepted as a middle

---

[16]See William Lane Craig, "Middle Knowledge: A Calvinist-Arminian Rapprochement?" in *The Grace of God and the Will of Man: A Case for Arminianism,* ed. Clark H. Pinnock (Grand Rapids, Mich.: Zondervan, 1989), pp. 141-64. It is interesting in this light that one of the figures most responsible for the renewed interest in Molina in contemporary philosophy of religion is Alvin Plantinga, a product of the Reformed tradition who holds a libertarian view of freedom.

ground position, "the Reformed would need to concede virtually all of the issues in debate and adopt an Arminian perspective."[17] It is clear, then, that Molinism, despite its strong account of particular providential control, does not represent nearly enough divine control for the truly Reformed.

Whether this is a weakness of Molinism depends on one's view of sovereignty. There is, however, another point where Molinism's weakness is more widely agreed on, even by its advocates. I am referring to the Molinist account of just how God has foreknowledge of our future free choices. Consider here Molina's explanation.

> Thus, while the full force of created free choice is preserved and while the contingency of things remains altogether intact in the same way as if there were no foreknowledge in God, God knows future contingents with absolute certainty—not, to be sure, with a certainty that stems from the object, which is in itself contingent and really able to turn out otherwise, but rather with a certainty that flows from the depth and from the infinite and unlimited perfection of the knower, who *in Himself* knows with certainty an object that *in its own right* is uncertain and deceptive.[18]

Notice for a start how strongly Molina describes the freedom of choice involved in "future contingents." These choices are as free and undetermined as if there were no foreknowledge in God, and yet God knows these choices with absolute certainty. There is nothing about prior circumstances and states of affairs that makes it impossible for Randy to do otherwise than murder Suzi. Determinists, of course, hold that prior circumstances and states of affairs make it impossible for us to ever do other than we do. Molina's rejection of this claim distinguishes his position from theological determinists.

But what is interesting for our present concerns is how Molina ac-

---

[17]Muller, "Grace," 2:265.

[18]Molina, *Divine Foreknowledge*, qu. 14, art. 13, disp. 51, no. 18 (emphasis in original). See also disp. 52, no. 29.

counts for this knowledge. His claim, notice, is that God's certainty concerning future contingents "flows from the depth and from the infinite and unlimited perfection of the knower." That is to say, because God is infinite and possesses unlimited perfection, he can know as certain that which is uncertain in itself.

As appealing as this is as a devotional expression, it is unhelpful as a theological or philosophical analysis. Insisting that God is the perfect knower does little to relieve our perplexity concerning how he could know the future free choices of his creatures, not to mention the countless free choices of persons who will never exist in the actual world. In the definition of middle knowledge cited earlier, Molina proposes that God "saw in His own essence what each such faculty [of free choice] would do with its innate freedom." The suggestion here seems to be that everything in the created order is somehow a reflection of God's own nature. Thus, by knowing his own essential nature, he can know the created order through and through.

This basic idea is intelligible enough and helps us understand how God can know the potentialities of his creatures and the range of possible choices they might make. But as for his knowing the actual, specific choices they would make on any given occasion, it leaves us in the dark. To see the difficulty here, we can probe the issue another way. A number of philosophers who are critical of Molinism have asked who or what makes true the things that God knows by middle knowledge. Consider again the children who would have been born if Bobby Knight's father had married another woman. Let's suppose that God knows that one of the grandchildren from this marriage would have been named Magic Michael Maravich Knight and would have become an all-American guard. God knows that Magic Knight would have then attended Notre Dame and in his senior year led them to a national championship. The question is who or what makes this true. It cannot be God who makes this true, because the choice in question is a free choice that is in no way determined. Indeed, it is as undetermined as if God did not foreknow it. Nor can it be Magic Knight who makes it true since he never exists in the real world.

In short, it remains mysterious on Molinist principles how God can have foreknowledge of our future free choices as well as the middle knowledge on which such foreknowledge depends. Now perhaps we simply need to embrace the mystery here. After all, there are many things we don't understand about God, including how he knows many other things we believe he knows. Even outside the realm of theology, many things about our world elude our comprehension. So perhaps it shouldn't concern us too much if we can't begin to fathom how God knows future free choices.

It is undeniable, then, that we inevitably come up against mysteries, concepts beyond our grasp, no matter what our worldview. The question is whether middle knowledge is one of those inevitable mysteries or whether it is sheer nonsense that can be avoided by other approaches. It is clear, at any rate, that Calvinistic determinism does not have to swallow a mystery here because it provides a readily intelligible account of how God can know the future, including our choices. This is one of the selling points of Calvinistic determinism for some thinkers such as Crabtree, whom we cited above. It is noteworthy that Crabtree criticizes Molinism precisely for failing to make rational sense of how God has middle knowledge and can know future free choices. Although it represents an ingenious attempt to make sense of how God can have rather particular providential control of the world without resorting to determinism, it is apparent that Molinism is not without its difficulties.[19]

THE OPENNESS VIEW

The Openness view has been the focus of considerable debate and contro-

---

[19]It is worth noting that Molinism is not altogether exempt from the sort of moral problems that Calvinists struggle with. The problem in brief is this: might there be persons who are damned in the actual world who, as God knows through middle knowledge, would have been saved if they had been placed in different circumstances? For detailed discussion of this problem, see Jerry L. Walls, "Is Molinism as Bad as Calvinism?" *Faith and Philosophy* 7 (1990): 85-98.

versy for the past few years.[20] Those who espouse this view intend to provide a biblical challenge to the traditional view of God. This is what makes their project interesting for evangelicals. The traditional view of God has, of course, been challenged in a number of ways by liberal and radical theologians of various stripes. But Openness theologians are evangelicals who accept the authority of Scripture. It is their contention that the traditional view of God has been shaped in certain crucial respects more by Greek philosophical categories than by sound scriptural exegesis.

Particular instances of this claim involve the traditional doctrines that God is absolutely immutable or unchangeable and that he is impassible. The latter doctrine, which holds that God never experiences sorrow or pain, is a specific aspect of immutability, for to experience sorrow or pain is to undergo a certain sort of change. Advocates of the Openness view argue that those biblical passages depicting God as sorrowful should be taken at face value rather than explained away in some manner that denies the straightforward reading of the biblical text.

For our present concerns, however, the most interesting aspect of the Openness view is its assessment of the traditional account of God's foreknowledge. In brief, proponents of this position hold that it is impossible in principle for future undetermined free actions to be known with certainty. Therefore, if we are free in the libertarian sense, our future free actions cannot be known with certainty, even by God. It's important to emphasize here that those who hold this view do not deny the claim that God is omniscient. However, they would insist that omniscience pertains only to what is logically possible to know.

An analogy is often drawn here between the attributes of omnipotence and omniscience. Most traditional accounts of omnipotence don't claim that God can do literally anything. Rather, they hold only that God can do anything that is logically possible and compatible with his perfect

---

[20]See Clark Pinnock et al., *The Openness of God: A Biblical Challenge to the Traditional Understanding of God* (Downers Grove, Ill.: InterVarsity Press, 1994). This book is most responsible for bringing this view to the attention of the larger evangelical world and sparking the debate that followed.

nature. Thus God can't lie or make a square circle. A square circle is by definition an impossibility, a nonsensical thing. The fact that God can't make square circles or married bachelors does not in any way detract from his perfect power. Similarly, it is argued, the fact that God can't know what is impossible to know doesn't detract from his perfect knowledge. If it is impossible in principle to know future free actions, then omniscience doesn't pertain to such actions.

To put the point another way, if an action is foreknown with infallible certainty, that action can't be free according to this view. William Hasker argues this point by asking us to consider Clarence, who is a noted lover of cheese omelets. Suppose that God has known before the creation of the world that Clarence will have a cheese omelet for breakfast next Sunday morning. If God has this knowledge, it is a fact about the past, and as such it is unalterable. Assuming that what God infallibly knows cannot possibly be mistaken, it isn't possible that things will turn out differently than he believes. So if the past cannot be altered, and if it's a fact about the past that God has infallible knowledge that Clarence will eat a cheese omelet, then it seems impossible that Clarence could decide to have a breakfast of a bran muffin and cranberry juice instead. And if this is impossible, then Clarence can't be genuinely free with respect to this choice.[21]

Now if libertarian freedom and infallible foreknowledge are incompatible, we must decide which of these we are more certain of and which one we are willing to give up. Faced with this choice, advocates of the Openness view argue that the traditional view of infallible foreknowledge is the conviction that should be dispensed with. They do not, however, see this as a choice that is forced on us by philosophical considerations, over and against the clear teaching of Scripture. Rather, they hold that Scripture itself gives us numerous indications that God doesn't know future free choices. Indeed, they hold that this is another place where the traditional

---

[21]William Hasker, "A Philosophical Perspective," in *The Openness of God: A Biblical Challenge to the Traditional Understanding of God*, ed. Clark Pinnock et al. (Downers Grove, Ill.: InterVarsity Press, 1994), chap. 4, esp. pp. 147-49.

view of God has been shaped more by alien categories of thought than by honest exegesis.

As an example, consider the famous story of God's testing of Abraham, when he asks him to sacrifice his beloved son Isaac. Look at how God responds to Abraham's obedience: "Now I know that you fear God, because you have not withheld from me your son, your only son" (Gen 22:12). If we take this passage at face value, it seems that God did not fully know whether Abraham feared him until after he had passed the test.

Of course, defenders of God's exhaustive, infallible foreknowledge interpret the passage otherwise. But that is just the point. It is a matter of interpretation, and there are several other texts that can plausibly be interpreted in favor of the claim that God doesn't know future free choices.[22] Theological interpretation requires that we make a choice. The first option is to take as most clear and compelling those passages that appear to teach exhaustive, infallible foreknowledge and then to interpret other passages in light of those. This is what traditional theologians have done. The second option is to do the reverse, namely, to take as most clear and compelling those texts that appear to teach that God cannot know future free choices and then to interpret other passages in light of those. This, of course, is the line taken by advocates of the Openness view. This issue should be decided in terms of which option makes the most exegetical and theological sense overall.

How does the Openness view construe sovereignty and related matters? In brief, the Openness view holds that sovereignty means God can create any sort of world that is logically possible and compatible with his perfect nature. If it is true that libertarian freedom and infallible foreknowledge are incompatible, then God had to choose either a world with creatures who are free in the libertarian sense or a world in which he has exhaustive, infallible foreknowledge.

---

[22]See the chapter by Richard Rice, "Biblical Support for a New Perspective," in *The Openness of God: A Biblical Challenge to the Traditional Understanding of God*, ed. Clark Pinnock et al. (Downers Grove, Ill.: InterVarsity Press, 1994), pp. 11-58.

Advocates of the Openness view readily agree that God could have created a world without libertarian freedom, in which he controlled everything in meticulous detail. If it is a question of power, certainly God has the power to create such a world. He has the power to determine everything if he chooses to do so. However, those who hold the Openness view believe it's apparent that we are free in the libertarian sense. Thus it's apparent that God made the sovereign choice to create a world where we are free in this sense rather than a world where he exercises meticulous control.

Note that God is no less sovereign in a world where he chooses to grant his creatures libertarian freedom than he is in a world where he determines everything. Sovereignty cannot simply be equated with meticulous control. Rather, sovereignty is the freedom to choose as one will and to accomplish one's purposes. If God chooses to create people who are free and to accomplish his purposes through their undetermined choices, it is his sovereign right to do so. Less control is not the same as less sovereignty if God chooses to have less control. A perfectly good and wise God will exercise just the amount of control appropriate for the sort of world he chooses to create.

Consider a parental analogy. Sometimes we hear of parents whose children are "out of control." This, of course, is a negative judgment that implies that the parents are not providing the proper amount of guidance and discipline for their children. It may also imply that the parents are at a loss and have no idea how to exert any sort of control over their children. Now consider parents whose children are said to be "under control." This does not imply that the parents completely dictate or determine every aspect of their children's lives, nor does it suggest that the children never disobey or displease their parents. But it does imply that the parents have both the resources and the will to discipline their children and that their children will remain accountable to them.

It's in this sense that advocates of the Openness view believe that God is in control of us and our world. He doesn't determine our choices or control every detail of our lives, but rather he gives us the freedom to make significant decisions, including whether or not we will trust and obey him. And he does not know beforehand how we will decide.

Does this mean that God might be surprised by our actions or that we might do things that would confound him? Although some representatives of the Openness view have suggested we might surprise God and that he took a risk in deciding to create this world, these are unnecessary conclusions. Even if future free actions are unknowable in principle, God could know all possible choices we might make as well as all possible scenarios the world as a whole might follow. Moreover, he could know how to respond to any possible situation to accomplish his ultimate purposes. Thus, no matter what choices we make or what course the world takes, God can anticipate them and plan the perfect response.

Here's a famous analogy. Think of a chess game in which a master is playing a novice. In this case, the chess master will surely win the game for the obvious reason that he knows all the moves of the game and how to counteract each of them; the novice does not. God is the chess master and we are the novices. Even if God does not know the exact moves we will make, he will have control of the game and will achieve his ultimate goals for his creation.

So nothing can catch God off-guard or confound him. The classic case here is the Fall. Advocates of Openness insist that the Fall was anticipated by God and that he will achieve his purposes through it. His aim in a fallen world is to reconcile the world to himself through Christ and to bring all persons to acknowledge his lordship. Since his creation includes free creatures, some may acknowledge his lordship only in their damnation. Although God is genuinely willing to save all persons and makes salvation available to all, freedom means that some may perversely decline the joy of being reconciled to him.[23] God doesn't unconditionally predestine particular persons to salvation. Rather, election is in Christ, and all are saved who do not knowingly and persistently refuse God's gracious offer of life.

---

[23]For insight into what might motivate such a perverse choice, see C. S. Lewis, *The Great Divorce* (New York: Macmillan, 1946). See also Jerry L. Walls, *Hell: The Logic of Damnation* (Notre Dame: University of Notre Dame Press, 1992), pp. 113-38.

The fact that God is sovereign over his creation means that he is glorified both in salvation and damnation, although in very different ways. This is not to say, however, that some persons are chosen to glorify God by receiving his mercy whereas others are chosen to glorify him by receiving his wrath. Rather, God loves all persons with perfect love. And given the fact that he has created us in his image, a relationship of perfect love with him is the only possible source of ultimate satisfaction and fulfillment for us. Those who accept his love experience joy and flourish under his care, and God is glorified in their flourishing. By sharp contrast, those who reject his love will inevitably be unhappy and fail to flourish in the long run. Their very unhappiness is an eloquent, although ironic, testimony to God's greatness and glory.

Let's consider how the Openness view would construe the events of Suzi's murder. In this view, God did not know before the world was created that Randy would murder Suzi. This is not to say that God was surprised or blindsided by the event, for he knew that such things were possibilities, if not probabilities, when he created the world. God ordained this event only in the general sense that he created a world with free creatures and that he allowed Randy to make this choice rather than prevented it. Once the choice was made, the Openness view would emphasize that God in his creative grace was able to bring good out of it. Randy's eventual repentance was one of the good things that came out of this tragedy. Again, this is not to say that God planned Suzi's murder knowing it would lead Randy to repent, as the Molinist might say. Instead, God has many creative moves he can deploy to bring good out of evil and defeat evil in the end.

Finally, before concluding this section, let us consider an objection to the Openness view often made by critics, both Calvinist and Arminian, who argue that it presents an overwhelming difficulty, namely, predictive prophecy. How can such prophecy be possible if God cannot foreknow future free actions? It would take us too far afield to deal with this in detail, but it is worth noting that advocates of the Openness view are well aware of this difficulty and have argued that their position can adequately account for predictive prophecy.[24] Interestingly, Openness advocates point out that some prophecy can be explained in terms of God's knowing his own intentions.

It's not clear whether Openness theologians intend for this to apply to prophecies concerning future human actions, but there is no reason in principle why it couldn't. That is, God could predict future human actions because he intends to cause those actions. For instance, consider the opening verse of the book of Ezra: "In the first year of Cyrus king of Persia, in order to fulfill the word of the LORD spoken by Jeremiah, the LORD moved the heart of Cyrus king of Persia to make a proclamation throughout his realm and to put it in writing" (Ezra 1:1). Notice in particular here that God moves the heart of Cyrus in order to fulfill the prophecy of Jeremiah (see Jer 29). It isn't altogether clear that the sense in which God moves the heart of Cyrus is deterministic, but if it were so, Cyrus's choice to make the proclamation would not be a free action in the libertarian sense. If the advocate of Openness interprets the passage in this way, he would agree with the Calvinistic explanation of some instances of prophecy.

Is this inconsistent? Not at all. It might be the case that God determines some events that he foretells, particularly if these events are crucial for his purposes of revelation or salvation. These would be exceptional events in which God makes known himself and his plan of salvation. God could perform such acts and still leave our libertarian freedom intact, especially with respect to the crucial matter of whether we will accept his revelation and salvation.

Look again at the analogy of parents who have their children "under control." This does not mean that the parents control all their children's actions. But they may control some of them rather directly while allowing considerable freedom most of the time. Similarly, advocates of Openness might consistently believe that God directly causes certain human actions while leaving future actions otherwise open.

---

[24]See Rice, "Biblical Support," pp. 50-53.

A BIBLICAL EXAMPLE

We will conclude this chapter by considering a classic biblical text that often figures in discussions of divine sovereignty, namely, the Joseph story. Sproul sees the Joseph story as a vivid illustration of the Calvinist view of God's providential control of the entire sweep of history. In the same vein, a number of Calvinist writers see this text as a prominent example of the compatibilist view of freedom. Particularly interesting here are the words of Joseph at the end of the story, when he responded to his brothers' plea for forgiveness for selling him into slavery: "You intended to harm me, but God intended it for good to accomplish what is now being done, the saving of many lives" (Gen 50:20). Earlier in the story, Joseph told his brothers that God had sent him to Egypt to save their lives (Gen 45:4-7). Although Joseph did not deny or minimize his brothers' guilt or wicked intentions, he nevertheless saw the hand of God in the event in retrospect.

D. A. Carson claims that Joseph was "assuming compatibilism" in his remarks to his brothers and goes on to insist that "compatibilism is a *necessary* component to any mature and orthodox view of God and the world."[25] In short, many Calvinists see this text as a clear instance of compatibilism and a strong support for their account of sovereignty.

As we pointed out in the introduction, Calvinists as well as Arminians rely on philosophical judgments at crucial junctures in their arguments. This is an excellent example of a case where Calvinism depends on both a controversial philosophical judgment and a contested interpretation of Scripture. It is highly misleading to claim that the Calvinist view is based simply on the clear teaching of Scripture.

To the contrary, this text can be read quite plausibly in terms of all three accounts of sovereignty and providence we have considered in this

---

[25]D. A. Carson, *The Difficult Doctrine of the Love of God* (Wheaton, Ill.: Crossway, 2000), pp. 52, 54 (emphasis in original). Carson's definition of compatibilism is philosophically imprecise, affirming only that "God's unconditioned sovereignty and the responsibility of human beings are mutually compatible" (p. 52). This definition could be accepted by those who hold that sovereignty and responsibility are an antinomy.

chapter. Carson's claim of Joseph as a spokesman for compatibilism is singularly unpersuasive. The text says nothing nearly precise enough to support a particular theory of sovereignty and human freedom to the exclusion of all other competing accounts. Since Carson is an astute interpreter of Scripture, we can only assume he does not intend his strong statements to be taken with full seriousness; rather he is exaggerating for rhetorical effect.

What would the text have to say to provide explicit support for compatibilism? It would have to say that God caused Joseph's brothers to have their feelings of jealousy (or at least that he moved their hearts to have those feelings, like he did with Cyrus) and that these feelings led the brothers to sell Joseph into slavery and so on. Or if God did not directly cause their actions, then he did so indirectly by allowing them to harm Joseph due to their jealousy. But their feelings of jealousy cannot be considered in isolation from earlier actions and events that produced those feelings. On the Calvinistic account, those actions and events are also determined by God.

Thus Joseph's brothers were determined to have feelings of jealousy, and they were determined in such a way that they couldn't do otherwise than they did when they sold Joseph into slavery. Nevertheless, the brothers were responsible for their actions because they willingly sold Joseph. Their actions flowed out of their own internal psychological states, even though those states were caused by God, directly or indirectly, for ultimately benevolent reasons.

We grant that it is *possible* to read the text in this way. However, the text doesn't come close to stating this explicitly, so we are hardly required to read it in a compatibilist way.

This text is quite amenable to a Molinist interpretation. On this reading, God's middle knowledge allowed him to know that Joseph's brothers would freely develop feelings of jealousy if Joseph received his coat, that they would freely (in the libertarian sense) sell him into slavery if placed in that situation and so on. Moreover, God foresaw the good that would eventually come out of this and (after considering all possible creatable worlds) he chose the world in which these circumstances and choices took place, and he allowed them for the sake of the good that would follow. This way of reading the story makes perfect sense of Joseph's claim that the brothers meant it for evil but God meant it for good.

Finally, consider how the text can easily accommodate an Openness interpretation. In this view, God has knowledge that can function similarly to middle knowledge. That is, God has perfect knowledge of all actual persons, including their characters, their beliefs, their tendencies and the like. Knowing this, God could know what all persons are likely to do in various circumstances. Granted, he could not know with infallible certainty what choices persons would make, but he could know the probability of all possible choices any person might make.

Armed with this sort of knowledge, God could orchestrate events like those in the Joseph story. Knowing the brothers' tendency toward envy, he could know how they would in all probability resent Joseph's colorful coat. Likewise, he could know that they likely would sell Joseph into slavery in the right circumstances. Again, God could not have the same degree of control over their particular choices as he does in Calvinism and Molinism, but he could still have sufficient control to orchestrate things to the degree necessary to get Joseph to Egypt, get him promoted to prime minister and so on. Given Joseph's understanding of God's purposes for the children of Israel, it would also make sense for him to say that God had sent him to Egypt to save lives and that God had meant for good what his brothers meant for evil.

We have tried to show that there is more than one account of sovereignty and providence that can do justice to Scripture. Calvinism is often particularly noted for its emphasis on God's sovereignty, but as we've shown, sovereignty is not a Calvinistic distinctive. Rather, it is a component of any orthodox biblical account of God that all Christians should recognize as a great source of comfort. God is in control and all things are indeed ordained and governed by him in some sense.

The difference is in the details. How minutely and particularly has God chosen to control things? It is not essential to biblical faith that God controls things as meticulously as Calvinists claim. What is essential is that he chooses as he will to accomplish his purposes and that he will certainly succeed in doing so. All of the views we have surveyed agree on that.

Each of the views presented has its strengths and difficulties. God's sovereignty and providential control of our world are surely matters that exceed our full understanding, so it's inevitable that we must allow for some mystery regardless of which view we take. It's our judgment, however, that the Calvinist account poses particularly severe difficulties, especially with respect to the problem of evil, and this is one preliminary but significant reason not to be a Calvinist.

5

CALVINISM
AND CONSISTENCY

❧

The year 1998 was the centennial year of the birth of C. S. Lewis, the most influential Christian apologist of the twentieth century. The annual theology conference at Wheaton College focused that year on the work of Lewis, and one of the featured speakers was the popular Calvinist author J. I. Packer. After his lecture, Packer took questions from the audience, and he was asked whether he thought Lewis was a Calvinist or an Arminian. Packer's response was most interesting. He offered the opinion that Lewis was a Calvinist, although an inconsistent one. Packer acknowledged that some of what Lewis wrote appeared to strongly favor an Arminian understanding of human freedom and is hard to square with Calvinism, but he noted that Lewis also affirmed God's sovereignty. His efforts to hold these truths together sometimes led him to tie himself up in knots, Packer observed, but his insistence on maintaining both of them made him a Calvinist for Packer.[1]

Packer's attempt to claim Lewis as a Calvinist (albeit an inconsistent one), despite Lewis's widely recognized Arminian views, is not overly surprising in view of some of Packer's perspectives on other famous

---

[1] One of the authors of this book (Jerry) was present at the Q and A session with Dr. Packer. For discussion of Lewis's views and how they contrast with Reformed theology, see Scott R. Burson and Jerry L. Walls, *C. S. Lewis and Francis Schaeffer* (Downers Grove, Ill.: Inter-Varsity Press, 1998), pp. 51-105; see esp. pp. 98-103.

non-Calvinists. It is noteworthy that Packer has offered a similar assessment of one of the most vigorous opponents of Calvinism in the history of theology, namely, John Wesley. In an essay surveying different views of predestination, Packer wrote,

> In the eighteenth century a confused Calvinist named John Wesley (pardon me! but truth will out) muddled the discussion in a rather grievous way. He insisted that he was an Arminian because he wished to affirm the universal invitation of the gospel and the love of God expressed in the gospel. Well, Calvinists do that too![2]

As Packer sees it, Wesley's powerful preaching on grace was Reformed in substance, but Wesley was confused because he did not believe Reformed theology truly teaches that God loves all persons and desires to save them. Moreover, his insistence that our free cooperation is necessary for salvation led him into hopeless contradiction. His efforts to hold these claims together were, in Packer's view, as futile as attempts to make a square circle.[3]

Packer's leveling of the charges of inconsistency and confusion is particularly interesting in light of his own appeal to the notion of "antinomy" to explain the relationship between divine sovereignty and human freedom. As discussed in chapter three, Packer defines *antinomy* as something that appears to our understanding to be a contradiction. We are faced with such an antinomy when confronted by two claims that we can neither deny nor see as compatible. In the same article where he charges Wesley with inconsistency, Packer reiterates his view that God is sovereign in such a way that there is no "contingency or indeterminacy" in human choice, and yet human beings remain responsible for those choices. A bit later he writes, "The reality of human moral agency and responsibility in a world where God is Lord is one of the mysteries of cre-

---

[2]J. I. Packer, "Predestination in Christian History," in *Honoring the People of God: The Collected Shorter Writings of J. I. Packer* (Carlisle, U.K.: Paternoster, 1999), 4:215.

[3]J. I. Packer, "Arminianisms," in *Through Christ's Word,* ed. W. Robert Godfrey and Jesse L. Boyd III (Phillipsburg, N.J.: Presbyterian & Reformed, 1985), pp. 143, 145.

ation, which we reverently acknowledge, but do not pretend to fully understand."[4]

Packer's retreat to mystery here is not an uncommon move among Calvinists. Notice, moreover, that the willingness to concede that we can't make logical sense of these matters is construed as a sign of true reverence and piety. The same attitude is suggested in the words of John MacArthur: "How can God choose some, offer salvation to everyone, and hold people responsible who weren't chosen? I don't know. But it is a mystery only to us. I don't know how God resolves it but I am content to leave it with Him."[5]

This obviously raises questions, despite these postures of piety. How can Packer make charges of inconsistency and confusion on the one hand and then turn around and defend himself with appeals to "antinomy" and "mystery" on the other? Are Packer's opponents really guilty of something that he is not? Are his antinomies and mysteries legitimate in a way that his opponents' views are not? If so, just what is the difference?

Some of Packer's fellow Calvinists have been concerned that his appeal to antinomy has left him open to serious misunderstanding, that it may be understood as suggesting that there are actual contradictions in divine truth. R. C. Sproul, for instance, insists that truth would lose its meaning if contradictions of any kind were affirmed. If contradictions can be true, we would be at a loss to separate truth from falsehood. Sproul distinguishes a genuine *contradiction* from a *paradox,* asserting that Packer surely must mean that to affirm both divine sovereignty and human responsibility is paradoxical but not contradictory.[6]

Calvinist philosopher Paul Helm is critical of Packer for similar reasons. He points out that if statements seem to us to be contradictory and we have no hope of reconciling them in this life, then we have no way to distinguish seeming contradictions from real ones. He asks, "In these circumstances, what is the difference between an apparent inconsistency

---

[4]Ibid., p. 147.
[5]John MacArthur, *Body Dynamics* (Wheaton: Victor, 1982), p. 28.
[6]R. C. Sproul, *Chosen by God* (Wheaton, Ill.: Tyndale House, 1986), pp. 43-46.

and a real one? How do we know that what is called an antinomy might not turn out to be a real inconsistency?"[7] To avoid such difficulties, Helm believes some effort should be made to show how the Calvinist account of sovereignty can be logically compatible with human freedom and responsibility. And not surprisingly, Helm opts for a compatibilist account of freedom to achieve this.

We fully agree with Helm and Sproul that logical consistency is nonnegotiable. And happily, many other Calvinists agree as well. While some Calvinists make a hasty retreat to mystery when faced with charges of inconsistency, most of whom we have read are committed to logic and would reject out of hand the claim that divine truth contains contradictions. Of course, this is not to deny that divine truth contains mysteries that elude our understanding. But mysteries are very different from logical contradictions. It isn't a sign of true piety for one to be willing to dispense with logical coherence in the name of mystery.

While logical consistency may not be a sufficient condition to show that a theology is true, it is a necessary condition. When inconsistency is exposed, we know that something is awry. It isn't surprising, therefore, that Calvinists have attempted to saddle Arminians and Wesleyans with inconsistency and that the latter have returned the favor; to succeed in showing that a theology is inconsistent is to show that it can't be altogether true as it stands.

In this chapter, we will examine Calvinism with respect to consistency. It is our contention that there is at least one version (and perhaps two) of Calvinism that is consistent, but that other variations are not. In order to pursue this question we need to get clear on just what it means to be inconsistent. How does *inconsistency* differ from *mystery, paradox* and other related notions that are often confused with it? Let's define these terms with some precision so we can differentiate among these concepts.

---

[7]Paul Helm, *The Providence of God* (Downers Grove, Ill.: InterVarsity Press, 1994), p. 65. Helm's full critique of Packer is found on pp. 61-65.

CONTRADICTIONS AND MYSTERIES

Perhaps the most straightforward of these concepts is what we call *real contradiction*. A real contradiction occurs when a statement is simultaneously affirmed and denied. One thing is at the same time and in the same sense both affirmed and denied. Consider the following specific example:

Statement 1: Bach is a bachelor.
Statement 2: Bach is not a bachelor.

Assuming that Bach is the same person in both statements and that both sentences are asserted at the same time, we have a clear contradiction and an obvious impossibility. It would not, however, be a contradiction to say that Bach is a bachelor the day before his wedding and then to deny it the day after. But Bach cannot both be a bachelor and not be a bachelor at the same time. Let us call an example like this an *explicit contradiction*.

But not all real contradictions are explicit in this fashion. Sometimes they are hidden but can easily be exposed. Consider the following statements, which are obviously contradictory, though not as explicitly as those above.

Statement 1: Bach is a bachelor.
Statement 3: Bach is a married man.

In order to show these two statements are contradictory, all we need to do is add a description of all bachelors, one that is necessarily true. Then by using the rules of ordinary logic, we can deduce a contradiction, as follows:

Statement 4: All bachelors are unmarried men.
Statement 5: Bach is an unmarried man. (This follows from assertions 1 and 4.)

Now the contradiction between statements 3 and 5 is explicit. Statements like 1 and 3 are implicitly contradictory. Not all implicit contradictions are as easy to make explicit as this one. Nevertheless, when statements are contradictory in this manner, both of them cannot possibly be true.

Now we turn to what we call *apparent contradictions*. These are not actual contradictions (i.e., they are not statements that couldn't possibly be true at the same time), but at first glance they appear to be so. One type of apparent contradiction is what is commonly called a *paradox*.[8] A paradox is a sort of verbal inconsistency or puzzle, but the inconsistency is merely verbal rather than real, so it does not involve the simultaneous assertion of incompatible claims. Once the meanings of the terms are clarified, the inconsistency is resolved. For a striking example, consider the following lines from the apostle Paul (see Gal 2:20).

Statement A: I am crucified with Christ.
Statement B: Nevertheless I live.

Anyone remotely familiar with Paul's thought will recognize that he is not claiming to have been literally crucified. Rather, he means that his old sinful self is dead as a result of his faith in Christ. And since he has died to his sinful self, he truly lives. So in order to "live" he had to "die." This is paradoxical at the level of language but perfectly coherent at the level of meaning.

A second sort of apparent contradiction is generated when we encounter seemingly incompatible facts. In this case, the conflict is not rooted merely in language but also in empirical data. As such, the data cannot be dismissed but must be accepted as an entrenched part of reality. The classic case here is the nature of light as disclosed in progressive discoveries in the field of physics. The most outstanding achievement of nineteenth-century physics was to establish that light behaves in a wavelike fashion. Then in the early part of the twentieth century it was shown just as certainly that light also behaves like particles, and this

---

[8]For another discussion of these terms, see Burson and Walls, *C. S. Lewis*, pp. 85-88. In that volume, the term *paradox* is defined (following David Basinger) as an actual contradiction. Here we follow the more common usage of the term in defining a paradox as an apparent contradiction.

created a serious difficulty, for no one could understand how something could be both a wave and a particle. But as physicist John Polkinghorne observes, for some time scientists simply had to live with the dilemma because both pieces of data were well established.

Polkinghorne goes on to point out that the story had a happy ending. In 1928, after living with the tension for around twenty-five years, physics was relieved of this problem when Paul Dirac invented what has come to be called *quantum field theory*. Polkinghorne explains:

> This provided an example of a well-understood formalism which if interrogated in a particle-like way gave particle behavior and if interrogated in a wave-like way gave wave behavior. . . . Since that day of Dirac's discovery the dual nature of light as wave and particle has been free of paradox for those in the know.[9]

The kind of *apparent* contradiction generated by seemingly incompatible data seems to be the sort of case Packer has in mind when he appeals to antinomy. Indeed, Packer appeals to the particle-wave problem as an illustration of an antinomy.[10] We will consider below whether this move helps Packer's argument, but for now the point is that apparent inconsistencies of this sort have clear and definite resolutions. Further insight, information or new discoveries provide the means to understand as perfectly coherent what seemed contradictory before.

Finally, let's distinguish the concept of mystery from the concepts of real and apparent contradictions. The best example here is the fundamental Christian doctrine of the Trinity, which says God exists in three persons. Notice in the first place that this is not a contradiction. Christians do not say there is one God and three gods, nor do they say God

---

[9]John C. Polkinghorne, *The Quantum World* (Princeton: Princeton University Press, 1985), p. 7. Polkinghorne expresses irritation at those who continue to invoke the particle-wave duality as a great mystery, as if it has never been resolved.

[10]J. I. Packer, *Evangelism and the Sovereignty of God* (Downers Grove, Ill.: InterVarsity Press, 1961), p. 19. Packer's comments on the particle-wave duality suggest he was not aware the antinomy had been resolved.

exists in three persons and one person. Rather, there is only one true God. But the *one God* exists in *three persons*. This is not simply a paradox that can be readily resolved once the meaning of the terms is made clear, nor is it the sort of thing that can be cleanly explicated by a mathematical formalism, like the wave-particle duality of physics. The nature of God is a mystery that eludes our full understanding. Our finite minds can understand enough of this to enable us to believe it with intellectual integrity, but even with our best insight, we realize we are dealing with a reality that is far beyond our comprehension.

With these distinctions before us, we are in position to examine different versions of Calvinism and evaluate them for consistency.

CONSISTENT CALVINISM

There is one version of Calvinism that can clearly be held without contradiction. This is the view that holds with open-eyed consistency that God not only knows the future completely but also controls it in every detail because he has determined everything that will ever happen. Whether he does this by constant direct management or whether he arranged the world in the beginning in such a way that things would inevitably unfold in a particular way does not matter. What is essential, however, is not merely the claim that everything happens just as God intended, but also the assertion that he could have caused things to happen differently if he had wanted. In other words, God's will for things to occur in a certain way is a sufficient cause for them to occur in precisely that way. Given his will, things could not possibly happen differently than they do in any respect.

The only kind of human freedom that can exist in a world like this is compatibilist freedom. If God has exhaustive foreknowledge of the future precisely because he has determined everything that will ever happen, then he has also obviously determined our choices. Our freedom must consist essentially in that we willingly do what God has determined us to do, even though it is strictly impossible for us to do otherwise. This means that we are responsible for our actions even though we cannot—and never could—do differently than we do.

If freedom and determinism are compatible in this way, then it follows that God could determine everyone to accept his love freely and be saved. However, the consistent Calvinist holds that God's perfect goodness is in no way challenged if he leaves many persons in their sins to be damned—persons he could just as easily determine to be saved. Though this seems unfair, not to mention unloving, on God's part, the Calvinist insists that God is under no obligation to save anyone. It would be perfectly just for God to damn everyone because all of us willingly sin, and this is sufficient to make us guilty and responsible, even though we were born in sin and cannot possibly do other than sin. Moreover, we are God's property, and as R. K. McGregor Wright writes, it is "the prerogative of a sovereign Creator to do what he wills with his own property."[11] God's reasons for saving some but not others is not for us to understand. Wright gives this point a starkly personal touch when he remarks that God may have reasons, unknown to Wright, for choosing him for salvation but for not choosing his father, who, so far as Wright knows, died as an atheist.[12]

While some may balk at the implication of unconditional election if it means God may choose not to save their beloved relatives, consistent Calvinists recognize this conclusion as part of what is required for those who submit to their view of sovereign grace. Perhaps an even more poignant example comes from the popular Calvinist pastor John Piper. He was engaged in debate over the question of how a sovereign God loves. His opponent in the debate, Thomas Talbott, had argued that if God chose not to save his daughter, then it is hard to imagine how her mother could consider God worthy of worship. Piper replied by referring to his own sons and expressing his own hopes and prayers that they will join him in Christian faith and service. Then he concluded his essay with these moving words:

---

[11]R. K. McGregor Wright, *No Place for Sovereignty: What's Wrong with Freewill Theism* (Downers Grove, Ill.: InterVarsity Press, 1996), p. 119.
[12]Ibid., p. 102.

But I am not ignorant that God may not have chosen my sons for his sons. And, though I think I would give my life for their salvation, if they should be lost to me, I would not rail against the Almighty. He is God. I am but a man. The potter has absolute rights over the clay. Mine is to bow before his unimpeachable character and believe that the Judge of all the earth has ever and always will do right.[13]

At one level, we admire Piper's efforts at consistency. For him to pledge to bow in adoration even when facing the prospect that God might have chosen not to save his sons bespeaks resolute commitment to his principles. His is not a merely intellectual affirmation of unconditional election that is far removed from his life.[14] It is not a speculation about persons halfway around the globe who may not be elect because they have never heard the gospel. It is a principled commitment to be true to what he believes Scripture teaches even if this becomes extremely uncomfortable at a personal level. Calvinists who are fully prepared to do likewise cannot be faulted with inconsistency or evasion, at least on this point. Few Calvinists, however, are this consistent. Most labor under varying degrees of inconsistency.

"MOLINIST CALVINISM"

Consider another version of Calvinism that *may* be consistent. We haven't seen this version explicitly articulated, but some of the Calvinists we have read seem to be saying something like this, so it is worth spelling out as an option. We have in mind Calvinists who are reluctant to embrace a thoroughgoing determinism, or who overtly deny that their view is deterministic, but still hold to unconditional election. How might this view go?

---

[13]John Piper, "How Does a Sovereign God Love? A Reply to Thomas Talbott," *The Reformed Journal* 33 (April 1983): 13.

[14]In one sense, of course, this is merely theoretical. The true test would come if Piper had good reason to believe his sons were, in fact, not elect.

In the first place, this sort of view would have to account for divine foreknowledge in a manner other than the one used by the Westminster Confession if it wants to maintain that God has exhaustive and infallible knowledge of the future. Something like Molinism would be needed to do the trick, for then Calvinists could consistently hold that God ordains many things in the sense that he permits or allows them. That is, he would know by way of middle knowledge the choices all of us would make in every possible circumstance, even though he did not determine those choices. God would then control things in the sense that he brought about those circumstances and allowed the choices he knew would be made.

Given the reality of the Fall, sin is inevitable for all persons, and none can do good without grace. But if God does not determine all choices, even fallen persons might have a range of freedom with respect to which specific sins they commit and when they commit them. Moreover, they might have something like libertarian freedom in the realm of morally indifferent choices. Unless God has something like middle knowledge, he could not know such choices and exercise providential control over them. Given middle knowledge, however, he could know the particular sins each person would commit, and he could decide which of these to permit for his providential purposes. Moreover, given original sin, the Calvinistic view of unconditional election could be maintained. God could choose to save certain persons by making them willing to believe and by leaving all others in their sins. He would thus permit, but not determine, the specific choices of those who continued to persist in sin and unbelief, with no intent to save such persons.

We think this is a consistent possibility for Calvinists to consider, but it is doubtful whether it coheres with historic Calvinist commitments. In other words, while it may be an internally consistent position, it clashes with essential Calvinist convictions. Molinism is a variation of Arminianism, so Calvinists would have to revisit their rejection of the Molinist option and be willing to embrace it as a way of accounting for God's foreknowledge of choices he does not determine but does exercise providential control over. It is not for us to say whether Calvinists who are uncomfortable with determinism should adopt this position, but it would provide them with a way to avoid a thoroughgoing determinism while holding to unconditional election in the realm of salvation.

We have now identified two versions of Calvinism that can be held with consistency if its defenders are clear on the following points. First, they must be explicit about which choices are determined. (Are all choices determined? Or is only the choice of salvation determined?) Second, they must acknowledge that if a choice is determined, it can be free only in the compatibilist sense: that is, the person who performed it could not do otherwise. One's freedom and responsibility for one's choice consists essentially in the fact that one willingly does what one has been determined to do. Third, they must recognize that the ultimate reason why anyone is finally damned is because of God's sovereign choice not to save them. God's sovereign prerogative, even in the case of beloved relatives and friends, may be to leave them in their sins to experience eternal misery. It's not for us to understand his sovereign will; we must only adore him.

INCONSISTENT CALVINISM

While we've shown that there are consistent versions of Calvinism available, more often than not the versions of Calvinism presented are inconsistent, though not usually explicitly so. Typically, the inconsistency involves the nature of human freedom. We contend that Calvinists often vacillate between compatibilist and libertarian views of freedom in a way that is neither clear nor consistent with their other commitments. We are not alone in this judgment; Wright has made the observation that many of his fellow Calvinists "are not clear on the idea of free will" and "often sound partly like Arminians."[15]

This inconsistency is not confined to versions of Calvinism espoused by contemporary Reformed spokesmen. Rather, it appears in classical

---

[15]Wright, *No Place*, p. 78.

sources as well. Indeed, perhaps the inconsistency in contemporary Reformed writings is a reflection of confusion in the classical sources.

DOES DIVINE ENABLEMENT INCLUDE DETERMINISM?

Let's begin with the Westminster Confession. This document can be read in a coherent way if freedom is understood in the compatibilist sense. Previously, we cited passages that clearly seem to support a compatibilist reading. There is, however, more to the story.

Let us reexamine the key passage we cited above and consider it in light of its larger context:

> All those whom God hath predestinated unto life, and those only, he is pleased, in his appointed and accepted time, effectually to call, by his Word and Spirit, out of that state of sin and death, in which they are by nature, to grace and salvation by Jesus Christ; enlightening their minds spiritually and savingly, to understand the things of God; taking away their heart of stone, and giving them an heart of flesh; renewing their wills, and by his almighty power *determining them to that which is good,* and effectually drawing them to Jesus Christ, *yet so as they come most freely, being made willing by his grace.* (art. 10.1, emphasis added)

This describes the effectual call that goes out to the elect by enlightening their minds, giving them a new heart and renewing their wills. Those who are acted on by God in this fashion are said to be determined to the good and effectually drawn to Christ "yet so as they come most freely, being made willing by his grace." A bit later, the Confession explicates the effectual call as follows:

> This effectual call is of God's free and special grace alone, not from anything foreseen in man, who is *altogether passive therein, until, being quickened* and renewed by the Holy Spirit, he is thereby *enabled* to answer this call, and to embrace the grace offered and conveyed in it. . . . Others, not elected, although they may be *called* by the

ministry of the Word, and may have some of the common operations of the Spirit, yet they never truly come to Christ, and therefore cannot be saved. (art. 10.2, 4, emphasis added)

Immediately striking is the different language used here to describe the effectual call. Notice the italicized words in the passage. Those who receive this calling are said to be altogether passive until they are renewed by the Holy Spirit. Then they are said to be enabled to do something they could not before, namely, to actively embrace the grace that is offered.

Now the notion of being enabled is quite different from that of being made willing. The one who is made willing to do something will surely do that thing. His will is controlled in such a way that he wills just what he has been determined to will. But to be enabled to do something is another matter altogether. It implies that one has been given the ability to do it but that how the ability will be exercised is undetermined.

Consider an example. Suppose there is a big basketball game coming up. We think our friend might want to go to the game, but we know he can't afford it. We might *enable* him to go to the game by purchasing his ticket, arranging his transportation to and from the game and so on. He is now able to go to the game. He has been empowered to do something he couldn't do before. However, it doesn't follow that he *will* go to the game, only that he can go if he wants. Perhaps he doesn't really want to go because he would prefer to stay home and watch MTV.

This example shows that ability is not the same thing as willingness. One may be enabled to do something without being willing to do it. This distinction is important because the notion of being enabled, unlike that of being made willing, is compatible with libertarian freedom. Indeed, it implies such freedom. To enable someone to do something is to make it possible for her to do it but not to determine her choice. It is up to her whether she will do what she has been enabled to do. This means that effectual calling is described in two ways: one implies a compatibilist view of freedom and the other implies libertarian freedom. These appear to be inconsistent accounts.

Now a defender of the Westminster Confession might contend that the concepts of being made willing and being enabled are in fact compatible. That is, it might be argued that fallen sinners lack both the will and the ability to obey God. It's not enough for God to make us willing to do right; he must also enable us to act rightly. For willingness doesn't imply ability any more than ability implies willingness.

Consider again our friend who might want to go to the basketball game. Suppose that now we convince him that basketball is the most exciting game on the planet, that it is a great way to spend an evening and so on. Now he is willing to go to the game. But suppose he still can't afford it and, moreover, lacks transportation. Now he's willing but not able. In order to go to the game, he must be enabled in addition to being made willing. Thus the concepts of being made willing and enabled are perfectly compatible.

Certain definitions of these concepts are indeed compatible, as this example suggests. The question, however, is whether the notion of being made willing that is found in the Westminster Confession implies that the ability is still lacking and must be added once willingness is established. The answer to this can be easily ascertained by examining the passage in question. Those who are described as having been made willing are clearly not lacking in the ability to do what they are made willing to do, namely, to come to Christ. Rather, they have been determined to the good in such a way that they actually do come to Christ, and do so "most freely." So the concept of being made willing here entails being determined to willingly perform the action in question.

This is very much at odds with the notion of being enabled to do something and being free in the libertarian sense to choose whether or not to do it. That is the ordinary meaning of the term *enabled* and the natural way to read it in the passage cited above. An earlier section of the Confession says that when God converts a sinner, he "enables him freely to will and to do that which is spiritually good" (art. 9.4). A later passage says that the elect are "enabled to believe to the saving of their souls" (art. 14.1). Again, it is natural to read these texts to mean that God provides through grace the ability to will and to do good and the ability to believe. But here there is no suggestion that those who receive such grace are determined to believe, to do good and so on. At best then, the use of enablement language is highly misleading in light of the deterministic language that precedes it; at worst, it is inconsistent.

Now consider *calling,* the other term we have highlighted in the passage above—namely, the calling that pertains to the non-elect. This calling is produced simply by the fact that the preaching of the gospel goes out to all persons, elect and non-elect alike. In addition to receiving this general call, the elect also receive the effectual call that moves them to respond positively to the invitation of the gospel. But notice that even the non-elect are said to experience something similar to saving grace: "the common operations of the Spirit." Unfortunately for them, though, this is not enough to save them, for they "never truly come to Christ, and therefore cannot be saved."

This is an interesting account, but it raises obvious questions. In particular, does it suggest that the non-elect actually could come to Christ but refuse to do so, and that is why they are not saved? Although it is easy enough to infer that the non-elect have refused grace they actually could receive, this reading is inconsistent with other claims in the Confession. Since the non-elect have not been chosen for salvation, it is impossible for them to be saved. God hasn't bestowed on them the effectual grace that makes it possible for a fallen sinner to believe and to will and do good. So it would be more accurate to say of the non-elect that "they *cannot* truly come to Christ, and therefore cannot be saved." But the actual language of the Confession obscures the hard truth at this point and suggests that the non-elect could come to Christ.

Compare this with John Calvin's description of the difference between the *general call* and the *effectual call* (which he calls the "special call"), where we find more than just a suggestion that the non-elect could respond to the grace they receive:

There is the general call, by which God invites all equally to himself through the outward preaching of the word—even those to whom he holds it out as a savor of death [cf. 2 Cor. 2:16], and as the occasion of severer condemnation. The other kind of call is special, which he deigns for the most part to give to the believer alone, which by the inward illumination of his Spirit he causes the preached Word to dwell in their hearts. Yet sometimes he also causes those whom he illumines only for a time to partake of it; then he justly forsakes them on account of their ungratefulness and strikes them with even greater blindness.[16]

This is a remarkable passage, but it is difficult to make sense of it on Calvinistic premises. Notice, Calvin says that God causes some of the non-elect to partake of the inner illumination of the Spirit but only for a time—because of their ungratefulness.

Surely it is natural to infer that these persons *could* actually respond favorably to the inner illumination they receive. Otherwise, it is hard to make sense of how their ingratitude can be the just cause of even more severe condemnation. In other words, Calvin appears to imply that these persons have been enabled to believe and pursue the good but have perversely refused to do so: they could have, but they freely chose otherwise.

However, this reading does not square with Calvin's doctrine of election. For if these persons are not among the elect, they simply cannot respond with this sort of gratitude. But if they were among the elect, they would surely do so; God would cause the word to dwell deeply in their hearts, and they would believe it and obey with thankfulness. Again, the point is that Calvin's language suggests a freedom and ability to respond that is incompatible with his other commitments.

IS THE OFFER OF SALVATION TO ALL PERSONS GENUINE?

The sort of inconsistency and misleading language that we have seen in classic Calvinistic texts also appears in contemporary Reformed writ-

---

[16]John Calvin, *Institutes of the Christian Religion,* ed. John T. McNeil, trans. Ford Lewis Battles (Philadelphia: Westminster Press, 1960), 3.24.8; see also 3.2.11.

ings. Take, for example, Packer's proposal that divine sovereignty and human responsibility are an antinomy, an apparent contradiction—two truths that seem to us to be contradictory but are not really so.

How does Packer understand human free agency and responsibility? That is the important question. He is clear on his view that human choice is determined, particularly the choice of salvation for the elect. God not only invites the elect but also "takes gracious action to ensure that the elect respond."[17] Moreover, God foreordains not only the "destinies" of the elect, but also their "doings."[18] But what about the non-elect? Is their destiny also sealed, or do they have a genuine opportunity to be saved? While Packer's answer is not altogether clear, he is quite emphatic that God gives everyone a bona fide offer of salvation.[19]

> Everyone in the Reformed mainstream will insist that Christ the Savior is freely offered—indeed, freely offers himself—to sinners in and through the gospel; and that since God gives all free agency (that is, voluntary decision-making power) we are indeed answerable to him for what we do, first, about universal general revelation, and then about the law and gospel when and as these are presented to us. . . . But Calvinism at the same time affirms the total perversity, depravity, and inability of fallen human beings, which results in them naturally and continually using their free agency to say no to God.[20]

So how does Packer understand the God-given free agency he invokes? Does he mean that God gives all sinners the ability to respond positively to the offer of the gospel, and therefore all are answerable to

---

[17]J. I. Packer, "The Love of God: Universal and Particular," in *The Grace of God, the Bondage of the Will,* ed. Thomas R. Schreiner and Bruce A. Ware (Grand Rapids, Mich.: Baker, 1995), 2:421.

[18]Ibid., 2:420.

[19]Ibid., 2:421-22. In this passage Packer insists that a "bona fide" offer of the gospel to all who hear does not distinguish Arminianism from Calvinism, and on the next page he cites with approval Louis Berkhof's use of the term for the same purpose.

[20]Ibid., 2:422.

him? Does grace make it possible to respond positively, even for those who end up responding negatively? Or does he mean only that everyone willingly (voluntarily) chooses as they have been determined to choose? The first sentence quoted above implies the former view of freedom, whereas the second sentence is more in line with the latter view.

Packer does not precisely state the nature of human freedom and responsibility, so his meaning remains uncertain. However, if Packer held to a compatibilist understanding of freedom and did so in a clear and principled way, he would not need to appeal to the notion of antinomy. For if we are free only in the compatibilist sense, then it is not difficult to reconcile freedom and determinism.

It is doubtful, however, that Packer meant to affirm compatibilism. He appears to have a stronger view of freedom in mind when he appeals to antinomy. For surely the rhetorical force of his insistence on a bona fide offer of the gospel for all sinners requires the understanding that sinners really could accept the offer that is freely extended. It is a safe guess that virtually anyone not trained to detect the true meaning of Reformed rhetoric would take it this way. Indeed, this is the normal meaning of the phrase "a bona fide offer."

This obviously poses problems for Calvinism. The unvarnished truth for Reformed theology is that any sinner who is not elect simply cannot respond positively to the gospel. Granted, the non-elect do not *want* to respond and inevitably say no to the offer because in their fallen condition they cannot possibly see the truth about what is good for themselves or where their true happiness really lies. Moreover, Christ knows they cannot respond in their fallen condition. As a committed Calvinist, Packer must recognize all this, but the offer of the gospel to all sinners is a bona fide offer nevertheless, as he sees it.

But what do we make of an offer that can't be *accepted* even though the one making the offer knows this is the case or—to make matters worse—could make the receiver able to accept but doesn't? Christ could move the hearts of the non-elect and make them see that the gospel is the truth that fulfills them. He could move them to gladly own the truth that sets them free. He does this for the elect, yet for the non-elect he does not. When all of this is on the table, Packer's insistence that the non-elect receive a bona fide offer of the gospel has the ring of a used-car salesman who assures you he is making you a great offer but doesn't want you to read the fine print. Even worse, he withholds the pen you need to sign the contract.

Packer, then, faces a dilemma. On the one hand, if he believes the non-elect really could accept the offer of the gospel and be saved, then he is at odds with the Reformed teaching that no one can be saved apart from electing grace. On the other hand, if he doesn't believe the non-elect can truly respond to the preaching of the gospel and be saved, his insistence on a bona fide offer of salvation is hollow and misleading.[21]

Let's take Packer's statement at face value and assume the natural meaning of a bona fide offer. When we do this, things only get worse. On this understanding, Packer's position can be shown to be hopelessly contradictory, although implicitly so. This can be seen from the following propositions, all of which Packer apparently accepts. The first two of these are basic tenets of Calvinist orthodoxy, and the third is a clear implication of them.

> *Statement 6:* Only the elect can actually accept the offer of salvation and be saved.
> *Statement 7:* Not all are elect.
> *Statement 8:* Not all persons can actually accept the offer of salvation and be saved.

Next, we have Packer's claim about a bona fide offer, followed by a definition of what is involved in such an offer and, finally, an obvious implication from these.

---

[21]Calvinists might attempt to avoid this sort of difficulty by stating more carefully the offer of the gospel as they understand it. They might say something like this: Christ died for sinners and if you repent of your sins and believe, he will forgive you and give you the Holy Spirit. Strictly speaking, this is an accurate statement of Calvinist convictions, but it is still likely to be misconstrued by the uninitiated. Listeners would likely understand this to mean that Christ died for all sinners and all are able to come.

Statement 9: God makes a bona fide offer of salvation to all persons.
Statement 10: A bona fide offer is one that can actually be accepted by the person to whom it is extended.
Statement 11: All persons can actually accept the offer of salvation and be saved.

Here we have a clear inconsistency between statements 8 and 11. When we make explicit what Packer's position entails, it leads to a straightforward contradiction.

The only way Packer can avoid this unhappy conclusion is by appealing to his notion of antinomy. Will this resolve the problem for him? The answer depends on whether there is any intelligible way that the contradiction can be seen as only apparent instead of as real. Consider again the following pair of statements:

Statement 8: Not all persons can actually accept the offer of salvation and be saved.
Statement 11: All persons can actually accept the offer of salvation and be saved.

Is this merely a paradox or verbal puzzle that can be easily resolved once we understand the meaning of the terms? Clearly it is not. Is this a matter of having two pieces of seemingly incompatible data from the world of empirical reality forced on us—data that we must accept until further discoveries are made, like the wave-particle duality? No. It is a contradiction that cannot possibly be true any more than statements 1 and 2 about Bach were, above. If Packer means to affirm both statements 8 and 11, his consistency problem is decidedly real and not merely apparent. If he does not mean to affirm both of these, his insistence of a bona fide offer is deceptive at best. So either he is profoundly misleading or he is simply inconsistent. As before, we assume Packer is not dishonest, so we conclude he is inconsistent. (Could it be that Packer is a confused Wesleyan?)

IS DIVINE COMPASSION FOR THE LOST SINCERE?

Let's turn to a more intensive effort to show that the offer of salvation for all persons can be sincere for Calvinists. This challenge is met head-on by Piper, who affirms both that God unconditionally elects who will be saved and that he yet has compassion for and desires all people to be saved. Piper begins by citing some of the well-known texts that seem to teach God desires the salvation of all persons, such as Ezekiel 18:23, 1 Timothy 2:4 and 2 Peter 3:9. Unlike many Calvinist exegetes, Piper does not attempt to circumvent the straightforward meaning of these texts by saying that *all* means "all the elect" and not all persons without qualification. But by conceding this point, Piper has set for himself a formidable project.

So how does he tackle it? He appeals to the notion that God has two wills with respect to the damned. In some sense he truly desires the salvation of and has compassion for the damned, but in another sense he does not. Piper realizes that this sounds like nonsensical double talk, but he believes Scripture drives us to this conclusion. As he points out, Arminians also face a difficulty when they ponder texts like 1 Timothy 2:4, because they believe all are not saved despite the fact that God is willing to save them. They too judge that God has commitments that may prevent him from saving all persons, and explaining this can be difficult. Piper remarks, "Both Calvinists and Arminians feel at times that the ridicule directed against their complex expositions are in fact a ridicule against the complexity of the Scriptures."[22]

So where does the difference lie, according to Piper? Arminians, he says, value what we have called libertarian human freedom and the relationships this makes possible more than they value the salvation of all people. If God cannot save all persons without overriding freedom, it is better for all not to be saved. Calvinists give a different answer. In their view, "the greater value is the manifestation of the full range of God's

---

[22]John Piper, "Are There Two Wills in God? Divine Election and God's Desire for All to Be Saved," in *The Grace of God, the Bondage of the Will*, ed. Thomas R. Schreiner and Bruce A. Ware (Grand Rapids, Mich.: Baker, 1995), 1:125.

glory in wrath and mercy (Rom 9:22-23) and the humbling of man so that he enjoys giving all credit to God for his salvation (1 Cor 1:29)."[23] The idea here, it seems, is that God's full glory is not manifested unless his wrath is displayed, so some persons must be eternally damned for their sins in order for humanity to be properly humbled and give God the glory he deserves. This idea goes back at least to Calvin, who wrote that the reprobate "have been given over to this depravity because they have been raised up by the just but inscrutable judgment of God to show forth his glory in their condemnation."[24] This reality produces two wills in God. At one level, he desires to save all; at another, his will to save all is restrained by his desire to manifest his full glory.

Still, the question persists: can God's offer of salvation to all people be genuine if he unconditionally elects some and not others to salvation? Piper himself poses the question thus: "Is it made with real heart? Does it come from real compassion? Is the willing that none should perish a bona fide willing of love?"[25]

Piper answers his own question using an analogy from the life of George Washington. The story concerns a certain Major Andre, who had rashly performed some treasonous acts that endangered the young and fragile nation. As president, Washington had the somber duty of signing Andre's death warrant. Concerning this event, John Marshall writes, "Perhaps on no other occasion of his life did the commander-in-chief obey with more reluctance the stern mandates of duty and policy."[26] His choice not to pardon the traitor even though he had the power to do so was in no sense an indication that his compassion was not deeply felt and sincere. Rather, it was a reflection of Washington's overriding commitment to justice and the well-being of the nation.

---

[23]Ibid., 1:124.

[24]Calvin *Institutes* 3.24.14.

[25]Piper, "Are There Two Wills," 1:127.

[26]John Marshall, *Life of Washington,* cited in John Piper, "Are There Two Wills in God? Divine Election and God's Desire for All to Be Saved," in *The Grace of God, the Bondage of the Will,* ed. Thomas R. Schreiner and Bruce A. Ware (Grand Rapids, Mich.: Baker, 1995), 1:128. This analogy was first used to defend Calvinism over a century ago by Robert L. Dabney.

Piper sees this as a helpful image of the complex emotions God feels toward those persons for whom he signs the eternal death warrant by not electing them for salvation. His pity for them is real, but it is restrained by superior motives. Although he has a genuine desire to spare those who have betrayed his kingdom, he has holy and just reasons for not acting on this desire.

This is an ingenious move, and we acknowledge its appeal and emotional force. However, we think it fails badly as an analogy for the notion that God has deep compassion for and even makes a bona fide offer to save sinners he has not elected for salvation. The analogy breaks down at so many relevant points that it does not begin to illustrate the relationship between God and the damned.

In the first place, Andre was not one among a group of other traitors who had performed similarly heinous actions but who were graciously pardoned while he was condemned. That, however, is precisely the situation with the damned. They are no better and no worse than other sinners who are pardoned and spared the fate of eternal misery. If Washington had singled Andre out among other equally treacherous persons, the claim that he felt genuine sorrow and compassion for him would lose all credibility.

Second, there is nothing in the story that is comparable to the notion that God makes a bona fide offer of salvation to the damned. It was not the case that Washington offered Andre pardon but he perversely refused to accept it.

Third, for Andre's crime to be comparable to the sin of the damned, his treason would have to match up with the sin of persistent unbelief and refusal to accept the grace offered in the gospel. After all, that must be what finally seals the fate of the damned if the Reformed claim that God makes a bona fide offer of the gospel to all persons is to make any sense at all. For all who repent and believe are spared whereas those who do not are finally lost.

But with Piper's analogy, the problem becomes even more acute: God has the power, according to Piper, to act on any sinner in such a way that the sinner will not persist in sin and unbelief. God can bestow electing grace on anyone he wants and transform any sinner into a saint who joyfully desires God. Washington had no power to control Andre in such a way that he would have become a patriot for whom treason would have been unthinkable. But if Washington could have done this and yet refrained from doing so, then again, the claim that he had profound compassion for Andre and was pained at signing his death warrant would ring hollow.

To put the point another way, if one assumes that sinners have libertarian freedom, then it makes sense to say that God makes a bona fide offer of the gospel that they refuse. It makes sense to say that he has genuine compassion for them and sincerely desires that they accept his offer of grace. But if sinners have no such freedom and God could save them without destroying their freedom but chooses not to do so, then there is no meaningful sense in which he truly desires their salvation. Piper's analogy has force on the assumption of libertarian freedom, and no doubt many readers take it that way. But again, this is an instance of implying a view of freedom that Piper cannot consistently maintain.

Of course, no analogy is perfect, so it should not surprise us if this one breaks down at various points. But perhaps we can salvage something here that will support Piper's main point. Recall his claim that Arminians explain the complexity involved in holding that God wills that all be saved, even though they are not, by appealing to human freedom, whereas Calvinists invoke God's desire to reveal the full range of his glory in wrath as well as mercy. Perhaps Piper's main point is that God has something like a duty to display his wrath in damnation and that this is what constrains his genuinely felt compassion for those he does not elect to save. For otherwise he would somehow be robbed of his full glory.

Anything that robs God of his full glory is unacceptable, so if God's full glory can only be displayed if some persons are unconditionally passed over and consigned to damnation, then Piper may have a case. But is this really required for God to be fully glorified? In response to this question, let's consider another passage where Piper ponders the question of whether God's concern for his glory is at odds with his love.

But is it loving for God to exalt his own glory? Yes it is. And there are several ways to see this truth clearly. One way is to ponder this sentence: *God is most glorified in us when we are most satisfied in him.* This is perhaps the most important sentence in my theology. If it is true, then it becomes plain why God is loving when he seeks to exalt his glory in my life. For that would mean that he would seek to maximize my satisfaction in him, since he is most glorified in me when I am most satisfied in him. Therefore God's pursuit of his own glory is not at odds with my joy, and that means it is not unkind or unmerciful or unloving for him to seek his glory. In fact it means that the more passionate God is for his own glory, the more passionate he is for my satisfaction in that glory. And therefore God's God-centeredness and God's love soar together.[27]

We resonate more deeply with this passage than with any other passage we have read from Calvinist authors. Piper echoes a theme central to the Christian hedonists who preceded him—from Blaise Pascal to John Wesley to C. S. Lewis.

He is fully glorified when his holy love is manifested most clearly, and it is precisely this love that seeks our fulfillment and happiness. Given that Piper heartily affirms this, it's puzzling why he believes God isn't fully glorified unless some are consigned to damnation. Does God have a duty to damn some persons in some sense analogous to Washington's duty to sign Andre's death warrant? If so, to whom could he owe such a duty? Washington's authority is not even remotely analogous to God's sovereignty, and God is beholden to no one and nothing higher than himself. How could he be duty bound to damn some persons?

Perhaps what Piper is thinking here is that God owes it to himself since wrath is a part of his nature; if none are damned, a part of his nature is not manifested, and he is being untrue to himself. But if this is what Piper is thinking, we think it betrays serious confusion. For wrath is not an essential aspect of God's nature like holy love is. Rather, wrath is entirely a contingent matter: *Wrath is the form holy love takes in response to sin and evil. If there*

---

[27]John Piper, *Let the Nations Be Glad!* (Grand Rapids, Mich.: Baker, 1993), p. 26.

were no sin and evil, there would be no need for wrath ever to be displayed. But when sin occurs, God responds in wrath to demonstrate the truth both about himself and about those who sin. Yet his purpose is always to show his holy love. He desires the best for his sinful creatures, and what is best for them is that they acknowledge their sin and repent of it.

God's love is not sentimental or indulgent, even though it is tender and gracious. If sinners will not repent, they still must deal with the truth about God and themselves. The result is that they can never experience the happiness and joy they were created to enjoy so long as they persist in their sins. Even the damned glorify God in this way. They are unwilling witnesses to the fact that we can't make ourselves happy by our own resources. But those who suffer this fate do it entirely of their own accord, despite the fact that God loves them fully and does everything possible (given their own natures as free creatures) to promote their flourishing. Remarkably, however, some may persist in evil even in the face of that kind of love.[28]

For Piper, however, human freedom is not the explanation for why some are lost even though God is willing to save all persons. For God can move anyone to respond freely and positively to his grace. So far as human freedom is concerned, he could move all persons to accept his bona fide offer of salvation. But in the end he can't do so because, Piper argues, it would compromise his glory.

This claim seems profoundly inconsistent with what Piper says is the single most important sentence in his theology, namely, "God is most glorified in us when we are most satisfied in him." Those who are saved surely experience more satisfaction in God than the damned! And God himself is satisfied when sinners repent and believe the gospel. Indeed, Jesus tells us that there is rejoicing in heaven when sinners repent. Interestingly, Jesus makes this point in a parable of a shepherd who has one hundred sheep and loses one of them. Jesus doesn't say that the shepherd is willing to con-

---

[28]Does this mean that God is somehow defeated if all are not saved? No. See Jerry Walls's reply to Talbott in *Universal Salvation*, ed. Robin Parry and Christopher Partridge (Carlisle: Paternoster, 2003). See also Jerry L. Walls, "A Hell of a Choice: Reply to Talbott," forthcoming in *Religious Studies*.

sign the lost sheep to its fate. Rather, he seeks the lost one even though he has ninety-nine who are with him. "I tell you that in the same way there will be more rejoicing in heaven over one sinner who repents than over ninety-nine righteous persons who do not need to repent" (Luke 15:7).

What an amazing thought! Heaven rejoices when a single sinner repents! If God is anything like this shepherd, then it is hardly credible that he needs or desires to damn some of his lost creatures to glorify himself. Quite the contrary, he glories in showing mercy and rejoices when his lost human creatures return to the fold.

If God can save all persons without overriding anyone's freedom, then surely he would be fully glorified thereby. Damnation is not necessary to display God's full glory unless we are free in the libertarian sense and some persons simply won't accept God's grace (which is not the Calvinist position). Piper then is no more successful than Packer was in providing a consistent account of how God can be sincerely willing to save persons he has not chosen to favor with electing grace.[29]

---

[29]Arminians may face an issue that is in some ways parallel to the problems in Calvinism we have just been discussing, namely, the fate of fallen angels. According to the Arminian, while fallen human beings are offered salvation, which they are free to accept or reject, no such offer is apparently made to fallen angels. If this is so, doesn't it present a scandal similar to unconditional election? For if God chooses not to save any one of his creatures that he could just as easily save, whether angels or men, it raises questions about the genuineness of his love for them. Unfortunately, however, we have few resources to answer this question, for Scripture says little about it. So we are left to infer and speculate, based on what Scripture clearly teaches.

The important point is that this objection assumes that fallen angels could be saved and that at least some of them would freely accept salvation if it were offered to them. But it's precisely this assumption that can't be taken for granted. Indeed, Aquinas argued that fallen angels would not accept salvation, and this is part of his explanation of why Christ assumed human nature but not angelic nature. In his view, angels, as purely spiritual beings, have an immediate grasp of truth. As such, an angel has such clarity of understanding that when he makes a choice, it is unchangeable. "Accordingly, he is either not fixed upon evil at all, or, if he is fixed on evil, is fixed so immutably. Hence, his sin is not subject to expiation." (Thomas Aquinas, *Summa Contra Gentiles,* trans. Charles J. O'Neil [Notre Dame: University of Notre Dame Press, 1975], 4.55.7.) Unlike human beings, who can be restored to good, angels cannot, according to Aquinas. If he is correct in his reasoning, then fallen angels do not pose the same sort of problem for Arminians that is posed for Calvinists by human beings whom God chooses not to save.

DOES GUILT DEPEND ON LIBERTARIAN FREEDOM?

Let's examine one more contemporary Reformed spokesman who has some interesting things to say about human freedom and responsibility: R. C. Sproul. In the passage we will consider below, Sproul is responding to the objection that it seems unfair for God to hold us accountable for failing to be righteous since we were born with original sin. After all, given original sin, we can't be righteous apart from grace, so how can God hold anyone accountable who is not given saving grace?

Sproul answers this question with an illustration. Suppose there were a gardener who is told by God to trim the bushes by a certain time. He is warned, moreover, that there is a large open pit at the edge of the garden and is clearly instructed to stay away from it. Perversely, however, as soon as God is gone, he jumps into the pit. When God returns at the set time, the bushes aren't trimmed. When he calls for the gardener, he hears a muffled cry for help. Sure enough, he approaches the pit and there is the gardener, trapped helplessly inside. When God asks why the bushes aren't trimmed, he responds with indignation that he couldn't work because he is stuck in the pit, and he blames God for leaving the pit exposed!

Sproul sees this as a fitting illustration not only of the Fall but of our current predicament as well. He elaborates as follows:

> Adam jumped into the pit. In Adam we all jumped into the pit. God did not throw us into the pit. Adam was clearly warned about the pit. God told him to stay away. The consequences Adam experienced from being in the pit were a direct punishment for jumping into it. . . . Adam didn't simply slip into sin; he jumped into it with both feet. We jumped headlong with him. God didn't push us. He didn't trick us. He gave us adequate and fair warning. The fault is ours and only ours.[30]

Interestingly, this passage has a strongly libertarian tone. Sproul is quite

---

[30]Sproul, *Chosen by God*, p. 98.

clear that before the Fall, Adam had libertarian freedom. "Before the Fall Adam was endowed with two possibilities: He had the ability to sin and the ability not to sin. After the Fall Adam had the ability to sin and the inability not to sin."[31] Just a few pages before this passage, Sproul affirmed the compatibilist view that our choices are determined by our desires.[32] Adam's choice to "jump in the pit," however, is apparently an exception to this, for he is clearly depicted as free in the libertarian sense, which gives credence to Sproul's insistence that Adam, and Adam alone, was fully to blame for his predicament.

It is also noteworthy that Sproul suggests that all of Adam's descendants are guilty for the same reason. Even though we do not have libertarian freedom now and can only sin without grace, we are still fully to blame because we jumped headlong into the pit with Adam. In some sense, all of us apparently had libertarian freedom but lost it in the Fall. Sproul attempts to make sense of this by endorsing the view, popular among Calvinists, that Adam was the "federal head" of the human race and as such represented all of us perfectly in the Garden.[33]

What we find most interesting here is Sproul's heavy reliance on libertarian freedom to give moral credibility to his view that sinners are to blame even though they cannot do otherwise than sin. Like the Arminians he repudiates, he can't swallow the idea of moral guilt without libertarian freedom. Although the non-elect can't do other than sin, their eternal damnation seems more fair if they gleefully jumped into the pit when Adam did, in defiance of God's clear and adequate warning.

It is also significant that in the same context, Sproul excoriates as "dreadful" and "repugnant" the view that God predestined some people to be saved and others to be damned, and then decreed the Fall to assure that some would perish. He characterizes this view as an "insult" and in-

---

[31]Ibid., p. 65.
[32]Ibid., p. 54.
[33]The notion of federal headship that Sproul endorses is controversial and makes little sense to many.

sists it "has nothing to do with Calvinism."[34] This is a curious comment since Sproul is obviously referring to one of the best-known controversies within Calvinism, namely, the dispute between the supralapsarians and the infralapsarians. He sharply rejects the former and enthusiastically supports the latter. The crucial contention of the infralapsarians is that God elects sinners for salvation in view of the Fall. Of course, God's eternal decree of election precedes the creation of the world *temporally* speaking, but *logically* it is made in light of the Fall. Fallen sinners, not unfallen people, are elected for salvation.

Why does Sproul think the notion of unconditional predestination before the Fall is repugnant while unconditional predestination after the Fall is glorious? In both cases God chooses not to save people he could save and thereby consigns them to eternal misery.

The all-important difference for Sproul is that sinners not elected in light of the Fall fully deserve eternal misery even though they can no more do good or escape their terrible end than those sinners predestined for hell in the supralapsarian scheme. Again, it is striking how much of Sproul's argument rides on a single act of libertarian freedom along with his controversial claim that all of Adam's descendants in some sense exercised similar freedom when Adam fell. Without this claim the infralapsarian view is even harder to distinguish from the supralapsarian. For if Adam was not free in the libertarian sense, it is hard to muster much outrage at his choice to jump into the pit or to insist that "the fault is ours and only ours."

It is far from clear that Calvinists have a historic claim to a libertarian view of the Fall. For one powerful piece of evidence that they do not, consider these words from Calvin himself:

> They say that he [Adam] had free choice that he might shape his own fortune, and that God ordained nothing except to treat man according to his deserts. If such a barren invention is accepted,

---

[34]Ibid., p. 96.

where will that omnipotence of God be whereby he regulates all things according to his secret plan, which depends solely upon itself? Yet predestination, whether they will or not manifests itself in Adam's posterity. For it did not take place by reason of nature that, by the guilt of one parent, all were cut off from salvation. What prevents them from admitting concerning one man what they willingly concede concerning the whole human race? . . . If there is any just complaint, it applies to predestination. And it ought not to seem absurd for me to say that God not only foresaw the fall of the first man, and in him the ruin of his descendents, but also meted it out in accordance with his own decision.[35]

Calvin is rather impatient with those who affirm unconditional predestination but balk at saying that the Fall was determined. Notice also that Calvin says it isn't the natural consequence of the Fall that everyone was cut off from salvation. Rather, this is also a matter of God's choice. He determined the Fall and the consequence that everyone would be cut off from salvation.

We conclude this section with a question that Calvinists must answer for themselves: If there is no libertarian freedom even at the point of the Fall, is unconditional election repugnant, even for many who consider themselves truly Reformed?

CONCLUSION

While not all Calvinists fail when examined for consistency, we have seen a recurring theme among those versions of Calvinism that do fail this test. In each case we have observed inconsistency, confusion or misleading language where human freedom and responsibility are concerned. In particular, the Calvinists we have surveyed are not clear on this matter and often vacillate between compatibilist and libertarian freedom without acknowledging or perhaps even being aware of what they are doing. Calvinists are particularly prone to slip into libertarian

---

[35]Calvin *Institutes* 3.23.7.

freedom in a way that is incompatible with their other theological commitments when they are accounting for unbelief or attempting to explain how God can make a bona fide offer of salvation to persons he has not elected to save. This suggests that a morally satisfactory theology requires a more principled commitment to libertarian freedom than they can consistently allow. Their very inconsistency indicates they recognize this at some level, though they haven't fully acknowledged it. This freedom, of course, is not natural to our fallen condition; rather, it is a gift of grace that enables us to embrace the good news of the gospel and be saved.

But if libertarian freedom is rejected and Calvinists want to be consistent, they should face unflinchingly the implications of their position. They should follow Piper when he says the potter has absolute rights over the clay, and if God chooses not to save some persons it is not for us to understand but simply to adore. This position is more forthright than his unconvincing attempt to argue that God has deep compassion for persons he has consigned to damnation. Wright, who is both more consistent and more straightforward than most Calvinists, puts the matter with unswerving honesty when he says, "God never had the slightest intention of saving everyone. That is what the doctrine of election means in the first place: God chooses some, but not all."[36]

Calvinists who believe election is unconditional in this sense do not serve anyone well by obscuring this claim with confusion, ambiguity or inconsistency. Nor does it serve the cause of clear thinking and truth to confuse contradiction with mystery or to suggest that it is a mark of superior piety to be unworried about logical consistency. While the truth about God is beyond our full comprehension, it doesn't contain contradiction. Calvinists can't eliminate the contradictions in their theology by fleeing into mystery or appealing to notions like antinomy. To the contrary, the contradictions we have identified are a telltale sign that something is profoundly awry at the heart of Reformed theology.

---

[36]Wright, *No Place*, pp. 131-32.

6

CALVINISM AND THE
CHRISTIAN LIFE

ॐ

Several years ago, D. A. Carson wrote a helpful and pastorally sensitive book dealing with the difficult issue of suffering and evil. One of the pastoral situations he discussed concerned a young woman who came to him seeking help and comfort because her father had died and, so far as she knew, had gone to hell. Such a case brings the hard realities of life and death into focus. It reminds us that Christian faith is far more than a matter of abstract doctrine. The teachings of Christianity concern us vitally for they pertain to our most deeply felt hopes and aspirations for meaning.

Christianity teaches that every single human being will eventually experience either eternal happiness or eternal misery, depending on whether one has received salvation through Christ. Death—particularly the death of a loved one—reminds us of this with brutal efficiency. The young woman who came to Carson was right to ask the questions she did and to struggle with the facts about her father's apparent unbelief. But what is interesting for our purposes is Carson's account of what he might say when faced with this question:

> I could say that none of us knows for certain what transpires between any person and God Almighty before that person is ushered into eternity. I could say that the final proof of the love and goodness

of God is the cross. I could say that we know far too little of the new heaven and earth to have any idea what consciousness we shall have of those who have chosen to live and die independently of God. I could add there are times when, in the confusion, it sometimes helps to think of all that we know of the character of God and ask, with Abraham, the rhetorical question, "Will not the Judge of all the earth do right?" (Gen. 18:25).[1]

Carson shows himself here to be a wise and sensitive pastor, but what is striking about this bit of pastoral counsel is that it is totally void of any trace of distinctively Calvinist thought. The doctrine of unconditional election, which is most relevant to the question at hand, is nowhere in sight. Rather than appeal to the mystery of God's eternal will in election, Carson appeals to the mystery of what transpires between a person and God before he or she passes into eternity. There is nothing here to suggest (reminiscent of R. K. McGregor Wright's frank acknowledgment concerning his own father) that God, in his sovereignty, may not have elected the young woman's father for salvation. There is nothing here resembling John Piper's resolute conviction that God has absolute rights over us as a potter has rights over his clay, and that God may not have chosen her father precisely in order to highlight his mercy toward her and other believers. Nothing here even hints that God simply may not have loved her father in the sense necessary to secure his salvation, although if he is lost, that is the ultimate reason why.

It is our conviction that pastoral theology should flow naturally out of systematic and biblical theology. If we have achieved even a measure of integration with respect to our theological commitments, then our central convictions should not disappear into the background or become invisible in a pastoral context. To the contrary, those beliefs should come into sharpest focus in those difficult seasons of life when the integrity of our faith is tested.

---

[1] D. A. Carson, *How Long O Lord? Reflections on Evil and Suffering* (Grand Rapids, Mich.: Baker, 1990), pp. 105-6.

Of course, there is a time and a place for emphasizing particular theological truths, and we are not obligated to discuss every doctrine in every context. The question here, however, is whether what we do share is true to our beliefs and accurately represents our deepest theological convictions.

In the preceding chapter we explored the logical consistency of Calvinism. In this chapter we will probe Calvinism at the point of what we might call practical consistency. That is, we will ask whether Calvinists forthrightly and consistently apply their theology in the rough and tumble of daily life and ministry or whether they tend to cloak their distinctively Reformed commitments in those contexts.

EVANGELISM

The first issue we want to explore pertains to the practical consequences for evangelism that follow from what we argued in the previous chapter. There we argued that Calvinists can't make coherent sense of their claim that God makes a bona fide offer of salvation to persons he has not elected for salvation, nor can they explain how God can truly have compassion for such persons (Jn 3:16). The consequences for evangelistic preaching are profound indeed.

At issue is whether Calvinists have a message that is truly good news for all persons. If Calvinists can't make coherent sense of how God can have genuine compassion for persons he has not elected to save, this should be reflected in their preaching. Not surprisingly, some Calvinists worry over this and wonder how to be true to their convictions in their evangelistic work. Carson, for instance, reports that he is often asked in Reformed circles whether he feels free to tell unbelievers that God loves them. Based on distinctions he had drawn earlier in his book, he informs us that he answers this question affirmatively: "*Of course* I tell the unconverted that God loves them."[2]

The reason Carson can say this will not be surprising to readers who

---

[2]D. A. Carson, *The Difficult Doctrine of the Love of God* (Wheaton, Ill.: Crossway, 2000), p. 78 (emphasis in orginal).

have followed the argument of this book so far. Like J. I. Packer and John Piper, he wants to insist that God's love is extended to all sinners in offering them salvation. Like many other contemporary Calvinists who want to distance themselves from the traditional Reformed notion of limited atonement, he holds that Christ died for all in the sense that his death is sufficient for all and that all are invited, indeed commanded, to repent and believe. Moreover, God's love is also shown in the material blessings that are providentially bestowed on all, believers and unbelievers alike.

Also like Packer and Piper, however, he holds all of this while insisting that election to salvation is unconditional; beneath their rhetoric of God's universal love and his desire for all to be saved remains the essential Calvinist conviction that electing love is unconditional. So Carson maintains that Christ died for the elect in a significantly different sense than he did for the non-elect; that is, he died "effectually" for those he chose from eternity to be saved. Since they are elect, God moves them to accept the offer of salvation so that it effectively saves them. Those who are not elect, of course, cannot will to accept the offer, so the death of Christ is not effectual for them.

When all of this is properly taken into account, it is difficult to see how Carson can say that "of course" he tells the unconverted that God loves them without being profoundly misleading. Presumably Carson doesn't know who among the unconverted have been privileged with the "particular, effective, selecting love toward the elect"[3] that is unconditionally reserved for them alone. For all he knows, many of the unconverted he encounters are persons whom God has chosen to pass over with respect to salvation rather than to favor with electing love. Since Carson can't know otherwise, how can he with honesty and integrity assure all unbelievers that God loves them, unless he forthrightly qualifies this in a way that does full justice to his beliefs about unconditional election?

---

[3]This is Carson's phrase describing what we have called *electing love*. See ibid., p. 18.

To see the force of this question, let's assess more carefully just what God's love for the non-elect amounts to according to Carson. First of all, consider his understanding of Jesus' dictum that God's love is displayed in the fact that the rain falls on the just and the unjust alike (Mt 5:45). For Carson, such material blessings are proof of God's love for the unconverted. We agree. But if this teaching of Jesus is wedded to the Calvinist doctrine of unconditional election (according to which some who enjoy such blessings are excluded from salvation), then we are at a loss to see how material blessings are a genuine expression of love. How do such gifts show any kind of true love for sinners if they aren't accompanied by electing love?

The ultimate context for evaluating any good from a Christian perspective is eternity. How can anyone say with a straight face that temporal goods, no matter how lavish, are proof of God's love if God chooses to withhold salvation, the one thing that really counts (Mk 8:34—9:1)? Reflect for a moment on Paul's confident hope that the sufferings of this world can't compare with the glory to be revealed in eternity for those who believe (Rom 8:18; 2 Cor 4:17-18). He can say this because he is certain that no earthly misfortune or loss could possibly even begin to compare in value to the unsurpassable good of eternal life with God (Phil 3:8-11). Indeed, comparatively speaking, any such tragedies are trivial and insignificant in light of eternity. A parallel point can be made about non-elect sinners. The goods and blessings of this world are not worth comparing to the future misery for the unconverted who are not elect. Eternal damnation and loss of all that is truly good surely makes any temporal benefits utterly trivial.[4]

---

[4]Have we have underestimated the value of God's temporal gifts to the non-elect? After all, isn't the psalmist sometimes scandalized that the wicked receive so many blessings in this life? While this is true, we must recognize that the hope of life after death was uncertain and tenuous in the Old Testament. If there is no certainty of life after death, then the prosperity of the wicked is troubling indeed, especially if the faithful often languish by comparison. The resurrection of Christ and the clear hope of eternity puts merely temporal blessings in an altogether different light.

Jesus made this point most memorably when he asked, "What good will it be for a man if he gains the whole world, yet forfeits his soul?" (Mt 16:26). It makes no sense to say God loves people if he gives them the whole world while withholding the grace they need to save their eternal soul.

Consider the love of God displayed in offering the gospel to the non-elect—persons who God knows can't will to accept the offer without the very electing love he has chosen to withhold from them. Apart from electing love, the offer of the gospel only serves as an occasion for condemnation, since sinners who aren't elect will inevitably reject it and thereby add to their record of disobedience.

All of this makes it painfully clear that the non-elect are not loved in the only way that can promote their ultimate well-being. God has not chosen to give them the only thing that can possibly provide true flourishing and fulfillment. For all Carson knows, many of the unconverted he interacts with are in this unhappy state. Therefore, he should make clear in what sense he can say with integrity that God loves them, being careful not to make claims that his theology will not underwrite.

In short, Carson should frankly admit to the unconverted that he doesn't know whether or not God loves them in the crucial sense that is absolutely necessary for them to experience eternal joy and flourishing. God may only love them in the sense that he provides them with earthly benefits and in the sense that he makes them an offer that in their fallen condition they can't begin to appreciate. When God's love to the world is reduced to this, it is difficult to see how it can be relished as the astounding good news Christians believe it is.

Let's turn to the second issue we want to consider regarding Calvinists' motivations for sharing the gospel. On the surface, Calvinism appears to undermine motivation for evangelism. For if God has unconditionally chosen who will be saved and who will be left in their sins for eventual damnation, then surely the persons so chosen for salvation will in fact be saved. And if this is so, there is little reason for us to worry about evangelism—nothing we do or fail to do will in any way thwart God's sovereign purposes in election.

In fairness to Calvinists this objection is often misguided, because their position is easily distorted or misunderstood on this matter. Many often overlook that God determines means as well as ends. Any critique that fails to grasp this point will invariably end up making a caricature of Calvinism. Reformed theologians have been careful to explain that God not only elects certain persons to salvation, but he also ordains the means to their salvation (e.g., our prayers and the preaching of the gospel). Consequently, we can't excuse ourselves from praying for the lost and sharing the gospel with them, precisely because we may be God's ordained means to lead them to faith.

C. Samuel Storms uses this example: Suppose that God has decreed that Gary will come to saving faith in Christ on August 8. Moreover, it is God's will to regenerate Gary in response to Storms's prayer on August 7. Does this mean that God's decree to save Gary on August 8 might fail if Storms neglects to pray on August 7? Storms answers as follows:

> If I do not pray on the seventh, he will not be saved on the eighth. But I most certainly shall pray on the seventh because God, determined to save Gary on the eighth, has ordained that on the seventh I should pray for him. Thus, from the human perspective, it may rightly be said that God's will for Gary is dependent upon me and my prayers, as long as it is understood that God, by an infallible decree, has secured and guaranteed my prayers as an instrument with no less certainty than he has secured and guaranteed Gary's faith as an end.

Storms argues that this view should not make us careless or indifferent precisely because we don't know what God may have ordained to do through our prayers. Indeed, he charges that it is "inexcusably arrogant, presumptuous, and disobedient to suspend my prayers on the basis of a will that God has declined to disclose."[5]

---

[5]C. Samuel Storms, "Prayer and Evangelism Under God's Sovereignty," in *The Grace of God, the Bondage of the Will,* ed. Thomas R. Schreiner and Bruce A. Ware (Grand Rapids, Mich.: Baker, 1995), 1:228.

This latter claim raises questions. Just how does Storms understand the arrogance, presumption and disobedience he denounces? In particular, is Storms here assuming that we have libertarian freedom with respect to prayer and evangelism, that we are free to pray or not to pray? That seems to be implied in his comment that it would be inexcusably arrogant for us to suspend our prayers based on our ignorance of who is or is not elect. However, his earlier comments clearly imply that we don't have libertarian freedom in this regard. That is, he insists that if God has ordained his prayer as the means to Gary's salvation, then it is a matter of infallible certainty that he surely will pray.

Does Storms mean that God ordains the prayer of the person who prays but not the arrogance of the one who chooses not to pray? Perhaps he does; he is not altogether clear. But surely his comments above imply that if God has ordained me to pray, I will not be arrogant or disobedient. So if I'm disobedient, my prayers have not been ordained as the means to saving faith. This seems clearly to follow from Storms's claim that God guarantees his ordained means will occur just as surely as will his ordained ends.

Of course, Storms's article itself could be God's ordained means to motivate certain believers to pray. If it is, they will surely pray. But those who aren't persuaded by his argument and who, even after reading it, feel indifferent about the need to pray or share their faith have not been ordained to pray or share. This conclusion seems undeniable from Storms's own claims. His tendency to slip into a libertarian view of freedom at this point is not surprising in light of what we saw in the previous chapter, but it isn't consistent with his account of how God ordains all things.

We conclude that Storms has not successfully answered the charge that Calvinism tends to undermine evangelistic motivation. This is not to deny the crucial claim that God ordains means as well as ends. Indeed, this very claim, consistently applied, easily leads to the conclusion that if a person is not inclined to pray or witness, that person must not be ordained to do so. This is not a matter of impersonal fatalism but of the logic of all-comprehensive determinism. For again, if God ordains means as well as ends, he will act to give us the inclination to pray and share our faith willingly if he has also ordained the end that someone be converted through our prayer and witness. And in such a case we will surely, and perhaps even gladly, pray and witness. But if God hasn't so ordained, then just as surely we won't pray or share our faith.

THE FATE OF THE UNEVANGELIZED

Another closely related issue is the question of what happens to those who have never heard the gospel. Countless persons around the world and even in North America have never heard the message that God loves them and that Jesus died and was raised from the dead to save them from their sins. Indeed, many of these persons have lived, and still live, in places where the gospel has never been preached.

This reality poses one of the most frequently asked apologetic questions. How can God be fair, not to mention loving, if he allows all such persons to be lost without ever hearing the name of Jesus? All of those who have lived in times and places where the gospel was not faithfully taught and proclaimed seem clearly to face an insuperable disadvantage concerning something of inestimable importance. They not only have no opportunity to receive the only thing that can give their lives true meaning and happiness, but they face the terrible fate of eternal misery when this life is over.

Let's briefly examine Piper's views on these issues. Piper has written at length about missions and the whole question of the fate of the unevangelized, and he defends traditional Calvinist views on these matters. He insists that none are saved unless they explicitly hear and believe the gospel in this life. Thus, he rejects the various versions of the "wider hope" view, which holds that saving grace is available to all persons, not just those who have heard the gospel in this life. C. S. Lewis concisely states the "wider hope" view as follows:

> Of course it should be pointed out that, though all salvation is
> through Jesus, we need not conclude that He cannot save those

who have not explicitly accepted Him in this life. And it should (at least in my judgment) be made clear that we are not pronouncing all other religions to be totally false, but rather saying that in Christ whatever is true in all other religions is consummated and perfected. But, on the other hand, I think we must attack wherever we meet it the nonsensical idea that mutually exclusive propositions about God can both be true.[6]

Let us emphasize that this view insists that everyone who is saved is saved through Christ (Acts 4:12). This view does not hold that all religions are equal or that Christ is just one of many ways to God. Rather, it holds that the grace made available by Christ is extended to everyone through the work of the Holy Spirit, even if they live in times and places where the gospel is not explicitly preached. In eternity, of course, all who are saved will explicitly own the name of Christ as the One who saved them.

This, however, is not acceptable for Piper. For him, anyone who has not heard and professed the name of Christ in this life is consigned to an eternity in hell. Piper also rejects the view, increasingly popular among evangelicals, that the lost are finally annihilated rather than made consciously miserable forever.[7]

Piper's Calvinism only exacerbates the difficulties in the view that all unevangelized persons are inevitably damned. The reasons are easy enough to see. Given Calvinist assumptions, all unevangelized persons are presumably not elected for salvation. Since God ordains means as well as ends, it is apparent that he hasn't ordained that the unevangelized hear the good news. If they were elect, God would ordain that they would hear the gospel as the means to their salvation.

---

[6]C. S. Lewis, *God in the Dock*, ed. Walter Hooper (Grand Rapids, Mich.: Eerdmans, 1970), p. 102.

[7]For Piper's views on these issues, see his *Let the Nations Be Glad!* (Grand Rapids, Mich.: Baker, 1993), esp. chap. 4. For a defense of annihilationism or conditionalism, see Edward Fudge's contribution to Edward William Fudge and Robert A. Peterson, *Two Views of Hell* (Downers Grove, Ill.: InterVarsity Press, 2000).

This means that God has chosen not to extend electing grace to whole generations and people groups. Entire cultures and nations have gone for centuries without hearing a single word of the gospel. Piper believes this is what Paul meant in the following passage from Acts 17:30-31.

> In the past God overlooked such ignorance, but now he commands all people everywhere to repent. For he has set a day when he will judge the world with justice by the man he has appointed. He has given proof of this to all men by raising him from the dead.

Piper says this passage means that God chose to pass over these generations rather than move them to repentance through the mission work of his people. God could have chosen to move his people to missionary zeal and used them to lead the nations to repentance. But for his own reasons he chose not to do so. As Piper reasons,

> There was a time when the Gentiles were passed over while God dealt with Israel and now there is a time while Israel is largely passed over as God gathers the full number of His elect from the nations. In neither case are the people of God to neglect their saving mission toward Jew or Gentile "that they might save some" (Romans 11:14; 1 Corinthians 9:22). But God has His sovereign purposes in determining who actually hears and believes the gospel. And we may be sure that those purposes are wise and holy and will bring the greatest glory to His name.[8]

Given what we discussed in the previous chapter, presumably Piper believes God has sincere and deeply felt compassion for all the lost generations he chose to pass over. But the full manifestation of his glory requires that he pass over them nevertheless. Elsewhere in his book *Let the Nations Be Glad!* Piper waxes passionate for the lost and urges that our love should extend to all persons. In this particular passage, he is com-

---

[8]Piper, *Let the Nations*, pp. 137-38.

menting on Acts 10:28, where Peter declares that God has shown him he should not call any human common or unclean. Piper writes, "Our hearts should go out to *every single person* whatever the color, whatever the ethnic origin, whatever the physical traits, whatever the cultural distinctives. We are not to write off anybody."[9]

This call for compassion toward every single person does not square well with the position that many of the persons we are called to love may not be elect. Seemingly it remains the case that any people groups or tribes who die today without hearing the gospel are persons God did not elect to save, for if he had, he would have determined them to hear the gospel. No doubt our hearts should go out to such persons since they face eternal punishment. But it remains practically difficult to both adore the purposes of God and let our hearts of compassion go out to persons he hasn't elected to save. But that is what Piper's Calvinism calls us to do.

All of this only magnifies the apologetic problem posed by the fate of the unevangelized. Of course, we should not modify the clear teaching of Scripture in order to make our apologetic task easier. It is our contention, however, that there are biblically grounded and theologically sound alternatives to Piper's Calvinism that put the good news of God's love to all persons in a far clearer and more attractive light than his Calvinism can begin to do.[10] For those concerned about the contemporary apologetic project, this is no small advantage.[11]

---

[9]Ibid., p. 145 (emphasis added).

[10]While Piper's views represent the dominant view among Calvinists, some Calvinist spokesmen have expressed cautious openness to the possibility that some could be saved without explicit faith in Christ in this life. For example, see Millard Erickson, "Hope for Those Who Haven't Heard? Yes, But . . . " *Evangelical Missions Quarterly* 11 (August 1975): 124; and J. I. Packer, "Good Pagans and God's Kingdom," *Christianity Today* 17 (January 1986): 22-25.

[11]For further defense of alternatives to the dominant Calvinist account of the fate of the unevangelized, see Scott R. Burson and Jerry L. Walls, *C. S. Lewis and Francis Schaeffer* (Downers Grove, Ill.: InterVarsity Press, 1998), pp. 226-34. See also John Sanders, *No Other Name* (Grand Rapids, Mich.: Eerdmans, 1992); and Jerry L. Walls, *Heaven: The Logic of Eternal Joy* (New York: Oxford University Press, 2002), pp. 63-91.

CHRISTIAN ASSURANCE

One of the hallmarks of Protestant evangelical Christianity is the assurance of salvation—the experience of knowing for certain that we are indeed redeemed from our sinful past. Evangelicals are noted for their joyful confidence that they are forgiven and regenerate children of God (1 Jn 3:19-21). To some this has seemed presumptuous, but evangelicals see it as a gift to be gratefully received from their loving and gracious heavenly Father.

As every pastor knows, however, this sense of assurance is vulnerable to periods of doubt and wavering. Times of adversity, moral failure or other sorts of struggle may send believers reeling and cause them to wonder whether they truly are in a state of grace or even whether God really loves them (Heb 3:6-14). This is a common yet profound pastoral problem that calls for theological discernment as well as for personal sensitivity.

Calvinists often claim that Arminians have no real basis for security and certainty with respect to their salvation. Since Arminians reject the notion that the regenerate person will inevitably be saved in the end, one's salvation must always be precarious and doubtful. The fact is, however, that Arminians have a doctrine of assurance that is similar in many respects to that of Reformed theology. John Wesley, in particular, had a well-developed and carefully worked out theology of assurance. Both traditions appeal to the inner witness of the Holy Spirit and to evidence that grace is working in one's life, evidence such as moral improvement and sincere devotion to God's will. Calvinists no less than Wesleyans urge believers to do all they can to "make [their] calling and election sure" in order to help ward off doubts and fears (2 Pet 1:10-11).

Still, Calvinists claim that the doctrine of unconditional election provides a depth of certainty that Arminianism lacks. This security of salvation rests in God's sovereign choice from all eternity that one will be saved. This allegedly provides a sense of security that believers who reject unconditional election can never enjoy.

At first glance, this argument may be appealing, but on closer inspection it's vulnerable to obvious difficulties. In brief, the essence of the problem is that Calvinist believers who struggle with their assurance can never know with certainty that they are one of the elect. Indeed, their theology entails at least the possibility, unthinkable as it is, that they may not be one of the chosen. For a vivid and memorable expression of this concern, consider the following lyrics from the popular band Caedmon's Call.

> Sometimes I fear maybe I'm not chosen
> You've hardened my heart like Pharaoh
> That would explain why life is so hard for me
>
> And I am sad Esau hated
> Crying against what's fated
> Saying father, please, is there any left for me
>
> Cast out my doubts, please prove me wrong
> Cause these demons can be so headstrong
> Make my walls fall, please prove me wrong
> 'Cause this resentment's been building
> Burn them up with your fire so strong
> If you can before I Baal, please prove me wrong.[12]

Now there are many things a wise Reformed pastor might say to believers struggling with the sort of anxiety expressed in this song. The pastor could remind the believers of the promises of the gospel and might even suggest that the very fact that they are concerned about their salvation is a good sign. But the one thing the pastor can't say without claiming knowledge that no finite human possesses is that God *certainly* loves them with *electing love*.

---

[12]Lyrics by Aaron Tate excerpted from "Prove Me Wrong," which appears on the CD *Long Line of Leavers*. As noted in the introduction, above, the members of Caedmon's Call consider themselves Reformed.

It's easy to deceive ourselves on the matter of our relationship with God. Consider in this light the Westminster Confession's chapter on the assurance of grace and salvation.

> Although hypocrites and other unregenerate men may vainly deceive themselves with false hopes and carnal presumptions of being in the favor of God and estate of salvation; which hope of theirs shall perish: yet such as truly believe in the Lord Jesus, and love him in sincerity, endeavoring to walk in all good conscience before him, may in this life be certainly assured that they are in a state of grace, and may rejoice in the hope of the glory of God; which hope shall not make them ashamed. (art. 18.1)

In the paragraphs that follow this one, the Confession explains that assurance rests on the divine promises of salvation, and the infallible certainty of this comes from the inner witness of the Holy Spirit. It urges believers to make their election sure and points out that cheerful obedience to God is one of the proper fruits of assurance. It also points out that even true believers may have periods of doubt and uncertainty for various reasons.

Now all of this is not only sound theology but also helpful pastoral advice. Notice, however, that among the crucial factors that indicate whether one truly believes are such things as cheerful obedience to God, endeavoring to walk before him with a good conscience and so on. These factors inevitably have an unavoidable degree of subjectivity about them, and it is at this point that believers who struggle with assurance typically find themselves torn and doubtful because their obedience has not always been perfect or cheerful and their conscience is sometimes clouded.

These sorts of spiritual battles are common for believers of all traditions that recognize moral and spiritual transformation as evidence of regeneration and true faith. (Catholics refer to such a season of doubt as "the dark night of the soul.") Calvinists no less than Arminians and Wesleyans must deal with this reality and cannot claim that their theology exempts them from such struggles. So does this mean that Arminians and Calvinists are on even ground here with respect to this issue that divides them?

We believe not. Here is the crucial difference. Calvinism deprives those struggling with their faith of the single most important resource available: the confidence that God loves all of us with every kind of love we need to enable and encourage our eternal flourishing and well-being.[13] Again, Calvinists cannot honestly assure such people that God loves them in this way without claiming to know more about God's secret counsels than any human being can know.

Look back at the passage we just cited from the Westminster Confession. The first sentence refers to hypocrites and other unregenerate people who deceive themselves with false hopes and carnal presumptions that they enjoy the favor of God. The notion of a false hope is based on ideas that go back at least to Calvin himself. Here again is the passage we quoted from him in chapter five, in which he describes how God sometimes causes non-elect persons to receive for a time the inward illumination of the Spirit:

> There is the general call, by which God invites all equally to himself through the outward preaching of the word—even those to whom he holds it out as a savor of death [cf. 2 Cor. 2:16], and as the occasion of severer condemnation. The other kind of call is special, which he deigns for the most part to give to the believer alone, which by the inward illumination of his Spirit he causes the preached Word to dwell in their hearts. Yet sometimes he also causes those whom he illumines only for a time to partake of it; then he justly forsakes them on account of their ungratefulness and strikes them with even greater blindness.[14]

What is truly remarkable here is that persons who receive this partial and temporary illumination appear for a time to be truly elect but in fact aren't. They are deluded by a false hope.

---

[13]See Ezek 18:23; Jn 3:16; Rom 11:32; 1 Tim 2:4; Tit 2:11; 2 Pet 2:9.

[14]John Calvin, *Institutes of the Christian Religion*, ed. John T. McNeil, trans. Ford Lewis Battles (Philadelphia: Westminster Press, 1960), 3.24.8.

This dreadful possibility is what haunts Calvinists who struggle with the assurance and certainty of salvation. Times of moral failure and depression can easily be construed as evidence that one is not chosen after all and that God is hardening one's heart for not responding more faithfully to his grace. This cannot be dismissed as an aberration of classic Calvinism that responsible teaching and preaching will prevent. Consider, for example, an account from no less impressive a figure than Jonathan Edwards, who is recognized as one of the greatest theologians America has ever produced—even by those who don't share his Calvinism. Edwards was a central figure in the noted eighteenth-century revival known as the Great Awakening. He recounts the events of this movement in *A Narrative of Surprising Conversions*. Included in this work are his detailed descriptions of the work of grace in the human soul with all of its mystery and complexity. For our purposes, one of his most interesting observations concerns the degree of assurance enjoyed by those converted under Edwards's preaching. While he notes that some converts consistently had a high degree of hope and confidence concerning their state of grace, he also reports the following:

> But the greater part, as they sometimes fall into dead frames of spirit, are frequently exercised with scruples and fears concerning their condition. They generally have an awful apprehension of the dreadful nature of a false hope; and there has been observable in most a great caution, lest in giving an account of their experiences, they should say too much, and use too strong terms. Many, after they have related their experiences, have been greatly afflicted with fears, lest they have played the hypocrite, and used stronger terms than their case would fairly allow of; and yet could not find how they could correct themselves.[15]

As you can see, Edwards says that most of the converted frequently

---

[15]Jonathan Edwards, *A Narrative of Surprising Conversions* (Wilmington, Del.: Sovereign Grace, 1972), p. 34.

struggled with the fear of a false hope; this was not an exceptional or unusual phenomenon. Rather, it seems to have been the norm.

In light of this, it isn't surprising that the desire to ward off the fear of a false hope and to make election sure has been a significant motivating factor in much of traditional Calvinist piety. Nor is it surprising that such piety can easily become legalistic and rigid. Later in his book Edwards relates the story of a precocious young convert of extraordinary sensitivity and devotion. Every night before going to bed she would say her catechism. One night she forgot it, and she began to cry and would not go to sleep until her mother came and said it with her as she lay in bed. As Edwards notes, she was sometimes worried about the condition of her soul and fearful that she was not ready to die.[16] Her fear of going to sleep without saying her catechism was an obvious reflection of that fear.

There is ample evidence in both Calvinism and Arminianism that legitimate piety and spiritual diligence can be twisted into stifling and demoralizing legalism. But Calvinism lacks the clear warrant to speak the most liberating word of encouragement available for persons struggling with their faith and doubtful of God's attitude toward them—the unqualified assurance that God loves them and is for them! His love is such that he would never sovereignly choose to pass over any of his fallen children and leave them without hope of escaping the eternal misery of their sins. None need fear that the grace they have received only *appears* to be the real thing. If any are lost it is not because the grace God has provided is not adequate to save them. It is because they persistently and continually reject the love of the One whose mercy endures forever, a mercy they could indeed choose to receive.

THE PROBLEM OF EVIL

This problem of evil is an age-old quandary that has challenged Christian thinkers and other theists for centuries. Indeed, the problem of evil

---

[16]Ibid., p. 47.

has been a favorite weapon in the atheists' arsenal as long as atheists have been doing battle with believers.

Critics of Christianity have often claimed that evil is simply incompatible with the existence of God. If there were a God who had the attributes Christians say he has—omnipotence and perfect goodness—then there would be no evil. For if he is omnipotent, then it seems he has the power to do anything possible, including eliminate all evil. If he is perfectly good, then he is opposed to evil and would want to remove it. But because there obviously is evil, there is no such God.

This intellectual challenge requires a rational response that will show God's existence is indeed compatible with the existence of evil. The attempt to do this is called *theodicy,* a term that comes from the Greek words for God and justice. Theodicy is the attempt to show the justice or goodness of God in the face of evil.

But evil is far more than a puzzle to be solved by logic or reasoning. It is also the profound experience of suffering and tragedy that can crush our spirits and cause us to wonder whether God really is good or whether he even exists. The cries of the psalmist and the prophets are eloquent testimony that evil in its various forms wrenches our souls as much as it baffles our minds. Thus it is important for our spiritual health to have some understanding of how evil fits into a universe created and governed by a sovereign God.

We don't think that we can ever master this problem in such a way that we eliminate all tensions, struggles and uncertainty. Paul reminded us that we presently suffer and groan as we anticipate the fullness of redemption. We live in a world that is still in "bondage to decay," but we hold on to the hope "that our present sufferings are not worth comparing with the glory that will be revealed in us" (Rom 8:18-21). But the reality remains that the glory we anticipate is in our future; in the meantime we have to make our way in a world where evil and suffering are still prevalent. What theological resources do we have to make some sense of evil and tragedy when we encounter them?

Because of their distinctive theological convictions, Calvinists sometimes dismiss the whole project of theodicy as a pointless one. Some argue that God no doubt has reasons for ordaining evil, but there is no way we could know those reasons. Others emphasize that we are God's property, and since he can do whatever he wants to do with his property, we have no grounds for complaint, regardless of how we suffer. Some argue that since God is the source and standard for what is right, anything he does is right by definition, even if it does not seem right or virtuous to us. The problem of evil simply cannot arise.

It would take us too far afield to discuss these matters in detail, but we do wish to address one specific issue: whether our grasp of goodness is reliable enough for us even to make judgments about what is evil and what is not. Some of the objections to theodicy we just mentioned assume that our understanding of goodness and evil may be so radically different from God's that we can't even begin to understand how his purposes are good.

We contend, by contrast, that our moral judgments are more trustworthy than this view holds. This is not to say that our moral judgments are perfect or that we can call God to account by some standard that is higher than God himself. But we believe that our moral judgments, at their best, are a reflection of God's own nature and as such are reliable. Of course, since we are fallen, our moral judgments are distorted by sin, so we need the benefit of revelation to correct and refine our perceptions. But we are still made in the image of God (Gen 1:26-27), and that is a deeper truth about us than our sin is. Calvinists acknowledge this reality in the doctrine of common grace, one manifestation of which is our legal system, which reflects our sense of right and wrong and a confidence in our best moral judgments and intuitions.

We should not think, then, that our best judgments about good and evil are radically at odds with God's goodness. If they were, we wouldn't know what is meant when we call God good. C. S. Lewis put it like this:

> The divine "goodness" differs from ours, but it is not sheerly different: it differs from ours not as white from black but as a perfect circle from a child's first attempt to draw a wheel. But when the

child has learned to draw, it will know that the circle it then makes is what it was trying to make from the very beginning.[17]

This means that when our moral intuitions are revised by Scripture, what we already know as creatures and image bearers of God will become deeper and more mature. It won't mean that we reject all our moral sensibilities and start from scratch.

Let's examine the views of Paul Helm, a Calvinist philosopher who agrees that the goodness of God's actions must bear some positive relationship with human goodness. Helm takes a more sympathetic view of the value of theodicy than some of his fellow Calvinists. His treatment of evil occurs within the context of a philosophically sophisticated account of providence that he authored. He rejects Openness views of providence, which he labels "risky," in favor of what he calls a "no-risk" view, which maintains that God exercises detailed control of all things, including human choices. Helm recognizes, moreover, that the most consistent way to maintain the Calvinist account of providence that he favors is to maintain a compatibilist understanding of human freedom.

Helm is a careful thinker, and he clearly recognizes the implications of holding a view of freedom that is compatible with determinism. Calvinistic writers often appear confused and ambiguous on this point, sometimes slipping back and forth between libertarian and compatibilist accounts of freedom. Helm, by contrast, is a self-conscious and informed advocate of compatibilism. As such, he recognizes that the appeal to human freedom in theodicy requires libertarian freedom, and Helm is generally forthright in sticking with compatibilism and all it entails. This is quite clear when he acknowledges that "if we suppose some form of compatibilism, then God could have created men and women who freely (in a sense compatible with determinism) did only what was morally right."[18]

---

[17]C. S. Lewis, *The Problem of Pain* (New York: Macmillan, 1962), p. 39.
[18]Paul Helm, *The Providence of God* (Downers Grove, Ill.: InterVarsity Press, 1994), p. 197.

Some Calvinists often lose sight of this implication, for their grasp of compatibilism is less clear than Helm's. Confronted by human rebellion, unbelief or wickedness, many Calvinists appeal to the freedom of those involved in such a way that implies they were able to do otherwise. They seem to forget that God could have determined these persons in such a way that they would freely, in the compatibilist sense, have obeyed and worshiped God. God, however, chose not to do so. This must be kept in mind by Calvinists who believe humans are free only in the compatibilist sense. They can't simply drop their compatibilism and adopt a libertarian stance when it is comfortable or convenient to do so.

Helm's commitment to compatibilism also leads him to reject a distinction between moral and physical evil that is common in discussions of theodicy. Moral evil is usually understood to be that evil that results from the choices of free moral agents, for example, the suffering caused by lying, stealing, rape or murder. Physical evil (e.g., hurricanes, floods and diseases), by contrast, is caused by the natural order. While this distinction is important for those who appeal to free will, it is less important for the approach Helm wants to take. As he puts it, all happenings, both natural events and human choices, "are finally attributed to the divine reason and will."[19]

Holding a consistent view on these matters has very practical consequences, as Helm is aware. He contends that his view of providence allows Christians to put their pain and suffering into a framework that is more meaningful than the views of others.

> How? By recognizing that the evil that they and others experience has been sent. It is not the result of a free-action of human beings who are temporarily outside the sovereign control of God; it is not the result of a basic dualism between God and evil that afflicts the universe, as the Manichees and other dualists believed. The evil that is being experienced is the result of the sovereign will of God.

---

[19]Ibid., p. 198.

While the reality of secondary causes, the immediate causes of the evil, is recognized, the evil comes from God, not as evil, the vindictive affliction of a malicious tormentor, but from one all of whose ways are just and good.[20]

The notion that the evils we experience have been sent by God has profound implications. Let's reflect on this claim by focusing on a couple of concrete examples.

Consider the instance of a teenager who is paralyzed in an automobile accident because the brakes in his car failed. Suppose he had done nothing irresponsible but that, unknown to him, there was a defect in the manufacture of his brakes that caused his accident. Now consider the case of a young girl who is sexually abused by her uncle. The experience is emotionally devastating and contributes significantly to a deeply negative self-image, which, among other things, leads her into sexual promiscuity. This makes it difficult for her to experience intimacy in marriage, and she continues to struggle with feelings of guilt and inferiority throughout her life.

These are hypothetical examples, but they represent the stories of countless actual persons, including many believers in Christ. Most of us probably know someone who has experienced something similar, either a tragic accident or some sort of treachery. How we should think about such cases and encourage those who struggle with similar experiences is a question of great personal and practical relevance.

Helm's position is fairly straightforward. He would say that such evils were sent by God for purposes that are just and good. In other words, God's intention in sending such evils is not evil, so he is in no sense the author of evil. However, he causes and determines evil for good purposes. Presumably then there is some good reason why God determined that the teenager's brakes would fail, even though we may have no clue what that reason is. Perhaps it is a punishment of some sort; perhaps there is a spiritual lesson

---

[20]Ibid., p. 231.

that his friends needed to learn and this was the best way to teach them. Or perhaps there is some other good that will eventually flow from it. Likewise with respect to the young girl's sexual abuse. God sent this evil for some particular reason or purpose. God could have caused her abuser to freely (in the compatibilist sense) love and respect her and help instill in her healthy and moral sexual attitudes. But instead God specifically sent the evil of sexual abuse into her life for some just and good purpose.

Part of Helm's case is that his view is encouraging and helpful from a pastoral standpoint, and we don't doubt that some persons find it so. When someone has experienced a terrible tragedy or is in the midst of prolonged suffering, it is perhaps comforting to see it as particularly caused by God with some specific good end in mind. If we see it as caused by God to serve some important role in his larger plan, it can ward off the despair that terrible tragedy sometimes leads to. This is especially so if the only alternatives are that evil and tragedy are outside of God's sovereign control or, worse yet, that they are merely painful but meaningless episodes in an absurd universe. The notion that evil is sent by God is certainly preferable to either of these alternatives.

We believe, however, there exist other options that are not only more existentially satisfying and encouraging but that also make more biblical and moral sense. We believe that a brake failure and the resulting crash that causes paralysis need not be understood as sent by God. Rather, the brake failure can be seen as a tragedy resulting from the fact that we live in a world operating by God-ordained natural law and that sometimes things designed by human beings fail. In this world, where God "sends rain on the righteous and the unrighteous" (Mt 5:45), all of us are recipients of good gifts from God's natural order even as we are vulnerable to the suffering it can cause. Gravity, like rain, is a good thing, but sometimes both of these contribute to tragic accidents. This is what is essentially involved in living as embodied beings in a physical world.

In the same vein, we don't believe the sexual abuse of the young girl was planned by God. Far from it! Rather, this tragedy results from our God-given libertarian freedom, and we often choose to use that freedom in terribly destructive ways. The same freedom that makes it possible for us to enter into a genuinely trusting and obedient relationship with God also makes it possible for us to go our own way and disobey him. God allows the latter in order to enable the former. The web of human choice is such that we are interdependent; our decisions can profoundly affect others, both for good and for ill.

Even though many of our choices displease God and make him angry, none of them fall outside the scope of his sovereignty. When we deny that God sent the evil of sexual abuse to a young girl, this doesn't mean it happened outside of his sovereign control. For nothing that happens to us, either from the natural world or from human treachery, can defeat God's ultimate purpose for us. Of course, we can reject God's purpose for our lives and choose self-destruction. But nothing else in the entire universe can keep us from reaching the ultimate good that God desires for all humans. This is what allows Paul to assure us that nothing can separate us from the love of God (Rom 8:35-39), neither natural disasters ("famines") nor instances of human cruelty ("persecution"). Paul even insists that in all things God works for the good of those who love him and are called to his purpose (Rom 8:28).

Romans 8:28 is one of the most famous and beloved verses in the New Testament, but its promise is often misunderstood. The good that Paul has in mind is identified in the next verse—that we will be conformed to the image of Christ. God promises that nothing, no matter how terrible or extreme, can defeat this purpose in our lives if we continue to trust him and allow his work to go forward. Nothing that happens to us is such that God cannot somehow weave it into the glorious pattern of the image of Christ he is working out in the lives of all believers. And when that pattern is completed, we will see our lives as things of great beauty and fully experience the joy and fulfillment we were created for. The perfectly good God who loves us is infinitely creative and has ways we cannot imagine of defeating the power of evil and overcoming it with joy and goodness.[21]

---

[21]For a very provocative discussion of these themes, see Marilyn McCord Adams, *Horrendous Evils and the Goodness of God* (Ithaca: Cornell University Press, 1999). See also Walls, *Heaven*, pp. 113-32.

This idea is at the heart of one of the most powerful and suggestive traditions in theodicy, which is named after the Latin phrase *O felix culpa,* which means "O fortunate crime." The fortunate crime referred to by this phrase is the Fall of Adam and Eve. The basic idea here is that the Fall, far from being a disaster, is fortunate in terms of the larger purposes of God because it led to the plan of salvation in Christ. In God's amazing plan of salvation we are privileged to know him and his love in ways we never could have without the Fall. John Wesley, an enthusiastic advocate of *O felix culpa,* put the point like this.

> So there would have been no room for that amazing display of the Son of God's love to mankind. . . . We might have loved the Author of our being, the Father of angels and men, as Creator and Preserver; we might have said, "O Lord our Governor, how excellent is thy name in all the earth." But we could not have loved him under the nearest and dearest relationship, as "delivering up his Son for us all." . . . If God so loved us, how ought we to love one another! But this motive to brotherly love had been totally wanting if Adam had not fallen. Consequently we could not have loved one another in so high a degree as we may now.[22]

Now *O felix culpa* is a controversial theme. Indeed, not all theologians even agree that without the Fall, the incarnation would not have occurred. Some have argued that the incarnation would have occurred anyway and that we would have come to know the fullness of God's love even if we had never fallen.

Our concern here is not to defend *O felix culpa,* but we do want to underscore that Helm is an advocate of that theodicy. More specifically, Helm appeals to *O felix culpa* as a version of the more general strategy called the *greater good theodicy.* This theodicy claims that God permits (if you are a libertarian) or causes (if you are a compatibilist) evil for the sake of some greater good that could not occur without the evil. Helm

---

[22]John Wesley, *Works* (Nashville: Abingdon, 1984), 2:426-28.

invokes this notion after pointing out that if one is a compatibilist, then God could have created persons such that they freely always did only what was right. The obvious question this raises is why did he *not* do this if he could have done so?

Helm's answer is that God determined evil to occur for the sake of the greater good that could then result. The Fall makes it possible for God to both pardon and renew us and thereby to reveal himself more fully than he could have otherwise. In a universe without evil there is nothing to forgive, and in a universe without ruined sinners, no one needs renewal. The Fall allows God to display his mercy and grace by lavishing his love on fallen sinners and to make of them something even more glorious than they could have been without the Fall. Thereby not only is God glorified more fully, but we also benefit accordingly.[23]

Helm lays these points out in an attractive way, but one thing is conspicuously absent—the doctrine of unconditional election. Is it unfair to object that he does not address unconditional election in a book about providence? We think not. Our understanding of election is closely related to how we understand providence. Moreover, the whole issue of election can hardly be avoided in a discussion of the problem of evil, since hell and eternal damnation are often considered the most difficult and intractable aspects of the problem.

Helm's choice to ignore the doctrine of unconditional election is perhaps understandable given that it makes his task more challenging, but the issue can't simply be evaded. The notion that God chooses not to save persons he could save without in any way overriding their freedom (of the compatibilist variety) poses severe and widely recognized difficulties for *O felix culpa*. Remember, the heart of *O felix culpa* is that we are better off with the Fall than without it. The glaring question that must be faced by Calvinists who invoke this move is how this can be so for those persons who are not elect. If God chooses not to save many, perhaps even most, persons who are born into sin and thereby consigns them to eternal

---

[23]See Helm, *Providence of God*, pp. 213-15, for his discussion of these points.

misery, how can this be a greater good than determining everyone freely to do right from the beginning?[24]

O felix culpa makes sense if the greater good resulting from the Fall is made freely available to all persons in such a way that they are truly able to take advantage of it. Those who freely receive it can thank God for the lavish grace shown in the incarnation, while those who refuse it have only themselves to blame. If God allows some to be lost by their own persistent choice of evil in order to make possible a greater good for those who freely accept it, then *O felix culpa* makes moral sense. The choice of evil by some shouldn't limit what God can make available for others. But if many are far worse off, indeed infinitely worse off, as a result of the Fall—that is, if they are never given the grace needed to escape their misery—it is difficult to see how the Fall can be seen as a fortunate crime. Moreover, it is most difficult to see how God could be good in any ordinary sense of the term if he ordained or allowed the Fall knowing that it would have such consequences.

Recall that Helm is committed to the view that God's goodness is not fundamentally at odds with human goodness and that theodicy aims to demonstrate how God can be good in this sense.[25] It is worth asking whether we would be considered good if we arranged things in such a way that many persons suffered greatly, even though we could have relieved their suffering. I think most persons would readily agree that we would not be good. So Helm has not succeeded in showing how God is good in a way that is consistent with human goodness at its best.

At this point the Calvinist can revert to the argument that God needs to damn some people to glorify himself fully. We have argued against this claim in chapter five and will not repeat those arguments here. But one of the fundamental divides between Calvinists and Arminians (including Wesleyans) concerns what best reveals and displays God's glory. It is our

---

[24]For more on this, see Jerry L. Walls, " 'As the Waters Cover the Sea': John Wesley on the Problem of Evil," *Faith and Philosophy* 13 (1996): 534-62.

[25]For Helm's statement about God's goodness in relation to human goodness, see *Providence of God*, p. 201.

contention that God's holy love can radiate in all of its splendor without hell as a necessary contrast. God is genuinely merciful to all his fallen children and is truly willing to pardon and renew all of them. His mercy and grace would be no less evident if all responded positively to the invitation to salvation.

Sadly, we have good reason to believe that not all will do so. Damnation is the ultimate human tragedy, but even the damned will glorify God by demonstrating that none of us can achieve happiness and fulfillment on our own. It is a strict impossibility for creatures like ourselves to be happy apart from a right relationship with God (Ps 16:11). The tragic reality of human evil is the failure to understand this.

We don't pretend to have given a full or complete account of evil or of our position on it. That is itself a book-length project, and even after that book is written evil will continue to baffle us and test our faith. There are no simple explanations for evil, and it poses a serious challenge to any theology that affirms the existence of a perfectly good God. It is our contention, however, that with respect to evil, Calvinism only magnifies a difficult problem and creates further apologetic obstacles for heralds of the good news of the gospel to a lost and hurting world. Indeed, the Calvinist account of eternal hell turns a difficult problem into an insuperable one.[26]

PRACTICAL THEOLOGY?

In the introduction to this chapter, we maintained that our practical theology should flow naturally out of our biblical and systematic theology. The hard realities that commonly confront us in everyday life force us to realize that our theological convictions bear quite directly on our lives. How should we counsel a young believer who fears her father has gone to hell? How should we answer the question of whether God loves the unconverted? What should we say to a woman who was sexually

---

[26]For attempts to make moral sense of hell that appeal to libertarian freedom, see Jerry L. Walls, *Hell: The Logic of Damnation* (Notre Dame: University of Notre Dame Press, 1992); Jonathan L. Kvanvig, *The Problem of Hell* (New York: Oxford University Press, 1993).

abused? How should we interpret this abuse theologically? Did God cause the perpetrator to freely abuse her even though God could have determined him to freely nurture her in a positive way? Or did God permit it as an undetermined choice? And how do our claims at this point square with our account of sovereignty and human freedom?

Calvinists are inclined to shroud and even misrepresent their central theological convictions at some of these crucial junctures where theology meets life. In chapter five we showed that Calvinism fails the test of logical consistency. Now we have seen that it fails the test of forthrightness in several arenas of Christian practice. In other words, Calvinism is beset with practical inconsistencies that mirror its logical contradictions. This is another powerful reason not to be a Calvinist.

CONCLUSION

W e have now explained in some detail why we are not Calvinists. As we noted in the introduction, there are several issues involved that require thoughtful attention before we can take an intelligent position on where we stand. The issue can't be reduced to whether or not we believe the Bible, whether or not we believe God is truly sovereign, or whether or not we believe in predestination. As we have tried to make clear, we accept the full authority of the Bible and believe any theological proposal must be judged first and foremost by its faithfulness to Scripture (Ps 19:7-14; Mt 7:24-27; 2 Tim 3:16-17). We also believe God is fully sovereign and that he has predestined who will be saved and the terms by which this will happen (Rom 8:29-30; 9:11-12; 11:29; Eph 1:3-14).

In a similar manner, most Calvinists insist that they believe God loves all people and offers all a genuine opportunity to be saved. Most also maintain that we are free and that we make meaningful choices, including whether or not to accept God's offer of salvation.

Arminians and Calvinists alike readily agree that the Bible is the supreme authority for our theology, that God is sovereign, that he is perfectly loving and that human beings are free and responsible for their actions. To the casual observer, it may appear that there is little if any real difference between the two positions. But agreement at the level of broad claims about sovereignty, love and freedom masks profound disagreements about how these matters are understood in detail.

It has been our purpose in this book to bring these differences into the light. Arminianism and Calvinism represent starkly opposing theological visions, at the heart of which are profoundly different views of

God. Consider the words of Baptist leader Albert Mohler.

> The God of the Bible is the holy, ruling, limitless, all-powerful God who makes nations to rise and to fall, who accomplishes his purposes and who redeems his people. Arminianism—the theological system opposed to Calvinism—necessarily holds to a very different understanding of God, his power and his government over all things.[1]

Mohler is surely right in underscoring the very different views of God in these opposing theological systems, but we believe he is mistaken in thinking that the primary difference pertains to how we understand the *power* of God. We believe the heart of the matter is how we understand the *character* of God. The issue is not how powerful God is but what it means to say that he is perfectly loving and good. This difference does indeed affect our understanding of God's "government over all things," but it is not most fundamentally a matter of how much power we think God has.

We are in full agreement with Calvinists and other orthodox Christians that God is supremely powerful. God's power has been displayed in unmistakable and breathtaking splendor in creation (Job 38—41; Ps 8:3-4; 19:1-6). The vast size and complexity of our universe, with its countless galaxies, are all the proof we need that God has supreme power and knowledge. Moreover, God has demonstrated his power on the stage of human history by his acts of special revelation, culminating in the bodily resurrection of Jesus (Ex 15:1-18; Josh 23:1-3; Jer 1:9-10; Rom 1:4; 6:4; Eph 1:20). Of course, sinful human beings are often oblivious to God's power and deny his awesome majesty (Ex 32; Num 14:20-23; Rom 1:18-23). But in the long run, God's power will be fully evident even to the most willfully deceived and obstinate, as every knee will bow and every tongue confess that Jesus Christ is Lord (1 Cor 15:25-28; Phil 2:10-11; Rev 20:1-15).

---

[1] R. Albert Mohler Jr., "The Reformation of Doctrine and the Renewal of the Church: A Response to Dr. William R. Estep," <www.founders.org/FJ29/article2.html>.

Furthermore, we agree that God *could have* created a world in which he precisely controlled and determined all things, including the choices of human beings. But we believe such a world would make true human love impossible. True human love requires libertarian freedom. God could make a world where the only freedom was of the compatibilist variety, but it wouldn't be a world of genuine love.

If we think of the issue only in terms of power, the question is naturally framed in terms of what God *could* do; but if we think of it in terms of God's character, the focus shifts to what he *would* do. And it is clear to us that if God determined all things, including our choices, he *would not* determine the sort of evil and atrocities that we have witnessed in history. Nor would many, perhaps even most, of the human race ultimately be separated from the love of God and lost forever. Indeed, if God determined everything, none would be lost (1 Tim 2:4; 2 Pet 3:9). Again, if it is a matter of sheer power, it is plausible that God could create a world in which many would be lost. But the God of holy love not only would not but could not.

Calvinists beg to differ. They believe God is perfectly good even though he has chosen to leave some persons in their sin and thereby consign them to eternal misery. Here is truly the major parting of the ways between Calvinists and their opponents. Let's probe this a bit further.

In a fascinating historical study, British theologian Colin Gunton identifies key points at which he believes some central Christian doctrines got off track. One particularly interesting development is that in Western theology since Augustine, "the theme of love becomes subordinate to that of will."[2] Gunton sees this manifested in the way the doctrine of double predestination is understood in some traditions. Part of the fundamental problem, Gunton believes, is a deficient understanding of the doctrine of the Trinity. The doctrine of the Trinity above all shows that God necessarily exists in an eternal relationship of perfect love be-

---

[2]Colin E. Gunton, *The One, the Three and the Many* (Cambridge: Cambridge University Press, 1993), p. 120.

tween Father, Son and Holy Spirit. God's will must always be understood as an expression of his essential nature of perfect love (Mk 1:11; Jn 3:34-35; 5:19-20; 17:20-26). Because he has such a nature, he genuinely loves all persons and genuinely invites them to share his love (Jn 3:16; 14:19-21, 23; 1 Jn 2:2; 4:7-12).

As we saw in chapter five, Calvinist John Piper recognizes the possibility that God may not choose his sons for salvation, but he insists that he would adore God even in that case. We acknowledged that we have a certain admiration for Piper, although we profoundly disagree with his understanding of the character of God. This, we suggest, serves as a good test case for those who still may be trying to make up their mind on Calvinism. Does Piper's attitude reflect piety at its best, or is it deeply at odds with God's character revealed in Scripture? Interestingly, the title of the article in which Piper insists on adoring a God who might consign his sons to hell is "How Does a Sovereign God Love?" We believe Piper has the question backward and that his article reflects the unfortunate subordination of love to will that Gunton identifies. Given the full revelation of God in Scripture, the question we should be asking is, how would a God of perfect love express his sovereignty?

When love is subordinated to will, then the fatherhood of God, which is emphasized in the Trinity (Mk 1:11; Jn 1:18; 5:19-20; 17:20-26; 20:17; 1 Cor 15:20-28), takes a back seat to the image of God as King or Ruler.[3] God's essential relational nature as a being who exists in three persons becomes secondary to the notion that God is a sovereign monarch whose will cannot be thwarted.

Without the benefit of the New Testament, such a perspective is perhaps understandable. This is not to deny that God's love is revealed in the Old Testament (Lam 3:22; Hos 11:1). However, the full meaning that God is love was revealed in its clearest light only with the incarnation (Rom 5:8; Gal 2:20; 1 Jn 3:16; 4:9). In the brilliant light of the incarna-

---

[3]For an insightful study of the various roles of God in Scripture and their relation to each other, see Allan Coppedge, *Portraits of God* (Downers Grove, Ill.: InterVarsity Press, 2001).

tion, we learn that from all eternity there was love between the Father and the Son (Jn 17:24, 26). Moreover, the coming of the Holy Spirit at Pentecost revealed that God's eternal dance of love included the third person of the Trinity as well (Rom 5:5; Gal 4:6; 5:16, 22; Eph 3:16-19). That is why love is not merely an activity of God—it is his very essence.

In a nutshell, our case against Calvinism is that it doesn't do justice to the character of the God revealed in Scripture. It does not accurately portray the holy One who is "compassionate and gracious, slow to anger, abounding in love" (Ps 103:8), the God for whom love is not merely an option or a sovereign choice, but who is such that his eternal nature is love (1 Jn 4:8).

In the introduction, we posed the question this way: Does God love all of us and desire our well-being? We have shown that Calvinists cannot answer this question in the affirmative without equivocation and inconsistency. The breathtaking vision of God's trinitarian love is obscured by the Calvinist claim that God passes over persons he could just as easily save and thereby consigns them to eternal misery. The exhilarating message of the gospel that should be good news to all sinners is muted by the Calvinist claim that only the elect are truly able to join the dance. While Scripture teaches that not all will come, the Calvinist account of why this is so ultimately goes back to God's choice not to save those persons rather than their refusal to accept the invitation. Indeed, Calvinists hold that God's sovereign choice not to save some sinners enhances his glory.

God is truly and fully glorified when his nature is brought to clearest light and he is properly worshiped and adored. It is noteworthy that in the Old Testament when the temple was dedicated, the Levites praised God by singing of his goodness and everlasting love and mercy. As they did, the temple was filled with the glory of God (2 Chron 5:11-14; 7:1-4). This glory was shown most fully when the Son of God took on a temple of flesh and lived among us (Jn 1:14-18; 14:8-11; Phil 2:5-11; 1 Jn 4:1-12).

By subordinating love to will, Calvinism fails to glorify God as he has revealed himself in history and ultimately in the incarnation of his Son.

The love of God as revealed in the incarnation is not a matter of mere *words* but of the *Word made flesh* who actively seeks the well-being of his fallen children. A love that truly and passionately promotes the well-being of the beloved, even when it is costly, is the sort of love that has existed from all eternity in the Trinity and was revealed in the life of Jesus. This is the kind of love, moreover, that God commands his children to demonstrate by following his example (1 Jn 3:16-18). Because God loves all sinners in this fashion and actively works to promote their eternal well-being, there is rejoicing in heaven when one of them repents (Lk 15:7, 10). A God who commands this sort of love and who positively delights in the repentance of sinners surely has no need or desire to show his sovereign power by passing over some fallen humans, nor would he truly glorify himself by doing so.

This is why we are not Calvinists. Our reasons are not merely autobiographical or personal, but rather they are theological, philosophical and most of all biblical. As such, we believe they are also good reasons why our readers should reject Calvinism.

Names Index

Subject Index

Scripture Index